Covers

Front, front inside, back inside, back
The towers of the Bayon, a Buddhist monument at the center
of the royal city of Angkor Thom, built around 1200, are
carved with four faces, generally believed to represent King
Jayavarman VII as Lokesvara, whose special attribute is
compassion. (These photographs were taken by Serge Thion
in 1969. No conservation work has been possible since 1972.
A visit in 1981 showed no substantial damage, but the need
to maintain and repair the structures of the monument will
surely arise. For political reasons, UNESCO has been unable
so far to act as a neutral protector of the Angkorian sites. The
fate of many of them in the war zone forest is not known.)

Res 14 Autumn 1987

Anthropology and aesthetics

Contents

Res 14 Autumn 1987

Anthropology and aesthetics

EDITOR

Francesco Pellizzi

ASSOCIATE EDITOR

Remo Guidieri

EDITORIAL COUNSEL

Joseph Rykwert

EDITORIAL ADVISORS

Alain Babadzan	Adrienne Kaeppler	Marshall Sahlins
Edmund Carpenter	C. C. Lamberg-Karlovsky	Carlo Severi
K. C. Chang	Michael W. Meister	David Shapiro
Whitney Davis	Rodney Needham	Stanley J. Tambiah
Morton Feldman	Nora Nercessian	Gianni Vattimo
Oleg Grabar	Douglas Newton	Nur Yalman
John Hay		

PRODUCTION COORDINATOR	Mary L. Strother
ASSISTANT TO THE EDITOR	Rose Wax Hauer
COPY EDITOR	Nancy Bell Scott
DESIGNER	Richard Bartlett
LAYOUT	Deborah Sarafin Davies
COVER DESIGN	From a 1981 sketch by Dan Flavin

EDITORIAL OFFICE

12 East 74th Street, New York, New York 10021

DISTRIBUTED BY

Cambridge University Press, 32 East 57th Street, New York, New York 10022

PUBLISHED BY

Peabody Museum of Archaeology and Ethnology, Harvard University
11 Divinity Avenue, Cambridge, Massachusetts 02138

The iconography of an aniconic art

PAUL MUS
Edited by Serge Thion

Before his unexpected death in 1969, Paul Mus devoted much of his attention to the dramatic events then taking place in Vietnam. Most of his reflections, lectures, or essays on Vietnam were published at the time, or shortly after his death. See, for instance, "Traditions asiennes et bouddhisme moderne," published in the Eranos Jahrbuch 1968, printed in 1970, or Hô Chi Minh, le Vietnam, l'Asie, edited by Annie Nguyen Nguyet Hô (Paris, Le Seuil, 1971). But Vietnam was only a part and a facet of a global research, and his thinking never stopped dealing with the rich material he had brought together in his famous Barabudur, a study the subtitle of which may be rendered as "a tentative approach to a history of Buddhism based on the archaeological critique of the texts." In fact, for him all these topics were interwoven as he went, from the texts to the stones to the people, and from these back to the great classics. In so doing and as if by chance, he solved many a riddle that had vexed archaeologists who had limited themselves to comparing monuments alone.

In the sixties he had been asked to write a book on Angkor, which was in a way the site from which his professional career had started. Before the work was entirely finished the publisher realized the work would largely go beyond the limits he had had in mind. So, as in many other instances, Paul Mus dropped the project altogether and the unfinished text went forgotten in the box of abandoned manuscripts. Recently, however, Arma Artis, a small French publisher, decided to publish it. The editorial work I undertook is in the process of completion, and we extracted from this forthcoming book, which the author had named Les Masques d'Angkor, a chapter we thought would be of particular interest for the readers of Res. As usual, Mus, who wrote his first drafts very fast, hardly quoted his sources; we have added footnotes to track them down whenever possible. The English-speaking reader who might find this text sometimes difficult to penetrate in all its implications may take some solace in the fact that French readers do not have a much easier task and must be very careful in picking their way through Mus's effervescent thought, couched in a classical but complex style. Paul Mus was not only a great scholar but also a powerful writer.

The newly created Societé des Amis de Paul Mus is undertaking the publication of several of Paul Mus's important manuscripts. Applications for membership and other information can be obtained from the Société des Amis de Paul Mus, 1 Aubray, 91780 Chalo Saint Mars, France.

Serge Thion

* * *

Architects—and preeminent among them Henri Parmentier, who was for so long head of architecture at the Ecole Française d'Extrême-Orient—have never had a high professional opinion of those of their Cambodian colleagues to whom we owe the Bayon, its conception and execution. They have seen in it "a typical architectural monster." On this technical point, the learned author of *Pour mieux comprendre Angkor* [Coedès] has felt obliged to adopt the opinion of the specialists. And I am afraid that on this point alone, I shall have to differ with him. "To the keen eye of the architect," he writes, "the Bayon in its present state appears to be the result of a series of transformations, most of which occurred in the course of construction. We owe this important discovery to Henri Parmentier."[1] Here is the judgment of the professional on this point: "In its present state, the monument creates a strange impression of accretion and compression, towers and buildings huddled together with courtyards like airless, lightless shafts. . . . " Thus, Henri Marchal—who was perhaps closer than anyone else will ever be to these stones, given the length of time he was in charge of them and the life of labor he devoted to them—might have erred (according to Mr. Coedès) when he suspected an intention in the very oddity of the monument. In his *Guide archéologique aux temples d'Angkor*, Marchal wrote, "A muddled and strange mass," adding, however, "presenting the aspect of a sculpted rock, rising up like a veritable crag hewn and carved by men."[2]

Is this a relapse into "symbolism"? The generation of

1. Georges Coedès, *Pour mieux comprendre Angkor*, Paris, 1947, pp. 127–128, referring to Henri Parmentier, "Modifications subies par le Bayon au cours de son exécution," BEFEO, 1927.
2. Henri Marchal, *Guide archéologique aux Temples d'Angkor*, Paris, 1928.

Face of a *devata*, a minor goddess. Bayon. Angkor.

our masters—that of Louis Finot, Sylvain Lévi, and Paul Pelliot—purged our sciences of such symbolism when it took over from reliable, although perhaps too imaginative, scholars such as Max Müller, Senart, or Kern, all of whom championed the "solar myth." Actually, there are no myths to speak of which would call for such a term: in them the sun is a sign or an index of the cosmos. On a less scientific level, but with wider circulation, and with references readily borrowed from a rather "wild" Egyptology, one also had to be wary of what Littré, under the word "Symbolic," defines as the "system which considers polytheistic religions as a collection of signs or symbols encompassing natural, physical, moral or historical truths." Once this aspect of the findings of our disciplines had been appraised by philological rationalism—as enunciated in Renan's *Avenir de la Science*, itself following in Burnouf's tracks—the next step was easy: to exclude symbolism and the role of symbols, not only from the method but also from the very subject matter of our research. This meant, for example—and quite questionably, in this case— ascribing to ancient Indian religious art our own repudiation of symbols, in the name of rational principles that we regard, a little too hastily, as universal.

A striking example of this can be found in the great book by the famous archaeologist Alfred Foucher, *L'art gréco-bouddhique du Gandhāra* (as well as in a series of memoirs that preceded and followed it).[3] This penetrating scholar, who had acquired so much firsthand knowledge of Asia, where he had lived, in encountering at an early date a Buddhist art already fully figurative, even narrative, but in which the Buddha's place is filled in by "symbols," failed to recognize an evocatory cult that made use of the appurtenances of a being in order to convey his presence. That is, with the emblem of the stupa, the wheel, and so on, the Buddha was symbolized—at the peak not only of an evocation but also of a true collective incantation—on the major pilgrimage sites "blessed" in advance through his foreknowledge of what was to happen there. Thus pilgrims came in quest of something of him, through contiguity, in his footsteps.

Comparative ethnology demonstrates the identity

between this device and the one used in Asia in the past, and even today, by many a village evocatory cult with the "presence at a distance" of a spirit attached to a site, symbolized (there is no other word for it) in both its structural absence and its functional presence, by a concrete object in which it "participates." Nevertheless, as rationalism at the beginning of this century was naively projected onto the interpretation of the past of Asia itself—the very Mother of the Gods!— it led A. Foucher to write that while there were accurate and even vigorous representations of the other characters—kings, merchants, brahmins, courtesans, hunters, wild animals, and so on—the Buddha was represented only by symbols because there was no model for him, since India at that time and in the centuries immediately following did not have the use of images! This error has deprived us of what such a perceptive scholar might have told us of this remarkable piece of evidence that has come to us from the ancient past: the iconography of an aniconic cult. In fact, the imagery of Bhārhut or Sānchī shows us, in its compositions, a cult in which the sacred person was deliberately represented by "nonfigurative" symbols— doubtless so that it could be perceived only through a "communication" with it derived from the workings of Karmic Law, in accordance with past merits—a communication sustained, on the Master's part, by prescience.

Understood in this way, symbolism bears no relation to the kind of "symbolism" from which our studies may have suffered for a time. In fact, we are brought back to its etymological meaning. In Bailly's Greek dictionary, *Sumbolon* was originally "an object broken into two pieces of which a host and his guest each kept one half (cf. Lat. *tessera hospitalis*)"; the bearers could then be recognized by bringing together (cf. *sumballô*) the two parts, which served as proof of formerly contracted relations of hospitality. The workings of *Karman* are more subtle; they bring into play separations and encounters that can go on through an infinite sequence of lives for one being, unless he escapes from this cycle of transmigration through encounter with the Buddha and his teachings.

In strict doctrine, however, such a perspective makes use of formulas and modalities established earlier in Indian eschatology, particularly at the level of kinship. Among other things, each generation inherited previously established social relations of the kind transmitted and authenticated by the Greek *sumbola*. The whole cycle of the "Previous Lives" of the Buddha,

3. Alfred Foucher, *L'Art gréco-bouddhique du Gandhara. Etude sur les origines de l'influence classique dans l'art bouddhique de l'Inde et de l'Extrême-Orient*, Paris, EFEO: I, 1905, XII–626 pp.; II, 1918, XI–400 pp.; II2, 1922, pp. 401–809; II3, 1951, pp. 811–923.

which predetermines, in his very life as a Liberated Being, his relations with his various companions and interlocutors, rests on this same principle: the Master and his listeners, by their very meeting, bring together the two halves of a *common karman*. Hence it is a personal relation, one that, properly viewed, is even more authentic than the person himself, since in this system it is literally the relation that constitutes the person, who will be nothing but this relation. As the Pāli canon teaches: "This, o disciples, is neither your body nor anyone else's body: it is rather to be considered as the work of the past, given shape, realized by the will, and become palpable." Each "being" progresses thus through Transmigration with a "Debit and Credit" account, that is, a complex of debts and credits toward other similar accounts, which plays its part in the predetermination of his lives and his social and physical position, without, however, relieving him of responsibility for the deeds carried out in each new instance. Personality is only a signature, but a valid one. The Buddha himself, in his last existence, is not totally exempt from the process of canceling out his previous faults. For example, the rock that Devadatta had rolled over him in order to crush him injured his foot lightly. Accordingly, one may wonder what will happen, after his *parinirvāna*, to the creatures—in other words, the "transmigrant series" toward which he had contracted obligations in the past —if their merits have not been extensive enough for them to meet him face to face in the course of his life so that they can receive the teaching that might liberate them. There are two answers to this: in a remote future, Maitreya, the Buddha-to-be, will take over from Çākyamuni and, on the other hand, the Community inherits his Law, which substitutes for his person ("he who sees the Law sees me"): these heirs "of his," in a spirit very near to that of ancient Roman law, *are* he— just as in ancient Roman law one is *heres suus*. They will enhance, in his name, the value of the gifts received, by offering the Law in turn. In this case, as in the case of Maitreya, the solution is expressed in accordance with contemporary juridical forms. But better still: we have seen that in this perspective the person extends to his "appurtenances" elements from his body and things he used: a hair, nail parings, a little ash from the funeral pyre, or a bowl, a beggar's staff, the Preaching Wheel, and so on, symbolize this person, of whom they are mandatory extensions—or here too, signatures. The merit that leads a creature to see these

objects—in default of the one whose trustees, one might say, they are—comes from the previous "karmic relation," so that the two series, that of the Master transferred on his witness-relics, and that of the beneficiary, literally "symbolize together" in this encounter. The remote presence, or participation, of the Buddha—a notion that could conjure up many ethnosociological analogies—is thus of an order that is juridical rather than mythic, given this karmic bookkeeping. "Symbol" is not necessarily synonymous with ideology.

Surprise at the powerful historical cohesiveness and wide appeal of a religion allegedly "of nothingness" derives from looking for its driving force (*dharma*) in a metaphysics, rather than in the way it has used contemporary human institutions to express its own originality. Of such fundamental realism, sustaining the boldest speculations to which the doctrine has lent itself in its time, there is however an identifying mark, which might have provided modern interpreters and translators with useful food for thought: in Buddhism, the canonic description of the status of the Community, in its relations with the world, with the Law, and with the Master, in the absence of a formally expressed constitution, is one expressed through images. It has been expressed juridically, in the terminology and the spirit of the Indian doctrine of inheritance. The Buddha's disciples, particularly the monastic Community of the four (or ten) cardinal points, inherit the Master's law—and since, even in the oldest canonic texts we have, the Law is identified with his person, not in a metaphysical sense, but in terms of law (that is the point!), thanks to such unquestionable evidence, one gets a direct view, in concrete terms, of the notion of Body of Law (*dharmakāya*), which was to become the keystone of Greater Vehicle speculation. Paradoxically, and from the origin, in a religion that left no room to *ātman*—which we have to translate, although approximately, by the Self—this notion of *dharmakāya* is a transposition, within a moral and mental frame of a new kind, of the pilot-image of the Mahāpurusha, the total Self that envelops all those who know and understand its meaning. "He who sees the Law sees me!" Let us not proceed here from term to term, projecting our own values on each, but rather let us accord to them as a whole the values implicit in the time and place of their own historical occurrence. As an imagistic canon, archaeology is, in the present case, a precious guide for our explanatory hypotheses—

provided one succeeds in experiencing them in the specificity of their own site, as, so often and so fruitfully, Alfred Foucher has done elsewhere.

Thus, whatever its ultimate meaning, the initial formula for Buddhist art appears as a partial aniconism, revealing a hierarchy among styles in which the aniconic is more sacred than the figurative. Everything is represented, save for the central character, the Buddha himself, although these are episodes of his life. From this to that other extreme, in Angkor Thom—where not only is the Buddha represented, notably by the large statue sheltered under the central Tower, but also everywhere on the monuments, where architecture becomes face—is there a correlation? And even if such a correlation can be established in theory, is there anything to be gained from the comparison, when there are so many differences? However, it is not only in the history of art that long-term perspectives, aiming at some realignment, lose nothing; quite the contrary, even if it entails a reconsideration of the intervening steps.

The problem of the first image of the Buddha—which a profuse bibliography and abundant polemics have not, apparently, brought us closer to resolving—may cease to be a problem once we have resituated its terms within the historical and semantic context. The curious mixtures and overlapping just mentioned, this disparate assemblage of the figurative and the nonfigurative, each with its own domain and task, this iconography of an aniconism, before the Buddha's image arose, without further explanation, there where it was missing, suggest at least that this may not be a naive art, one that later would make up for its backwardness on the essential point by drawing inspiration from Hellenistic Apollos.

There will be no way out, until we ascribe to these manifestations their corresponding intent. As I attempted to show about thirty-five years ago in a memoir on the adorned Buddha (le Buddha paré),[4] two characteristics distinguish it from our own ways of thinking and acting. First, this art is the exact opposite of what, in our own art, is decorative. This art is always totally in earnest, involved in what happens (événement); it is itself a happening, a tracing of the first event that it thus renders present in a secondary way, rather than represent it, in the sense we would

give to this term. As Chavannes perceived with great insight, in the Buddha's image there is "something" of him; we shall return again later to this evidence and interpretation.[5] There are singular and instructive resonances with our expressionism: if the formula for Indian thought is that one understands only what one somehow becomes, then the corresponding formula for the artist is that he will create only what he has become "in spirit" or rather, through what Alain calls interior dance, outlining things within us by a movement that conjures up their presence. Lévy-Bruhl, for his part, in the most definitive aspects of his study of participation, clearly brought out the power of such a presence (which may be labeled affective) within the notion of representation.[6]

The second point—which, everything considered, can hardly be separated from the first—is that the iconography of the Buddha (first within India, later outside) has constantly referred to the great pilgrimage sites where, after a certain date, images of the Master replaced his scenic representation, with the nonfigurative restriction that testified to his presence where the composition as a whole was a projection of him in narrative form. For example, the two styles are juxtaposed in Amarāvatī. The collection of "explicit" images, as seen in Bodhgayā, Bénarès, Vaiçālī, and so on—in a way a map of those sites—fixed traditionally by what are called the stelae "of the Eight Miracles," served as a model for image-makers everywhere. Nonetheless, they did not draw inspiration from these models in order to represent in their own way the legendary scene that these prototypes commemorated. Striking details prove beyond question that their reproduction was only secondary; they consciously and deliberately represented, for example, not the Buddha triumphing over Māra in Bodhgayā but, almost as a tracing, the image which, in Bodhgayā, represented that scene at first hand. One cult—which is attested to by ancient images and is still alive in a country such as Siam, where "basic Buddhism" (known, rather inadequately, as "the Lesser Vehicle") lives on—included the adornment of the statues with detachable crowns, necklaces, and bracelets. The same images are represented sometimes with and sometimes without

4. Paul Mus, "Le Bouddha paré. Son origine indienne. Çakyamuni dans le Mahayanisme moyen," BEFEO, 1928, no. 1–2, pp. 153–278.

5. Edouard Chavannes, Mission archéologique dans la Chine septentrionale, II, la sculpture bouddhique, Paris, EFEO, 1915, pp. 261–614.

6. This might refer to Lucien Lévy-Bruhl, L'Expérience mystique et les symboles, Paris, 1938.

such ornaments; in traditional perspectives that have been preserved in the South, these could not be attributed to the Buddha himself in a direct representation of his life. While one may discuss the meaning of these ornaments, it is at the very least undeniable that they have to do with his images and not with his person. They are at the level of what I would call a secondary iconography—by repercussion or by rebound. Ancient Chinese inscriptions, studied by Chavannes in his *Mission archéologique dans la Chine septentrionale*, support this formulation.

It is essential to understand that—in relation to an art whose purpose is to place the viewer authentically in the presence of what it "represents"—all beings are classified according to the contact that they have deserved to entertain with the supreme model—the Buddha, in his glorious appearance marked by the thirty-two major, and eighty secondary, signs of the Mahāpurusha. In the forefront come the privileged ones who see him in person in the course of his last life; between him and them—if the person we understand, wrongly, as an "I" is at the least the symbol of his past actions, which make him that person today—there is, consequently, an encounter and an "adjustment" of their person to his, just as there was one between the two Roman tesserae that "symbolized" an alliance. All others will have to be content, at best, with the provisions, the "tokens" left by the Buddha for them—that is, the Law and the Relics corresponding, respectively, to the archetypal pair, *nāma*, the Word = the Law and *rūpa* = the visible Form. Further, and lower still, there is the crowd of those who have acquired no symbolic merit with respect to the Buddha's person of the present period. According to the ancient doctrine, they will thus not meet him, even if he wished to go to them: the conditioning for a meeting must be mutual. They have no karmic consistence before him nor he before them. Perhaps our least inadequate terminology for discussing these perspectives is that of customary law in relation to a "household"—kin and in-laws, servants, and clients revolving around a *consortium* [a term comparable to *sambhoga*, which in Sanskrit denotes the common enjoyment of a "legal" base]: the *dharma*—throughout past existences there has never been any karmic hospitality between them, passed on from one existence to another. Hence nothing concerning him can touch them, as comprising "something" of him, neither his Law nor his name nor even, in any way, his image. For at this level the intervention of an "external force"

(*force étrangère*), one, that is, not rooted in the karmic connection between two transmigratory sequences, is not admitted; a force that, to the contrary, will radiate from the Boddhisattvas of the Greater Vehicle: in this sense, it has been compared to Grace. As early as 1924, Mr. Paul Demiéville's fine memoir *Les Versions chinoises du Milindapanha* included all that was essential concerning this great turning point in the dogma and its consequences.[7]

In this field of study, one can thus come to a more reasonable understanding of the apparent paradox of an explicit iconography with regard to secondary characters, associated with an aniconism of the principal character. This imagery, rich and free though incomplete, shows us the Buddha's contemporaries exercising their privilege, and in the very anecdote of their meeting with him. But we do not share this privilege of seeing him face to face: he is visible for them, not for us. Such an arrangement would be absurd if the purpose of this art were simply to draw an image, and not to make the scene "actually" present—an attenuated presence, as if through repercussion, but of the same nature as its model, the difference corresponding to different levels of karmic retribution. If we do not physically, as it were, see the physical person of the Buddha, it is because we have not merited it. In times of degradation of the Law, before the images themselves disappeared, they obviously were a substitute for his person. Various later legends, by trying to trace those images back to the actual period when the Master lived and could delegate "something" of himself to them, show quite well that, in this perspective (which justifies the image of the Buddha a *posteriori*), the image "occupies his place" in his absence, as the ancient Buddhist epigraphy of Northern China explicitly states. But what about the "intermediate" period when the Buddha had disappeared, after the *parinirvāna* and when these substitutes had not yet been established on his path—a phase corresponding to the most ancient Buddhist art? As the existence of statues has been justified by carefully tracing them back to the time when their model was still on earth, one must not seek in those apocryphs any information about the early style of Bhārhut or Sānchī or Amarāvatī. One has to judge on evidence, taking into account both the monuments and the texts that throw light on them directly and indirectly.

7. Paul Demiéville, "Les versions chinoises du Milindapanha," *BEFEO*, 1924, pp. 1–258.

Let us follow this line of thought; it is revealing. Where indeed is this iconography to be found? Primitive aniconism is found on the sites, where the cult was addressed either to real objects taken as symbols of the corresponding event—such as the Bodhi tree or the *stūpa* of the Parinirvāna—or to symbols that were conventional figures of the Nativity —(a lotus), or of the Teaching (the Wheel of the Law), and so on. A second kind of aniconism then appears, as in the bas-reliefs on the oldest *stūpas*: at this level, the question arises of what is being expressed in this way. What is this that we are beholding? In the context of the time, there is no doubt about the answer: we are beholding the *dharma*. Indeed, one of the fundamental meanings of this term is "sacred text," the "Scriptures." In fact, this ancient iconography never is anything other than the direct and literal illustration—except for the omission of the Buddha's person—of these Scriptures: it is a true publication for the eyes, unfolding, on the other hand, in close relation to the *stūpas*, around their bases, beneath the massive dome that is a symbol of the *parinirvāna* and in which the relics are enshrined; the images cover the base, the railings, the pillars, and the porches. Therefore, their interpretation must not be fragmentary and sculptural, but wholistic; dramatic, scenic, in a word, architectural, in harmony with the ordinary structure and function of Indian architecture. The order and meaning of the monument illuminate the order and meaning of the bas-reliefs, and vice versa.

In this respect, two observations should be noted, their significance deriving from all that has preceded:

1. The pairing of the Word and the Form (*nāmarūpa*) is made all the closer, in the case of the *stūpas* and their illustration, as those monuments are related to the canonic writings, particularly in the Açoka cycle, just as the altar of the Brahmanic fire had been with the *Rigvéda*: and also because "scriptural relics"—literally, relics "of the *dharma*," texts or fragments of texts, which constituted the very "life" of these monuments —were enshrined in addition to the personal relics.

2. As already noted, the general disposition of the *stūpa* on its axis, which is in a way the essential part of it: symbolic worlds rise one above the other along an axial disposition, and surrounding it is the succession of the *Lives* that have led to the liberation. This general disposition reproduces the pattern that has remained the backbone of India's conception of the universe. The general rule for such a pattern seems to be the projective identification of this axis and its periphery. In the most ancient architectural Buddhist version, this comparison is one of the reserved mysteries, the Buddha having refused to reveal anything concerning the existence or non-existence of the Liberated One in the *parinirvāna*. In the plastic and architectonic order of the *stūpa*, the chain of the Buddha's existences, including the last, leads visibly to the "informal" symbol of this state (the term "informal," of the language of contemporary art, is useful here). Therefore, when the Greater Vehicle categorically formulated the equation Transmigration (*samsāra*) = *nirvāna*, it only stated openly what, in their way, the dispositions of the monuments had implied without explicit concepts. Let us not theorize on this point, but look instead at history!

In these two approaches, there thus appears an intimate relationship between the Law as Word on the one hand, symbolized, in the compact mass of the dome, by the enshrined *dharmaçarīra* and indeed by the architectural whole in its "cosmic" order; and, on the other hand, the Form deployed in a circle around the secret deposit of which these forms are but the illustration.

By reading the whole dramatically, one gets closer to the canonic proposition contained in it. According to a general rule of Indian artistic expressivity (a rule to which we will return, and which I have developed elsewhere),[8] in these traditions the ultimate artist, the one who puts the finishing touches to the work—just as, for instance, and even more so then than today, the keyboard player in J. S. Bach's time—is the spectator: it is he who, as he circumambulates a four-faced Brahma, transposes it from a four-headed monster into a sequence in four phases. Here, as spectator, he sees the Buddha's contemporaries see him. And if the ultimate end is a communication with the Master, what is *his* part in this? He enters into the play, and as actor *he himself sees* the *dharma*. Then, not on the stone but on the site, dramatically, with his person and not as an image, he illustrates the fundamental text: "He who sees the *dharma* sees me." It is an informal suggestive art akin to drama and, beyond the scenario, to the "figurative" power [*puissance "figurative"*] of *yoga*. However, on the canonic level which we consider, what is involved here is not—or not yet—a free exercise in *yoga*, but rather, the efficacy of *karman*, and of the classification of beings and their perceptions

8. Paul Mus, "Un Cinéma solide. L'intégration du temps dans l'art de l'Inde et dans l'art contemporain: pourquoi?", in *Arts Asiatiques*, 1964, reprinted in *L'Angle de l'Asie*, Paris, 1977, pp. 141–154.

—or better, the classification of beings by their perceptions—which appraises their karmic standing ["balance"] and allows them to determine their position in samsāra.

* * *

Consulting with Chinese pilgrims on these beliefs and practices is highly instructive, given their first-hand experience in front of the images and, I dare say, outside the text. No doubt in their time there had long been sacred statues everywhere. It is all the more remarkable that Fa Hian, for example, was able to note down the legend of the Buddha's Bowl, which is to remain among us as a symbol of the juridical capacity of the Buddha and of the Community (pātra, bowl, hence pātratva, "the capacity to receive and to multiply the 'merit' of the gift''; we recall that the stūpas are in the shape of the Buddha's bowl, upside down), until the other relics have disappeared. At that moment all the creatures that Çakyamuni was called to save (through the karmic correlation with him of their past lives) will have been saved, and the bowl will go to the Tushita heaven where the Buddha-to-be, Maitreya, awaits this sign that the times are ripe for him, in his turn. One can also read in the biography of the famous Hiuan Tsang a moving account of this great pilgrim's visit to the Grotto near Nagarahāra, known as the Cave of the Shadow Left Behind: the shadow of the Buddha could be seen on a wall of the cave, but only by those whose good karman allowed them this indirect communication with the Master; the distinctness of the shadow was the gauge of their merit. To his despair Hiuan Tsang almost failed to see it, and it was only with great difficulty that he finally distinguished anything of it at all.[9] The emotional intensity of such an impression on the part of this powerful defender and exponent of the Greater Vehicle is striking. There is no better way to understand—not at the level of scholarly polemics, but in actual religious and everyday life— that for those not linked to the Buddha by karmic "symbolism," in times of Cosmic darkness the "external force" [force étrangère] itself at first appears only as a substitute for the historical Buddha's power to save.

Father Lamotte writes: "In ancient times [before there were figurative images of the Buddha] the 'joy one could derive from contemplating the Buddha' came not from contemplating the images, as is the case today, but from contemplating attentively the cetiya [a commemorative, and in particular a funeral, monument] or the sacred tree."[10] The fact is that the nescio quid that later on was found in the statues used to be encountered on the site formerly "impregnated" (in the exact spirit of the pre-Aryan and pre-Chinese cults of monsoon Asia) with the Master's presence and related to him through some appurtenance of his. Atharvaveda, the Veda of Magic, is rich in such pre-Buddhist indications.

One sees the angle: one searches for oneself, one gauges oneself, one confirms one's faith at the pilgrimage sites and in front of their monumental illustrations, which are at once the religious map of the country and the backbone of legend and history, and consequently of the religion itself. Collective and individual experiences of an obvious sincerity, on the other hand: see Hiuan Tsang and the Shadow! Doubtless it is here that we must look for the explanation of certain features—what I would call the art of polished stone, cave walls, or "Açoka pillars"— which are well attested to and still visible in continental India. The pilgrim's training in aesthetics and in legend enabled him to play his part as the "ultimate artist," fixing the indispensable affective impression of a real presence on the moving reflection that gradually, through attention and concentration, stabilized in front of him. It is a psychotechnical art. I would be inclined to carry thus far the remark so full of insight made by my learned colleague Father Lamotte. Clearly, he perceived the emotional values that became "liberated" in this way: Lucien Lévy-Bruhl's affective category of the supernatural, but in keeping with a conception of nature that in India, particularly with Buddhism, is broad enough to integrate, in a sense, rationally, what we call the supernatural. What one comes to experience (if one can attain it) is not so much "the joy to be felt in contemplating the Buddha" as in this very joy, which acts as a detector of something of his presence, the certainty of having encountered him karmically. His prescience, and the projection of his acceptance of the homage, were sufficient, in such an emotional perspective, to ensure its canonic validity. Here perhaps, although not in the case of Hiuan Tsang —who was so direct and profound in everything he

9. Hiuan Tsang, translated into French by Stanislas Julien, Mémoires sur les contrées occidentales, Paris, 2 vol., 1857–1858, and in English by Samuel Beal, Si Yu Ki, Buddhist Records of the Western World, Boston, 2 vol., 1885. Also in Chinese Accounts of India, vol. III, Calcutta, 1953.

10. Mgr. E. Lamotte, Histoire du bouddhisme indien, Louvain, 1958. Bibl. du Muséon no. 43.

A Royal Face. The four faces are meant to cover the entire horizon. Their measures are between 170 and 240 cm. Bayon. Angkor.

was and did — we may also consider the German tale of the *Emperor's New Cloak*, which was so wonderful that it was invisible, at least to the eyes of the crowd. No one dared admit that he could not see it. Thus it existed through the power of social hypocrisy, hence with a density and weight of human feeling, with a semantic realism that ordinary reality cannot approach — until the naiveté of a child revealed that there was nothing there. And all awoke to that truth. Buddhism, at least in its phenomenology, is expressed through this apologue. In the natural and human landscape of the great pilgrimages that constitute it, one was not judged solely through one's own eyes, but through one's reactions one was assigned a category in the eyes of other men. What a powerful source of conviction, even inwardly! Yoga has manifold aspects.

Let us proceed to analysis. If the artists of Sānchī and Bhārhut had represented the Buddha, they would have shown signs of a communication with him sufficient to enable them to transpose him, with a lesser degree of reality but with reality all the same, to stone; in sum, as ultimate artists: it would have meant trespassing on the magico-religious attributions of their public. Leaving the place vacant, representing the Master by his absence, meant setting the stage for future viewers to attain, beyond the convention of the work of art, the realism of an evocatory religious act. Tree, rock, empty throne: this cultural material, it has often been noted, seems to have been borrowed by Buddhism from the immemorial heritage of monsoon Asia — so much so that the homage, in fact, to the Buddha, that early sculptors felt "sufficiently" represented, for example, by the Bodhi fig-tree, was interpreted by some as the adoration of a tree. We have just perceived what devices were used to extract him out of it.

At this ancient level of the traditions, however, all this is to be enunciated in values of karmic actions and reactions, if one may be allowed such a pleonasm. The faith that comes to the site, and the material apparel that awaits it there—infused with the Buddha's anticipated blessing (adhisthāna), addressed to those with whom, in the night of the past, he has contracted a karmic alliance—these are the two halves of a symbol that are brought together, testifying to the authenticity of the benefit thus acquired. One can be bold enough, then, to give its full force to the image drawn from customary law: it gives life to this semantic of the monuments and Scriptures. If everything that we are is accomplished by our past actions and if these are measured according to their repercussion on our partners in the action, and vice versa, then one may say that every being receives the others in himself, makes them be, and nourishes them into what they are and thus become through him, pending the reciprocal. The Buddha, however, destroys the house. This is the lesson of the Dhammapada:

I strayed vainly on the path of many a rebirth,
Seeking the builder of existence; it is a great pain
to be born ever anew.
Now I have found thee, builder of the house;
thou must not
rebuild the house.
All your beams are broken, and the ridge of the house
is destroyed.
Having escaped from this ever-changing world, the soul
has reached the end of desire.

As for him, nothing holds him back any longer:

Disciples, the body of the Perfect One endures without communication with the power that leads to becoming. As long as his body endures, the men and the gods will see him; if his body be broken and his life gone, the gods and the men will no longer see him.

While everything is karman and the product of karman, and karman binds the future inevitably, this is no longer so for the Buddha; his balance "closed" on a credit; on the debit side, however, there is still a remainder. It is on this very point that the infinite capital of merit accumulated and still surmounted by the Bodhi concentrates, so that there can be no further accounting of this credit. Yet certain beings—some of the karmic series that we hold as beings—still have an open account with the series that ended with the Buddha, and they carry it forward. It is this that enables these beings, and no others, to encounter the Buddha, or his path—that is, the various expressions of the Law inherited by the community, which must see to it that these debts of reciprocity (hospitalité) are gradually extinguished.

Following this line of thought, one may perceive the meaning of a text in the Mahāvamsa capital: the dialogue between King Dutthagāmanī and the head of the Sinhalese community on the occasion of the erection of the Mahāthūpa, Ceylon's great "metropolitan" stūpa. The king orders it built, but the Church alone can provide the relic, the "life" of the monument. All the world's merit lies in building this stūpa, which is in itself a world, the world, in Ceylon. On a relatively minor scale, it evokes the famous example of Açoka. The building is one half of the symbol; the relic is the other half—the Buddha's part, given by the Church, his heir, in this solemn karmic alliance of the temporal and the spiritual, or better still, of the brahmanic "dual" of religion and politics, as it appears in brahmin and king, each being his partner's other self. The Vedic texts have an expression in which this reciprocal causality—a single existence between two or more beings—is, typically, condensed: anyonyayonitva, the capacity, in each, to form the others into what they become in the totality. Before and beyond all metaphysics, it is a juridical category, denoting solidarity, but of a singularly intimate and creative nature; Aristotle's philotès is, in our world, a beautiful and profound parallel to this. Buddhism has preserved and in many ways strengthened this category, through the reciprocal symbolic play of karman, while it eliminated the belief in ātman, which had been its support during the preceding period.

"An object cut in two, of which two hosts each preserved one half, which they passed on to their offspring." Isn't all the secondary aniconic art there, that of the images in Sānchī and elsewhere, where the earth's part is represented exactly while the Buddha's part, facing it, is not? The object here, the concrete object, is the tale, consigned to the texts—that is, to the dharma—where the Master's place is always explicitly designated, with a detailed explanation of his relations with each of his listeners, often going back to their past contacts, which "inform" the present encounter. But this total object is cut in two in the "symbolic" imagery. The other half is missing. The other side of the implicit karmic contract is not the material tokens left by the Buddha, but the life which, projected by him in advance, can come to give them life. And in accordance with the very rules of the genre, this can happen only as an answer, destined for the rightful receiver and shaped to his just measure. This eliminates the sculptor and awaits the pilgrim. All this is second to the event represented, and rests both on the invitation to the "concerned" viewer to put himself in the place of the Buddha's interlocutors, and on the idea of an analogy between their situation, requests, needs, and so on, and the pilgrim who, as his *karman* summons him before these images, and one image in particular, receives from it, according to a sort of rule of three, a blessing proportionate to theirs. The Buddha then comes to him, in thought, through the force of the solidarity of the *karman*, as once he went to his interlocutors. The term that expresses all this, *upāya*—a "device," a "practical approach," even a "stratagem"—is pre-Buddhist, and it will become one of the major articulations of the Greater Vehicle, covering all the compassion and activity of the great Bodhisattvas, the peers and emulators of Avalokiteçvara. But already the Pāli canon said:

> If three things did not exist in the world, o disciples, the Perfect One would not appear in the world, he who is the Saint, the supreme Buddha; the Doctrine and the Rule [*dharma* and *vinaya*] that he announces would not shine in the world. What are these three things? Birth and old age and death.

As Louis de la Vallée Poussin has shown, such texts take us close to what the West calls Docetism—the heresy according to which the Lord was born, lived, and died only in appearance, symbolically, so that his coming and going should edify the souls of men.[11] But this parallel also points to all that separates us from ancient Asia: our approach, here as elsewhere, remains essentially individualistic; for us the theme is the encounter between Christ and the faithful, each in person. The "opinion" (*doxa, dokèsis*), which the Christ intentionally arouses in the faithful, is at the same time a personal affair for each believer. Because of its own historical and sociological heritage, India, on the other hand, reabsorbs all persons within the "envelope" of cosmic *ātman* or Man, or it dissolves them all in the *karman* network, in this case objectively founding their existence on their relationships, which are considered to be more real than they themselves, and not the reverse. The Buddha during his life, and afterward, the Law and the Discipline which represent him, with the full juridical force of that term, exist only in correlation with one's need of them, within the infinite development of beings who make each other be, for better and for worse: that is, *samsāra*. By definition, such solidarity is also discriminatory. Even when the Buddha intervenes in a retributive series to amplify its "fruit," through his capacity to receive and multiply what he gives in exchange, it is impossible, at that level

11. Louis de la Vallée Poussin, *Bouddhisme*, Paris, 1925.

of the beliefs, that anyone other than the initial doer should taste of this fruit. Through the social and psychological realism of this adjustment, Buddhism thus introduced into the history of India a doctrine of collective salvation, that of the community of the Buddha, in the Law it inherits from him; a religious practice that confirms and guides the social and political collectivities, particularly at the level of the kingdom, but also, with Açoka and Harsha, of the Empire; and, on the other hand, in the absence of any metaphysical or divine personality, an ethics based on strict individual responsibility, with everything obviously proceeding from a deliberate referring of beings to their reciprocal conduct—more real than themselves, as it involves others, weaving everyone in a common web: that is *samsāra*, attachment and "flow" all at once. At this point of doctrinal development, the dominant characteristic is the personal specificity of the benefit that the world, the laity, find by the force of their own merits, in the encounter which these made possible for them with varying degrees of intensity and presence, with the Buddha, in his person, his Church, or his Law. Only the revolution marked by the adoption of the Greater Vehicle could break up these compartments and spread salvation and charitable assistance like a radiant light; but even so, such an action will remain an *upāya*, a "skill in the use of appropriate means," and will define its orientation according to the final goal. The big difference will be that past *karman* is no longer taken into account as such. Ultimately, this guiding of the "external force" by and toward each creature's need of it will lead to the famous paradox of Japanese Buddhism—the key to which seems to lie in this very word of "guiding"—i.e., that "if even the virtuous are saved, how much more surely [*a fortiori*] the wicked." Grace, and its peculiar logic toward sinners? "There is more joy in my Father's house. . . . "

*   *   *

Let us return to the iconography of the ancient *stūpas*. The specific reward of the Buddha's listeners and contemporaries was that they heard him in person; as for him, he undertook to be there. The two could be joined like mortise and tenon. The specific reward of those who, emerging from the formidable sea of transmigrations, set out on India's great pilgrimages and gain access to the monuments, which are the "effects" ("*effets*") of the Law—is that they see, secondarily, the iconography, although incomplete as to the essentials of the ultimate Life in which the Master found his

Cham warriors. They took and looted Angkor in 1177, about twenty years before the building of the Bayon began. Bayon, external gallery. Angkor.

realization, he who is their immemorial and thenceforth sublime karmic correspondent. Thus they see the *dharma*. In the admirable human balance [*équilibre*] of this ancient confession one should not see a seeking for magical help. The authentic teaching is formal, reconciling reason with the most powerful movements of affectivity, this magic of crowds. Here is the famous instruction from the *Majjhima Nikāya*:

> If now you know thus and see thus, o disciples, will you go and say: "we honor the Master and out of respect for the Master we speak thus"? — We shall not do so, Lord. — . . . What you say, disciples, is it not what you have recognized by yourselves, understood by yourselves? — It is indeed, Lord.

Although the conclusions may not reinforce the text dramatically, the prescription remains essential nonetheless.

Facing a First Preaching (identified by the first five regular Listeners, or by the symbol of the Wheel) the pilgrim — in the exaltation, often collective, often also felt at the end of a long journey, his mind full of the text, reciting it and hearing it recited — was familiar enough with the scene to follow it on the image. He saw, recognized, and grasped it by himself. Everything in these texts refers to the Buddha, is regulated and measured in relation to him, finds its meaning in him, in the attitudes described and in the words reported, all closely adapted to the specific situation that occasioned them. To thoroughly understand this theory of *upāya* and karmic symbolism, one can doubtless do no better than draw a parallel with the basic concept of *Gestalttheorie*, that is, that the contour of an object or of an event belongs both to the figure and the ground: another adaptation of the joining principle of the *sumbola*. The five listeners and the background of the first preaching, then, are at once half of it and the whole of it; for this receptacle awaiting the teaching totally determines the teaching, which responds to it; and reciprocally, the teaching bears, defines, and molds all that it causes to be what it alone could cause it to be. The incomplete Image is the container (*contenant*) awaiting the contained (*contenu*), the mortise awaiting the tenon. This contour is enough for one who understands the whole. This is as far as the sculptor and the viewer can go, the one helping the other along. The Buddha is present, since seeing the Law, understanding its application and applying it to oneself, is seeing the Buddha. Better still, such a vision prevails over that of his material body. Father Lamotte, in summing up the *pāli* doctrine, writes: "It is no use seeing the Buddha in his material body, in his body of putrefaction, one must see him in his *dharmakāya*, that is, in his Teaching."[12] But this classification, in its

12. Op. cit., p. 689.

materiality, is related to the object of such a perception, and not to the event of which this perception is a consequence: everything changes and takes on greater dramatic value and meanings when appraisal is made on the level of action. Seeing the physical body of the Buddha then is no longer anything but the sign of a merit great enough, of a karmic "alliance" close and potent enough, for him who has this privilege, to deserve this face-to-face encounter. In this presence there is more than can be gained through a clear understanding (essential though this may be) of his Body of Doctrine. Indeed, being a universal reference—as is shown in the majestic theme of the rays of light emanating from his smile, like a counterpart to the *Purushasūkta* of the Rigveda, the Buddha measures all other beings, but no one has ever taken his measure. There is something there that we could call an irrational residue, beyond all conception; and it is not only with the *Parinirvāna* that this problem arises, as the dialogue between Çāriputra and the monk Yamaka shows:

> What do you think, Yamaka, my friend? Is the Perfect One contained in the Name and Body . . . ?—It is not so, my friend.—Is the Perfect One distinct from the Name and Body . . . ?—It is not so, my friend.— . . . Thus Yamaka, my friend, even in this very world the Perfect One cannot be understood in truth and in essence. . . .

Thus one perceives what the Buddha puts into, what he alone can put into, and even conceive of putting into a real encounter—which, however, at this level in the system, the play of karmic retribution alone assigns to such or such a beneficiary. Then what about the second category of privileged beings, those who have not met him in all his glory, but come, however, to seek something of him, something like their karmic due, from the liberating instruments he predestined for them, in *pranidhāna*? Will the symbol which they bring on the site and which is themselves, not attain to something of him, that may be connected to it?

A textual fact, that has, surprisingly, gone unnoticed, to me seems to end the debate here. While everywhere the ancient monuments show us, in close connection with the *stūpa*, an iconography with blanks or a partial reserve awaiting the principal character just where he is known to sit or stand, walk and teach—in parallel fashion, all the traditions relating to the *stūpa* explicitly and solemnly give the relics the power to soar into space, out of the dome where they are enshrined, to manifest the Great Miracle of Crāvastī: assuming the

Buddha's appearance, they display his four basic attitudes as, later, the iconography represented them in the different episodes of his life: standing, walking, sitting, and lying. Let us look at the setting and the scenario, the stage and the action all together: this miracle is precisely the one called for in ancient times by the blanks on the bas-reliefs, or the symbols that filled them—figure and ground, tenon and mortise, act of faith and corresponding *upāya*. This is the part that the Buddha alone could fill in, at a distance and through foreknowledge. It is, literally, a form of expressionism: the believers as well as the object of worship must put something of "themselves" into it. It is a realistic (*réel*) art, in its way: entirely gauged in terms of karmic values, it distributes only on their account, with the addition, however, of the multiplying coefficient introduced by the Buddha—once again in the true line of Brahmanic antecedents: indeed, the *Doctrine du sacrifice dans les Brahmana*, by Sylvain Lévi, presents an admirable analysis of what the eminent Indianist called precisely "the coefficient of posthumous nourishment" (in the other world) of the sacrifices carried out in this world; by addressing them not to such and such a god but to the *ātman*, one achieves a final and fathomless liberation; ultimately, also, such is the retributive capacity of the Buddha.[13] Is he not "the true *brahman*," the ultimate form of *ātman*? In this, also, ancient Buddhism spoke the language of pre-Buddhist India—but to say something else.

To shed more light on this ancient aniconism we have had to bring together the doctrinal, artistic, and sociological elements (understanding by the latter a kind of psychology of social organization that orients personal reactions) in order to arrive at a more general view and interpretation of the whole. This was necessary because the intervening centuries were silent on this issue, even ignoring it, historically, in order to substantiate the various legends. Even though these were contradictory, they were nonetheless convergent in their effect, tracing the first image of the Buddha back to his own lifetime—thus enabling the Master to impress upon it, directly or indirectly, but always miraculously, a resemblance that artists reduced to their own resources could not have obtained, but which they had the leisure to copy later on.

As for the amazing growth of the cult of the Buddha's images after the first (doubtless evocatory) aniconism of the sites, which was, in turn, followed by

13. Sylvain Lévi, *La Doctrine du sacrifice dans les Brahmana*, Paris, 1898, 183 pp.

an iconography that enchased, as more precious than itself, an aniconism of the Buddha onto a representation where he alone was missing—the history of the religion and of its propagation has no difficulty in accounting for it. One must bear in mind that in India itself Buddhism announced its own disappearance, so much so that the course of events on several occasions compelled it to postpone the date, which it had considerably outrun. As we have seen, the heritage that the Buddha of our time left to his Church, for the good of the entire community of the faithful, gradually dwindled. Recourse to a karmic currency of himself, relics and so on, which constituted this provision, became more and more necessary, and more and more dramatic: toward the beginning of the Christian era and later on as the Greater Vehicle developed, century after century lived in the midst of historical disasters in an end-of-the-world atmosphere. This explains the prestige that the replicas of his person—which were deemed to derive, in active value, from this very person— acquired once they were established on the sites consecrated by his passage and prescience. Words such as *image*, *portrait*, *statue*, are inadequate in such a context. The Indian word, and at that level of the tradition the concept as well, was *pratimā*: "measure," literally "counter-measure." Imbued with the magical principle that the measure of a being is, secretly, this being himself (the notion on which rested the entire ritual of the vedic altar of fire), ancient Buddhist India could not think of anything other than a "presence" or a nonformal representation of the Buddha, in front of some pillars of Sānchī I, which are exactly the size supposed to have been that of the historical Master— that is, theoretically, twice the human size: evidently the legend was already flourishing, before it materialized in a formal iconography. In his valuable studies on the origins of Buddhist art,[14] Ananda K. Coomaraswamy effectively brings into evidence the silhouette—which was perhaps all the more real, in ancient Buddhist perspective, since it was mental. "All that one is, is the fruit of the mind, has mind for its essence, is made of the mind," the *Dhammapada* symbolically teaches—that seems to have been projected before pillars, in front of which the Buddha's footsteps were represented, carved in a stone, level with the ground, while behind the top of the pillar a

stone rosace, in the shape of a solar wheel, surrounded and identified the head, majestic at that size, of the invisible character. Everything was ready for the image to become embodied—or perhaps we could say, borrowing from the language of existentialism—for the imaging of the imaginary (*imager l'imaginaire*). In the land of Yoga, such expressions carry weight. Reread Heinrich Zimmer![15] "Life" (*jivita*) comes from the relics entrusted under the *stūpa* (the "container," in the shape of a bowl, of the exchange of symbolic gifts), first to the bas-reliefs with their illustrated aniconism images, to make the Master present, and then to his images, once they are established, in order to consecrate them. This is, indeed—but framing it within the complete setting, including architecture, sculpture, and "pictorial" elements (taking this term in the sense we have sketched earlier)—a transposition of a direct statement made by Father Lamotte, outside this "historical" setting: in Ceylon, as late as the fifth century A.D., that is, when the use of statues had spread everywhere, the worship was still addressed essentially to the *stūpa* and the *Bodhi* tree. "Damaging them would be a serious fault, whereas there is no threat of punishment against those who would destroy or damage a statue. The image is sacred only insofar as it contains a relic."

* * *

But here the entire principle of interpretation defended in these pages is at stake: that is, through the general scenario, all arts united not simply under the aegis of architecture, but also of the image of the world it reflects; functionally, in fact, beyond architecture, the structural framework. In this perspective the relics were not to be inside the statue, as they eventually were; more concretely, they were in the *stūpa* for the statue, giving it life, just as the statue, after the bas-reliefs, was added to the *stūpa* (notably in niches around it) in order to give body to the life that was inside them, in, and by the relics.

This general scenario can be found, decisively I believe, on the stelae known as the stelae "of the Eight Miracles." Two main topics—which, when better understood, are but one—overlap on these works, some of which are of remarkable composition and beauty: a map of the sacred places of Buddhism, identified by the corresponding statues, and, if we have seen rightly, facing the pilgrims, the soaring of the Buddha toward them (*upāya*, "approach") in these

14. Ananda K. Coomaraswamy, *History of Indian and Indonesian Art*, London, 1927. See also *Elements of Buddhist Iconography*, Cambridge, 1935, reviewed by Paul Mus in *BEFEO*, 1935, pp. 391–397.

15. Heinrich Zimmer, *The Art of Indian Asia: Its Mythologies and Transformations*, New York, 2 vol., 1955.

images—or yet more precisely, the motion of *something* of the Buddha, in them, through his foreknowledge (*pranidhāna*), a blessing from a distance (*adhishthāna*) and symbolic karmic conformity. There we have an explanation for something that has puzzled M. Foucher. On these stelae, which are a veritable catalogue of the sacrosanct models in the iconography of the Master, the images have become essential. The historical sequence is clear: these are ancient representations of the sites—originally essentially four: those of the birth, the enlightenment, the great miracle of the multiplication of the bodies, and the *parinirvāna* —through their symbols, in a fully developed iconographic style in which eight images speak through and for themselves, with the addition of four secondary scenes to the principal ones. However, a discordant element upsets this progression: after all the others, one symbol remains, extending the aniconism (which we have called secondary) into the very midst of a flourishing iconography: it is, crowning the stelae, the *stūpa*—nonfigurative expression of the *parinirvāna*.

It all becomes clear, as soon as one has learned to recognize that the nonfigurative, in this powerful strain of Buddhist expressionism, is not an inferior form, but the highest aspect of a *realistic* nondecorative art. Compare the traditions and the monuments. The stelae, crowned by the representation of a *stūpa*, and surrounded by the succession of the "miraculous" images of the Buddha, are the direct translation of the "Great Miracle" attributed to the relics; under the dome of the *stūpa*, these await their time to soar forth in the open sky, assuming all the forms and attitudes that the Master assumed in this world. What else does one see on these stelae? They have been designated "stelae of the Eight Miracles," but this conventional expression is fundamentally related to some confusion: there are eight sites and eight sacred images, but ultimately, only one miracle, if one wishes to call this a miracle: it covers the eight places, which are sacred; or rather, it "fills" them.

Let us go further. Does not the procession (in an almost Plotinian sense) of these forms, from the hidden shrine that contains them potentially (*en puissance*) also correspond to an architectural disposition of major importance in the development of symbolism and the plastic arts? I mean the representation, around the base of the *stūpa*, of images of the Buddha that "seem to come out of it." This leads regularly to a type of architecture in which four niches, at the four cardinal points, will contain four Buddhas, at first apparently in

the same attitude, but to which finally the sculptors will attribute the four *mudrā*, or symbolical hand-gestures, called Earth-witness, Setting the Wheel of the Law in motion, Protection, and Gift.

R. D. Banerji has given a clear summary of this evolution in his article "Stūpas or Chaityas," published in the *Modern Review* of Calcutta in February 1928:

> The addition of images of the Buddha or Bodhisattvas on the bases, pedestals and tambours of the Gandharian *stūpas* has to do with the history of Indian plastic art rather than architecture. But the addition of niches and chapels at the four cardinal points led to a truly architectural alteration of the aspect of the medieval *stūpa*. The first example of such niches on the four sides is a specimen of *stūpa* from Mathura, going back to the Kushana Period. The tambour is circular; around it there are four niches, each containing a small statue of Buddha sitting cross-legged. . . . Most of the time those niches were occupied by images of Buddha in a uniform posture, but gradually the gestures were differentiated and the four Buddhas had their hands in the conventional positions that Buddhists call *bhumisparça°*, *dharmaçakra°*, *abaya°*, and *varadamudrā°*.

This transformation is the starting point of one of the major developments of the iconography and Buddhology of the Greater Vehicle: the group and the transcendent category of the (five) Jinas or Buddhas of the Pure Lands, eternal elements ruling everything in the universe, from high and from afar, in the same way as planets in an astrological system; indeed they even control our senses and our "humours"—a term that corresponds approximately to what in India was successively called *pranas*, "breaths" (organic powers, J. Filliozat)[16] or *indriyas*, ruling or sovereign functions (as in our psycho-physiological notion of "capacity" [*ressort*]). On two levels of belief, one attested to in the representations of Gandharā and Mathurā mentioned by Banerji, and the second, the soteriology and mythic cosmology of the Greater Vehicle, the *stūpa* is, concretely, a common denominator. As for the Mahāyānistic dogmas, there is no difficulty in this: while in the most ancient times the images issuing forth from the *stūpa* naturally recall the historical Buddha, whose relics, personal or symbolic, give life to the edifice, the "flamboyant" Buddhology of the *Lotus of the True Law* teaches that the "celestial" Buddhas in their remote heavens are in the end nothing but

16. In section "Anatomie et physiologie spéciale du Yoga," *L'Inde classique, manuel des études indiennes*, II, Paris, EFEO, 1953, p. 161. Filliozat had been a physician himself.

manifestations, processions (*vigraha*) emanating from his body (*ātmabhāvanirmita*); in the customary style of these esoteric teachings, this formulation must be interpreted in direct relation with the symbolism of the *stūpa* as it appears in this capital work. Indeed, the miraculous *stūpa* of a Buddha "nirvanaed" from time immemorial, *Prabhūtaratna*, is described there as circulating invisible, underground, in order to "assist" in and to all the manifestations of the Dharma. An example (but in no way a limiting one) is the teaching of this same Lotus of the True Law by the Buddha of our time, Çākyamuni. Through the latter's supernatural virtue the dome splits in two, the extinct Buddha appears "in person," Çākyamuni sits down by his side, and from then on they stand, act, and speak together, each one half of the account, Buddhas in the "dual" form — a symbolism (and here it is indeed appropriate to use this term in the etymological sense) in two pieces, thus reunited.

This central miracle of the *Lotus of the True Law* is equivalent to a transfiguration of the historical Buddha. From the heights of the marvelous throne that he shares with Prabhūtaratna, in the *stūpa* that has been opened by the prodigy just described, he glorifies this new persona, which, as he himself proclaims, he has assumed at the end of his earthly career in order to deliver the supreme teaching. The dramatic narrative of this preaching — in the middle of Heaven, far from the reach of ordinary listeners who have not gone beyond the teaching of the Lesser Vehicle — shows the universe as full of Buddhas coming from the far end of nirvāna, to hear the Sūtra, like Prabhūtaratna himself. The interpretation of this element has been seriously distorted by our translators and interpreters, because the text presents these Buddhas as "factitious" (*factice*) (*nirmita, nirmāna*) forms created by the Tathāgata Çākyamuni; but this is only a kind of *rebus*, a discursive code for the message emanating from the whole scenario, that is, that at the precise moment when Çākyamuni attributes this miracle to himself, he is on a different level. He now speaks as the immemorial Buddha, the mythic "envelope" of all, himself included. It is one of the instances in which contemporary thought, art, and especially poetry, in formulating the paradoxes of a very new kind of anxiety, have brought us singularly closer to a more human comprehension of Asian expressionism. There is no better way to read the text of the *Lotus* (whose meanderings were regular stumbling blocks for Hendrik

Kern as well as Burnouf, to mention only these two) than to bear in mind the expressive dislocation of language resorted to by Arthur Rimbaud in his famous formula of transpersonalization: *"Je est un autre."* We must understand that Çākyamuni becomes everything and everyone as he towers over himself and the rest of the world from this *stūpa* where we are told, significantly, that "the Buddha's whole body is gathered" — meaning *this* Buddha who is all the other Buddhas and finally everything, as everything in the world is potentially Buddha. Spaces and Times then are but one, and so is their content. What has happened, what will happen, happens here at the same time: thus it is the relics enshrined in the mysterious *stūpa* which "soar" into space and display the phantasmagoria of the numberless Buddhas. Apart from the mythology, it is once again — but with limitless expansion — the miracle of the relics, near the *stūpas* of the Lesser Vehicle — or rather the *stūpas* as they are seen; for in fact on the great classical pilgrimage sites they remained common to the two schools of thought, as did the imagery itself, at least within the limits of this scene. The difference is that the Greater Vehicle named and personalized these wondrous forms.

Is there a more conclusive example than that of the Five Jinas or transcendental Buddhas who tower above everything from the pantheon? Their origins have been sought for everywhere but in India, with Iranian affinities attributed, perhaps a little too specifically, to one of them: Amitābha. When analyzing more closely their respective traditions and the making of their character, it is difficult not to recognize the divinization of the five major images that looked out over the near and closely associated sites of Bénarès and Bodhgayā. These are five episodes, five attitudes, five functions, one might say, and crowning all, five appellations of Çākyamuni (as for example, Akshobhya the Imperturbable, taking up the whole cycle of the Vajrasana and of the Victory over Mara) who have been made Buddhas, each in his own universe, like lesser currencies of our own Buddha in whom, according to the *Lotus*, all times and all regions had converged. Before that, they are to be found around the *stūpa*, where the Mahāyāna concretely translated its views on them — how can we fail to evoke the scenario of this great Sūtra, where, from mysterious "ashes" or "relics" that retain the shape of the whole body of the "total" Tathāgata (including, by anticipation, Çākyamuni, as well as Prabhūtaratna, by recurrence: for a Buddha,

Compassion is the main attribute of Lokesvara (or Avalokiteçvara), the main bodhisattva (near-Buddha) of the Greater Vehicle.

these three moments [*temps*] are all together), spring up all around, in all the regions of space, not anonymous vain forms but—and the text is positive—the Buddhas of all the Lands of Buddha in the Universe, and among them precisely Akshobhya and Amitābha?

The doctrinal paradoxes, the breaks and returns marked by the development of dogmas, become reconciled, then, through the course of history, which is retraced through the endurance of the images (even before there were any in stone) and the succession of texts—not of course with a unity that the Church itself failed to maintain, but with enough coherence and semantic affinities for there to be, in the end, only one Buddhism, and with a greater unity still when paired with Brahmanizing Hinduism.

The crucial moment—if one takes in this way the Buddhist happening [*événement*], where the Scriptures coincide with the archaeology—would lie in three stanzas, which sum up both the doctrine of the *Lotus* and the changing intepretation, from the Lesser to the Greater Vehicle, on the same sites and before the same sacred apparatus:

I make the site of my extinction appear, [thus] I present beings with a device the aim of which is to instruct them, although it is not true that I then become extinct and although on this very site I am [secretly] teaching the Law.

On this site I exert my power, on all beings and on myself. But mortals with deformed minds are deceived and do not see me though I am standing here.

Persuaded that my person has entered total extinction, they honor my relics, in many ways, but do not see me. [Yet, by this means] they get an impression which turns their minds towards the Good and the Truth.

Thus, on this essential point, on which all the artistic expression as well as the basis of the dogma revolve, there is no division between the two Vehicles but a partial overlapping. The transformation has been framed within a belief common to all the schools: the universal degradation of beings and of things, which announces in the convulsions of history and nature the end, if not of a world, at least of a cosmic era—which is about the same thing for those being then affected by it.

The final failure in Cambodia of the "revolution" signified by the Greater Vehicle and its replacement by the Sinhalese Theravāda obedience prevents its ways and means from being studied over a period as extensive as in India itself—with its abundant but erratically dated documents, or in China and Japan, with their much more accurate and reliable chronological apparatus. However, from the accumulation of facts—opinions and events—an impression emerges enabling us to correct what we might have thought of it at first approach. One might sense, for example, that the Greater Vehicle's apparatus of recourse and salvation, its promise of final liberation for all beings, the beauty, the marvels of its Heavens and Saviours who bring them within our reach, are signs of a change in perspective and imply a view of the world that is singularly more optimistic. In a museum, looking at the paintings and sculptures, and the literature, especially the Amidist texts—if one is particularly sensitive to this accumulation of Saviours and recipes for salvation—then those of the Lesser Vehicle as they are seen and still experienced in the South, from Ceylon to Thai, Burmese or Khmer Indochina, may seem narrow and restricted essentially to those whose firm vocation is sheltered by convents, already out of the world.

This would be overlooking a fundamental fact, or even two: the notion of karmic retribution, without which there are no Buddhists at all and, closely related to this, the consideration and interpretation of the signs, too often resorted to in Asia, of an oncoming "end of the world," with horrific detail, in the text and works of art. In this connection, the precise content of the documents—ranging from the Pāli canon and the basic *sūtra* of the Greater Vehicle to the Buddhist inscriptions of Central Asia and Northern China as well as the abundant Chinese and Japanese exegetic production— shows that in many respects the multiplication of those devices corresponds, on the contrary, to the ominous darkening of immediate and concrete perspectives. Everything was much simpler when the whole Law, concentrated in one person, spoke on earth and saved those whom it reached through the natural play of *karman* and the wondrous merit of the historical Master. Clearly, this is a striking example of psycho-sociological compensation. The development, the very extravagance of the promises of liberation, come as a response to the desperate need for these promises in

times of crisis, when such times were worsened and multiplied in the course of history, as was predicted in the ancient canonic prophecies. In a word, this is romantic excess, replacing a classical balance: such a change is not generally marked by social optimism. It is rather a semantics of crisis. Practically, the recourse of the Buddhist of the Lesser Vehicle lies in regulated behavior, the observance of the rule of the *dharma* in this world. In the hierarchy of beings (that is, the hierarchy of future rebirths) there are enough spiritual rewards that one can virtuously desire, such as the fruit of good deeds to be performed immediately for everyone—in a community oriented by a few saints guaranteeing the system from above, all the way down to the levels with which common beings must still content themselves—to draw moral inspiration, each according to his own worth. The game remains open as to the supreme fruit; [the Buddha], by ordering all other beings, determines the places and values within reach of those who cannot yet aspire to rise up to him. Contrarily, the Amidism of difficult times—before a society recovers its stability—as it occurred in Japan, compensates, by the splendor and universality of its promises, for the dramatic darkening of the immediate perspectives offered to the contemporary world. Such wonders, however, are within the reach of those who "have faith"—those whom Amitābha or Avalokiteçvara —his universal "right arm" everywhere secretly stretched toward us (symbolized in the images of the Great Compassionate One, under and in the radiance of his Buddha)—choose to inspire with this faith. But in the contemporary evidence of the dramatic centuries that are the origin of everything, the romanticism of the solution offered is revealed precisely in that the fruit enjoyed in its present reality, at the start, by such a small number, was called, in anticipation, the Greater Vehicle. Such apparent contradictions—with all the compensations, conscious or subconscious, that they released—explain better than a supposed metaphysics of nothingness or of total salvation, universally promised or even guaranteed, the force and human reach of this religion, whatever the school.

The real shift in points of view from one Vehicle to the other is indeed coherent with this: it concerns the intervention of what has been called "the external force" to make up for insufficient karmic merits in hard times. The concrete sequence whose artistic expression we have followed around the *stūpas* sustains and clarifies this historical evolution. To those who deserved it, and only to them, did the ancient reliquaries (the "life" of which lay in the personal relics, whether symbolic or "textual") open up to release for these privileged ones a blessing projected there in advance, which took the shape of the Master, seen in his *dharma* — all this without a tangible image, but by being inscribed in the "blanks" of an iconography of this spiritual aniconism. The next step was to give the miracle concrete form by showing, by an opening door or a niche, this transparency of the *stūpa* to its wondrous content. Here too there would be grounds for speaking of a secondary iconography: there is evidence that *stūpas* that opened were represented by these figurative means, before one built the *stūpa* in which the architectural disposition could make the event materialize, thenceforth permanently figured, and which then became a new type of monument. In the face of the stabilization of these apparitions, gathering reality and presence of themselves, and no longer the result of a mysterious symbolism between the *karman* of those who obtained them and the debit-and-credit handed down by the Master to the Church, its monasteries and *stūpas*, one came to a deification of these statues, sprung from the cosmic symbol to fill the world with images of their Heavens. As an answer to an inevitable question in the controversies raised by this stunning innovation, and actually recorded in the *Kathāvatthu* of the Pali canon, the Greater Vehicle conferred name, legend, and attributes to these multiplications of the historical Buddha. We have noted that in what concerns the most famous of these, the Five *Jinas*, a cycle was born, to this effect, on the holy site which drew pilgrims from the other end of the Far East from Bodhgayā to Bénarès — names, forms, and legends transposing five episodes of the Life of the Buddha and marking out five statues, which were worshiped and copied throughout the Buddhist world.

*   *   *

These ideas, adumbrated in a study of the great Javanese *stūpa*, the Barabudur, and familiar to my audience at the Institute of Art and Archaeology around 1937–38,[17] seem to have since received full confirmation in comparative Indian archaeology, in the great monograph of the Hindu Temple which we owe to Professor Stella Kramrisch.[18] On the field, and

consulting the texts, in front of the great monuments of continental India and among the architects and the faithful who have received the meaning of it, both technical and doctrinal, our learned colleague has shown how the exterior iconography, on the walls of those splendid monuments, springs from the image, figurative or symbolic (as, for example, the çivaite phallus), preserved in the secret cella at the heart of the temple; the niches, materialization of this miracle of the temple that opens — our "Open, Sesame!" — bear the significant name of *Ghanadvāra* "compact doors" (i.e., "openings that are not so"). If further argument were necessary, we could point out that in the case of the *stūpas*, the "miracle" that permits an exterior manifestation of the secret power of the "relics" (whatever their nature) is but the repetition — in reverse — of the miracle that in many a legend allowed their subsequent introduction into this solid mass.

Such are, in the end, the remote antecedents of the art of the Bayon. It remains true, as Mr. George Coedès wrote in 1943, that "before Jayavarman VII no one had thought of . . . ornamenting the towers of the central temple with the portrait of the King in order to affirm his omnipresence." But the formula that "paints" on the walls of an edifice the miraculous apparition of the god it contains has ancient and attested parallels in Indian art: on this common theme, the two presentations with their technical difference, one in symbolic niches ("solid openings") framing the miracle, the other as the direct representation in stone, constituting the raw miracle, correspond mainly to a classical formula and its romantic replica. In the doctrine and, one may add, in practical politics the striking feature is the personalization of this miraculous apparition of the Buddha in the actual proportions and features of the king; but here too this intercession is not without antecedents in India or even in Ceylon, where kings were seen to have statues of the Master made exactly in their own size ("the size is the man," and "image" in Sanskrit is *pratimā*: "counter-measure" rather than "counter-appearance"), or others appear among their court or their kin as earthly replicas of either Maitreya or Çākyamuni. The chronicle of the reign of Buddhadāsa in Ceylon, toward the end of the fourth century A.D., tells how he had given his eighty sons the names of the eighty disciples of the Buddha. "Surrounded by his sons, who bore the names of Sāriputa, etc., Buddhadāsa ["the Buddha's slave," an expression of complete self-renunciation, in order to assume, by the loss of a minor individuality, at least the

17. *Barabudur, esquisse d'une histoire du bouddhisme fondée sur la critique archéologique des textes*, Hanoi, *EFEO*, 2 vol., 1935, 1100 pp. Reprinted 1978, in one volume, by Arno Press, New York.

18. Stella Kramrisch, *The Hindu Temple*, Calcutta, 1946, 2 vol.

aspect of a superior being, to whom one thus becomes "transparent"] shone as if this king had been the Perfect Buddha himself."

The architectural expressionism of the Bayon, even if it is particular to the Khmer style and is legitimately its pride, is therefore at the crossroads of traditions that, far from diminishing its significance, ought to enhance it for us. For instance, they could suggest a slight amendment to the conclusions reached by Mr. Coedès in the chapter called "Le mystère du Bayon" in *Pour mieux comprendre Angkor*: "What the architect meant to represent is not so much a real being, an individual, as an abstraction . . . — it is 'royal might blessing the four orients of the country.' . . . "[19]

Certainly this interpretation, which I had a share in, is acceptable as a first approximation; these are not portraits at all in our sense of the word. This is a powerful kind of expressionism, in which abstraction plays a part, reacting in and on reality with its entire weight, with its maximum historical density. "Royal might"? We would tend to see a concept in this, and this kind of abstraction is, I believe, as far as it can be from the symbol's active, functional intent. Indeed, by means of the symbol it is quite a real being, an individual, who with his whole person projected in the open, facing his kin, confronts all the perils and tragedies of the time. Sanskrit is rich in semantic detours that act massively as proof and testimony: I cannot see the individualized portrait of the king— raised, as on an elephant throne, at the five gates of Angkor Thom, facing the world from where the Cham invasion had come—without considering the structure of his very name (Jayavarman). As Mr. Coedès has observed, it is applied to his monuments "whose ancient names when they are known to us always begin with *jayā°*, victory, a term meant to mark them as with a seal bearing the name of the founding king:"[20] *jayasindhu*, "ocean of victory," for the moats of the town; *jayagiri*, "mounts of victory," for the ramparts, and so on. Under the general symbolism of Indra's bow, rainbow, and bridge, or the gods' "causeway" to go up to Heaven or come down from there, the causeways with *Nāgas* are the king's bow, brandished against a possible enemy—all this for the benefit and protection of the kingdom, the sole preoccupation of the reign. Now, the sovereign's personal name completes adequately this panoply of symbols: the concrete meaning of *varman* is "armour," "coat of

mail," as well as "rampart" or, more abstractly, "protection." Placing the Armour of Victory near the Bow on the rampart in front of the Moat of Victory: does not this complete the political and military, as well as religious, sense of this architectural sentence in which names and shapes reciprocally assume and clarify each other? It is not only the king's person but the whole kingdom that is "shielded" by the "Armour of Victory" in this scenario. It transposes the negation of the Self (ātman)—now no longer accomplished through emptiness, with the individual purifying himself from this "false vision" (satkayadrsti) as ancient Buddhism contented itself with saying; but in full, by identification with him of all creatures whose charge one assumes, in a world whose saviour one claims to be: one and the same symbolic armour will shield the whole. Such is the case in stanza XXV in the TA Prohm stela, mentioned less often than the Edict of the Hospitals, but equivalent to it in doctrine as well as in intention. One can easily recognize in it the ancient theme of the Purusha, colored by Buddhist charity:

> Although the *ātman* was linked in various ways to the various beings, he nevertheless realized their unity in a manifest way, as he absorbed in his compassionate *ātman* [i.e., in himself] the joys and sorrows of those who have an *ātman*.

Thus the involved personality, individuality—as that of the Khmer people itself at that moment of its history —remains, contrary to any too abstract interpretation, the true meaning of the adventure. This is what, if one understands them correctly, the towers proclaim rather clearly, in contrast to so many kings who, for reasons of personal magical security, had hidden themselves so that they would become gods, at the heart of the powerful fortifications of their magic and their architecture.

If on the other hand, in the light of what was just said, we should reconsider the expressionist sequence —which goes from the ancient aniconism of the sites to the secondary aniconism of the ancient iconography, then to the fully figurative iconography of the Buddha and the Buddhas—but without losing sight of the relationship between this exterior imagery and the secret deposit of the Law with the monuments, and in the memory of men, and finally into a broad interpretation of the Supreme Unity of the Universe, we would find that, at each step, there is reason to talk of extraction, rather than of abstraction. The miraculous event that makes a Buddha or his glorious vision soar

19. G. Coedès, op. cit., p. 140.
20. Idem, p. 192. See also p. 102.

Some of the fifty-two towers, each bearing four faces. Bayon. Angkor.

forth from the varying kinds of deposits we have just discussed is all the less abstract, in fact, as it is strictly related to the person for whose benefit it occurs — either in ancient times and in the Lesser Vehicle tradition, through *karman* and its cosmic accountancy with the Buddha and the heritage held by his "sons," his "own" heirs — or, with the Greater Vehicle, through the Buddha's "devices" (*stratagèmes*) (*upāya*) of which ultimately the blossoming of the transcendent Buddhas and of the Pure Lands, in the depth of Heaven, is the final bouquet in an apocalypse of pure light,

> *Empruntée au foyer des rayons primitifs.*[21]

It is this eternal source of light that the Greater Vehicle, taking up and magnifying a more ancient term, names the Body of Law, common to all Buddhas, hence ultimately to all beings, as they gradually realize, in widening circles as the revelation gains ground, over the repentances, the relapses, and the tragedies of history. Thence come, and thither return, the forms of the Buddhas who appear in this world — as, for instance, through a great king entirely devoted to his task, that is, to the beings who are in his charge, within the province of his authority. Is this not a way of devoting oneself to the Buddha, and even being Buddha oneself, in the fulfillment that one provides for everything one touches? Through eight centuries and

doctrinal disagreements that, as we may see now, are more apparent than real — the very name of the Sinhalese sovereign, Buddhadāsa, echoes the active thought of his great Khmer parallel. The turn that Jayavarman gives to his personal onomastics and what it symbolizes is quite revealing of the disparity in problems and destinies between the two forms of worship and their circumstances.

These remarks could allow closer analysis of a name Mr. Coedès identifies as being that of a series of portrait-statues of Jayavarman VII with a particularly close relation to Khmer territory: *Jayabuddhama-hanatha*.

> Their name is made up on the one hand of the term *jayā*, "victory," which is Jayavarman's very name and marked all his foundations as with a seal, and on the other hand with the expression *mahānātha*, "the Great Saviour", which could apply to no one better than to Jayavarman VII since he had, ten years before [i.e., ten years before the erection of the Prah Khan stela, where these images are mentioned] saved the country by repelling the Cham invaders and carrying war into their own land.[22]

But this leaves the term *buddha* untranslated, even though it is very likely to be one of the principal elements — if not the essential element — in the combination. But in "the Great Protector with the

21. Charles Baudelaire. From "Bénédiction," the second poem of *Les Fleurs du Mal*. Quoted from memory.

22. G. Coedès, op. cit., p. 198.

Buddha of victory''—*nātha* being the ''refuge,'' the ''protector'' rather than the ''saviour'' (*trātar*), one fully recognizes the style of the reign and of its system of titles. The Protector adds a palladium, the Buddha, to his magical instruments, bringing him dramatically before his subjects, devoting himself jointly to them and to him; such a cult is transpersonal. At this point in the interpretation, by way of a parallel that does not seem hazardous, there appears a means of resolving the ambiguity that still marks the supernatural identification of Jayavarman VII, represented in the aspect of a Buddha under the central tower of the Bayon, but rather with the features and ornaments of the Bodhisattva Avalokiteçvara on all the external apparel of the temple and on the gates of the sacred town. Everything confirms the appellation Buddha-King chosen by Mr. Coedès for this great image. But how does it stand in the religious perspective of the reign and of the ''cosmic'' city? On the whole, despite a few secondary developments, the character of a Buddha preserves its original primacy over that of the Bodhisattvas. But is it necessarily so in the Angkor Thom setting? All this apparatus has a common denominator: the King. This, then, is no Buddhology in the absolute, but a local application; it is not doctrine, but action in line with this doctrine. Now, it is quite remarkable that Amitābha, the Buddha from whom Avalokiteçvara can be said to emanate, should not have a preeminent position in the epigraphy and the iconography of Jayavarman VII's reign: he is, for instance, second by far to the Buddha of Medicine, Bhaishajyaguru. Therefore, in this case the sequence Budda more than Bodhisattva is not prescribed by the context. Is the reverse order, Bodhisattva more than Buddha, in which the Bodhisattva as a basic principle would ''emit'' the Buddha, more likely to have been adopted locally with reference to the later magnified forms of belief, in which Avalokiteçvara becomes the Supreme Being? Here too epigraphic evidence hardly confirms the hypothesis, and nothing can be inferred from the material place granted to the Bodhisattva in this architecture-portrait since no other historical examples have been found. Yet the determining argument, which sets these various elements in proper perspective, is to be found in Chapter XXIV of the *Lotus of the True Law*, devoted, as the very title proclaims, to the metamorphoses of Avalokiteçvara, ''turned towards all directions (*Samantamukha*).'' He assumes at will all the shapes in which it is in the *karman* of beings to receive instruction or help. Thus he will appear under the features not only of Brahma, Indra, a King with the

Wheel (*çakravartin*), the head of an army, even a demon, but also of a ''Buddha-for-Oneself'' (*pratyekabuddha*) or of a perfectly accomplished Buddha. The unlimited efficacy of this universal compassion draws out of the sea of existences, for the benefit of creatures engulfed in it, precisely the appearances from which they can profit, thanks to this device (*upāya*) as much as, or even more than, to their own *karman*, which compels Avalokiteçvara to make such a choice.

We have just said extraction, and not abstraction: surely this is what one can see in Angkor, where all the material and moral conditioning of a redemptive victory is gradually ''churned''!—according to a great Vishnuite image expressing the action of royal Buddhism—out of a formerly desperate situation, through the transcendent merit and total devotion of the king: the ramparts, the causeways, the gates, the town, and finally the victory and the Buddha whose majesty consecrates it, come out of the symbolic sea of milk which has become a figure of *samsāra*. The truth which lies at the limits of these teachings can be glimpsed here: *nirvāna* is *samsāra* but it must be seen and acquired in *samsāra* through an external force that suddenly reveals itself as one's own. The fantastic artistic and mythological adventure of the Greater Vehicle, then, cancels itself by returning to the common good. Few epics have had such scope.

From Vedism to Buddhism and medieval Hinduism, from partially Iranized North-Western India, to the Hinduized kingdoms on the Pacific shores, these symbols have come a long way. It is their persistence more than the evolution of the forms of their expression which is puzzling, under the evolution of ideas and of history that is reflected in them. At the end of the series: symbols, visions, images—each step pointing less to a giving up of the previous pattern than to its readjustment—undoubtedly, we are beginning to be better prepared to approach the Angkor Thom of Jayavarman VII functionally and no longer only archaeologically. Under many guises, a face spontaneously appears everywhere, on the stone surface, just where nothing after all calls for it; this, for the external force is the surest way of being all gathered there, when the eyes turn to the symbolic edifices, with a prayer, in times of peril—whose extent had just been measured—or with thanksgiving in times of triumph and joy. The aegis of victory!

(Translated from the French by Martine Karnoouh-Vertalier)

The Hmong cross

A cosmic symbol in Hmong (Meo) textile designs

ERIK COHEN

The designs on Hmong (Meo) costume are renowned for their great variety, complexity, and richness. First noted by Bernatzik (124–126) in a study conducted prior to World War II, this has recently become fully manifest in two volumes on the crafts of the hill tribes of Thailand (Campbell et al.; Lewis and Lewis, 104 ff.). The very diversity of Hmong designs, however, apparently has hindered attempts at analyzing their cultural meaning. According to some authors, the nonrepresentational Hmong designs are stylized geometric representations of natural objects such as flowers and animals (Bernatzik, 124). This claim seems to find support from the names of some of the ornamental motifs as reported, for example, in a recent catalogue of Laotian Hmong refugee work in the United States (Dewhurst and MacDowell [eds.], 70–71; see also Campbell et al., 128–129). But the simple listing of names is unreliable: names can serve as mere identifiers, perhaps even conferred a *posteriori* simply as playful "interpretations" or "brand names" by which certain motifs are widely known, without thereby revealing either their origins or their hidden cultural meaning. Moreover, some motifs may have several different and unrelated names: in the above-mentioned catalogue, for example, one motif is called "seed," "chicken eye," and "water vegetable seed," another "rooftops," "snail," and "tiger" (Dewhurst and MacDowell [eds.], 71). This same multiplicity of names for motifs is found among the Yao, a tribal group culturally akin to the Hmong with whom the Hmong have many designs in common (Butler-Diaz, 14).

Students of Hmong culture seem to share a common, tacit assumption that the rich ornamentation of Hmong costume is merely decorative and devoid of more profound cultural meaning. All seem to deny that Hmong designs have a magical or religious significance. This has been explicitly stated for Yao designs (Lewis and Lewis, 138), despite the fact that these designs have been found to be closely related to Yao mythology (Butler-Diaz, 12–13). As a consequence of such assumptions, no student of Hmong culture has yet attempted to discern any general underlying regularity of form and symbolic meaning in the variety of Hmong motifs and ornamental designs.

In contrast to the prevailing tendency, this paper aims to demonstrate the existence of a significant relationship between basic Hmong designs and some wider magical and religious themes in Hmong culture. Specifically, I shall show

1. that underlying the apparently unlimited variety of Hmong textile designs, some common "ground forms" (de Beauclair, 205) can be discerned. I shall limit my discussion to one ground form that appears to be of particular significance, to be called here the "Hmong cross" (figs. 1, 2);
2. that this particular ground form has a magical and religious significance in Hmong ritual;

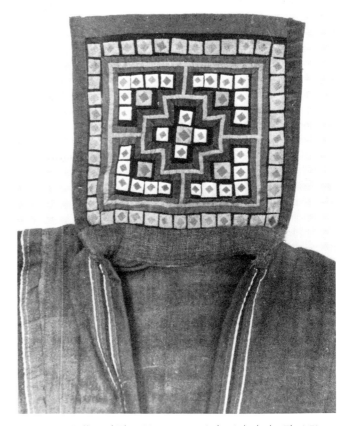

Figure 1. Collar of Blue Hmong man's burial cloth; Thai-Finn Handicrafts, Chiang Mai.

Figure 2. Sailor's collar of Blue Hmong woman's jacket (author's collection).

3. that the ground form of the cross is at root an iconic cosmological representation, possessing a deep-structural symbolic meaning in Hmong culture, of which, however, most or all members of the culture are generally unaware. Special attention will be paid to the designs on a most salient component of the Hmong woman's costume, the "sailor's collar" of her jacket (Lemoine, 1972b: 116–117; Lewis and Lewis, 108 and ill. on pp. 111–113);

4. that this ground form is preserved even in commercialized Hmong textile products, which are intended for an "external," mostly Western public that is unaware of and largely uninterested in Hmong culture.

The Hmong

The Hmong (or Meo in Thai, Miao in Chinese) are a partly sinicized (Walker [ed.], 19), semimigratory people, who in recent centuries have inhabited the higher altitudes of southern China, and the northern regions of Laos, Thailand, and Vietnam (see map in Lemoine, 1972a: 106). They practice swidden, or slash-and-burn, agriculture.[1] The Hmong are divided into about twelve exogamous clans; members of several clans usually reside in the same village (Lemoine, 1972b: 184–192). While in the past Hmong chiefs appear to have ruled over extensive territories, the village is presently the largest political unit. During approximately three thousand years of contact with and frequent persecution by the Chinese, the Hmong

acquired many elements of Chinese culture and incorporated them into their belief system.[2]

The main concentration of Hmong at present is still in southern China, where they number several millions. In Thailand and Laos, where they migrated only during the nineteenth century, they are much less numerous. In Thailand, there are about 58,000 Hmong living in villages (Lewis and Lewis, 10). Before the communist takeover in Laos, there were about 300,000 Hmong in that country (Yang Dao, 3); many of these, however, perished in the Indo-China war and a large number escaped to Thailand after the communist takeover in 1975. In 1971 about 60,000 Hmong still lived in refugee camps in Thailand, while about 100,000 have been resettled in Western countries (ibid: 18). Presently, there is only one camp left in Thailand—Ban Vinai in the province of Loei—with about 40,000 inhabitants. In this paper I shall be concerned only with the designs of the village Hmong in Thailand and the Hmong refugees from Laos.

The Hmong are divided into several major subdivisions, most of whose names are derived from the colors of the women's skirts. Thus, two main subdivisions of the Hmong in Laos and Thailand are the White and the Blue (Green)[3] Hmong. Here, our principal concern will be with the White Hmong, since more information is available to the author on their designs.

The Hmong have a complex religious system: they believe in and worship a variety of gods and spirits and practice a form of shamanism, whose major purpose is the healing of illnesses (Morechand; Chindarsi; Mottin, 1981). It is in the context of magic and religious ritual that the symbol of the Hmong cross is frequently encountered.

The Hmong cross

In the Hmong house there are usually several altars or "spirit platforms" devoted to a variety of spirits and other supernatural beings (Bernatzik, 202–205; Meo Handbook, 54; Chindarsi, 60–61; Mottin 1979: 24 ff.; Kasemani ill. 40, 42). The central altar in the house is decorated with three elongated papercuts (Mottin 1979,

1. On Hmong ecology, culture, and social structure, see Bernatzik; Binney; Schrock et al., 573–687; Geddes; Lemoine 1972b; Chindarsi; Cooper 1975, 1978; Tapp; Lewis and Lewis, 101–133.

2. On Hmong history, see Savina; Schrock et al, 579–586.
3. Most authors translate the self-appellation of this subdivision, Hmong Njua, as "Blue" Hmong: Lemoine (1972b), however, prefers "Green" Hmong (Hmong Vertue). The confusion stems from the fact that there is no distinction between our blue and green in Hmong color classification (cf. Lemoine 1972b: 116n).

ill. 6, opposite p. 24; Meo Handbook, 54, fig. 23, here reproduced in fig. 3). Referring to these papercuts, Lewis and Lewis (131) report that "the focus of the main altar in a Blue Hmong house is a piece of white paper about one hand-span square put on the wall opposite the doorway. At this altar, protection is sought for all of the people and animals of the household." Bernatzik (129, author's translation) similarly reports that Hmong altars are "decorated with bamboo-paper, into which simple ornaments are cut [by the Hmong] with their own punches." His meticulousness notwithstanding, Bernatzik appears to have paid little attention to the precise design on the paper; in his drawing (Bernatzik, 202, table 41) he renders it as a kind of stylized flower. This seems to be incorrect. A careful scrutiny of all available photographs of papercuts on Hmong altars in later publications indicates that they are invariably based on the ground form of the Hmong cross. This appears in three prototypes: a +-form, an ×-form and a double cross; the latter is obtained when the former two are superimposed upon one another (diagram 1.a1–3).

These prototypes of the Hmong cross do not appear on the altars in isolation. Rather, they tend to be repeated several times, over the elongated surface of the papercut; in some cases they form a simple row of +'s or ×'s (e.g., Kasemani, ill. on pp. 8, 40; Lewis and Lewis, 1984: 132, lower right ill.). On some papercuts, however, a more complex design of double crosses appears (as, for example, on the altar in fig. 3, also depicted in diagram 1.b1). This design is obtained when a piece of paper sized 1 × 2 is folded once (creating a square), then folded diagonally four more times, and the borders are cut out in a zigzag pattern. The design is of special importance for our study, since it presents a complicated, multistable image (Ihde, 66–79) that can be seen in at least three different ways: (1) as two rows of ×'s separated by horizontal and perpendicular lines; (2) as a series of three interlinked double crosses; or (3) as a middle double cross surrounded by a diamond-shaped square flanked by two halves of the same design (diagram 2.a–c).

The multistability of that design—which appears to be the most common one on Hmong altars—is of fundamental significance for the following exposition. This design harbors most, if not all, potential permutations of the Hmong cross and their variations in Hmong textile designs. It is therefore important to interpret the meaning of this prototype of the Hmong cross and the possible ways of seeing it.

It should be emphasized that my exposition of the different ways in which the design on diagram 1.b1 could be seen is not merely an arbitrary listing of possibilities derived from the visual characteristics of the design. Rather, the Hmong themselves also seem to see it in various ways, and to emphasize these differences in the manner in which they execute its permutations and variations. On the altars, they apparently see it primarily as possibility 2 above: as if to emphasize the way of seeing the design as three interlinked double crosses, each set into a diamond-shaped square, a small rosette sometimes appears in the central points of the crosses (as in fig. 3). This way of seeing the design is reinforced in another permutation, in which the diamond-shaped middle square is turned into a circle (e.g., in diagram 1.b2, taken from the papercuts on the altar in Lewis and Lewis, 132, lower left figure; the three encircled double crosses are thereby separated from one another and do not intersect, as they do in 1.b1). In other permutations, appearing particularly on the sailor's collars, the other

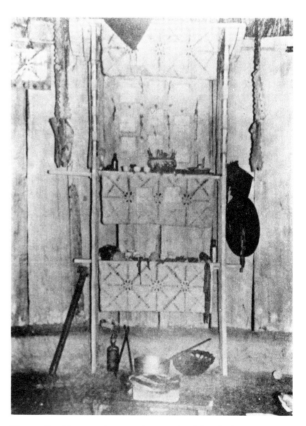

Figure 3. Hmong house altar or "spirit platform," from Meo Handbook 1969: 54, fig. 23.

DIAGRAM I : THE GROUND FORM OF THE HMONG CROSS & ITS PRINCIPAL
PERMUTATIONS ON ALTAR PAPERCUTS

a) The basic prototypes of the ground form

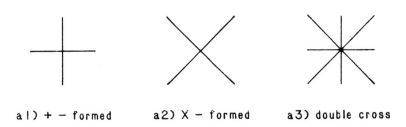

a1) + — formed   a2) X — formed   a3) double cross

b) Permutation of the prototypes on altar papercuts

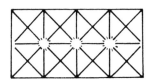   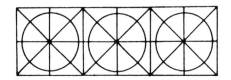

b1) Interlocking double crosses   b2) Encircled double crosses
(Meo Handbook, 1969:54,   (Lewis and Lewis, 1984:
Fig. 23)   132, lower left figure)

two ways of seeing the design of the multiple double crosses also appear, as we shall see.

To the fundamental question "What is the meaning of the Hmong cross and of its permutations in Hmong religion and worldview?" the voluminous literature on the Hmong offers no clues at all. I therefore propose my own interpretation, based on an analysis of the situations in which the cross is used in Hmong life. I shall first deal with the cross on papercuts on the altar and then refer to some of its other uses.

The Hmong probably acquired the custom of hanging papercuts on their altars from the Chinese. This is suggested in Graham's description of the altar in the houses of the Chu'an Miao of China. He reports that, while the Miao "completely reject the Chinese gods and their images" (Graham, 70), nevertheless "in some homes there is a family god representing the ancestors. It consists of a string of spirit money, hung up . . . in the imitation of, and a substitute for the Chinese house

god. . . ." (ibid: 71). The Chinese origin of the Hmong papercuts is further supported by the fact that they are made of bamboo paper (Bernatzik, 129; Campbell et al., 43), and that papercuts are a common Chinese folk art (e.g., Bewig 1978). In Thailand and Laos the paper used is white. Some Hmong in China and Tonkin, however, used red paper (de Beauclair, 101). This is a conspicuous color in Chinese culture; the Chinese usually use red paper for calligraphies to be hung up in houses on festive occasions (Graham, 145). The most important fact to note concerning the Hmong papercuts, however, is their location: they are hung in the center of the house altar, which itself is located on the wall precisely opposite the main entrance of the Hmong house (Graham, 71; cf. Lewis and Lewis, 131, and diagram of Hmong house on p. 122). The use of the papercuts is thus similar to the use of the magic "eight Diagrams" (or Trigrams, Chinese "Pa Kua") hung over the house door "as an emblem of felicity"

DIAGRAM 2 : BREAKDOWN OF MULTISTABLE IMAGE DESIGN ON
DIAGRAM I, FIG. b I)

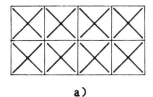 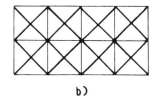 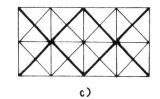

a)   b)   c)

(Williams, 149; Comber, plate no. 8). Magic mirrors too are similarly used in Chinese households: they are hung up on a wall or a roof "to reflect back evil influences" (Dennys, 45), and thus to protect the inhabitants. We can thus infer that the designs on the papercuts on Hmong altars serve essentially as symbols of protective magic.

This interpretation is corroborated by other situations registered in which the cross is used ritually among the Hmong. Following are some instances, related to shamanistic practices, which are reported in the literature.

The Hmong shaman, when practicing, wears the sign of the cross, made of white cloth, on his back. Bernatzik (177, table 40) renders it in the form of a +-formed cross. Schrock et al. (633), however, report that the "mark [on the shaman's back] resembles a cross or square ×"; and it also appears in the ×-form on an illustration in the Meo Handbook (57, fig. 24). The fact that the two forms of the cross, the +-formed and the ×-formed, here appear to serve the same function lends support to our contention that they are interchangeable prototypes of this basic Hmong symbol.

In another instance reported, the cross appears on the back of the jacket of a person who underwent a shamanistic healing ceremony; the symbolism here appears to be more complicated and differentiated. The fullest description and explication of this use of the cross can be found in Mottin's book on Hmong shamanism. His explanation of the drawing of two versions of the cross[4] is worth quoting in full:

Cross in several colors, about 8 cm in size, which the sick person preserves on his jacket until it falls to rags. It signifies that the route, or the routes, of reincarnation are

henceforth cut for the vital spirits of the sick. One of the stripes is black, the other white, the third red. The black is the color of the invisible world, the white, in opposition, is the visible world; with respect to the red, it frightens the demons and hence serves to cut the first two colors.

Mottin, 1971: 289, author's translation

The black-and-white cross thus, by preventing reincarnation, preserves the sick person's life. The red stripes form an additional protective device, which shelters the sick person from the demons. It is clear, hence, that the resulting double cross, as illustrated in Lewis and Lewis (111, lower right ill.), is a doubly protective sign. The single cross on the shaman's back can be interpreted, on the basis of Mottin's explanation, as a sign intended to frighten away the demons.

Other instances of the use of the basic prototypes of the Hmong cross have also been recorded. Thus, what seems to be a black-and-red ×-formed cross on a white square background appears on the back of the jacket of a male Hmong, on an illustration in Campbell et al.'s (57) book; the caption merely reads: "Jackets with appliqué cross to lengthen the life of the wearer." This is obviously another protective use of the symbol, but it is not clear whether it is identical to the preceding one.

It is thus obvious that the Hmong cross, as ritually used, is a protective magic sign, whether it appears on the back of the shaman's jacket as he engages in a perilous business, on the back of a sick or recently healed person, or elsewhere. The fact that in all these instances the cross is located on the back of the person is important, for the back is the most vulnerable part of

4. Unfortunately, Mottin's drawings are imprecise. He renders two versions of the Hmong cross, one a +-formed cross with a red vertical stripe crossing a black horizontal one, the other a black and

white ×-formed cross, over which a single vertical red stripe is drawn. I have never encountered the latter form of the symbol. The illustration in Lewis and Lewis, 111 (lower right ill.), appears to render its correct form: a vertical white stripe crossed by a horizontal black one, constituting a +-formed cross, and this in turn is overlaid by a red ×-formed cross; both crosses together form a double cross, as in diagram 1.a3.

the body. However, the Hmong cross is not merely an arbitrary magic sign; rather, it is an iconic symbol, whose meaning derives ultimately from Hmong religion and cosmology.

On a most general, "archetypal" level, the +-formed cross is a generic cosmic symbol, an iconic image of the basic structure of the world—its center and four cardinal directions (e.g., Eliade, 6–17); this virtually universal symbol can thus be interpreted to serve in Hmong culture, as it does elsewhere, as a microcosmic sign, whose function is to symbolize the basic homology between the cosmos, the house, and the human body. This interpretation helps explain the location of the cross either in the center of the altar opposite the main entrance to the house or in the center of the back of the shaman's or the healed person's body.

Our interpretation, based on the general meaning of the cross in many cultures, would be much reinforced if we found that the specific Hmong cosmological concepts also reflect the image of the cross. The literature on the Hmong, unfortunately, says little about their view of the world. The one explicit report on their cosmology, however—Chindarsi's study of the religion of the Blue Hmong—corroborates the above interpretation:

> The Miao believe that the earth is flat, and that four gods hold it up one at each corner. . . . The Hmong name four major directions: sunrise, sunset, upland and downland.

Upland

Sunset   Sunrise

Downland

> These four gods . . . are seen as largely responsible for the form of the earth as the Miao see it.
>
> Chindarsi, 19

This description of the Hmong view of the world and Chindarsi's diagram of it lends specific support to our general interpretation of the Hmong cross as a microcosmic symbol: the form of the Hmong image of the cosmos is obviously that of a cross. Moreover, Mottin's (1981: 289) statement quoted above—that the black and white colors of the stripes of the +-formed cross on the sick person's back represent respectively the invisible and the visible world—again clearly reinforces our interpretation: it suggests that the black-and-white cross is a Hmong variation of the Chinese Yin and Yang cosmic symbol.

The Hmong cross on costume: The ornamentation of the sailor's collar of the woman's jacket

The Hmong are adept at a variety of textile arts: they use the techniques of embroidery, appliqué, and batik with great skill and imagination.

All the literature on Hmong costume reports on the extraordinary richness and variety of its ornamentation (e.g., Bernatzik, 124 ff.; de Beauclair, 203–205; Lewis and Lewis, 104 ff.). However, the very variety of techniques of ornamentation, of motifs and their variations, and of colors and color combinations on Hmong textiles seems to have precluded any attempt at their systematic analysis. Only de Beauclair, dealing with the Pa Miao, a subdivision of the Hmong in China, has attempted a rudimentary stylistic classification. She distinguished two basic styles: one, which she considers as the original Pa Miao style, is essentially "geometrical"; the other consists of patterns representing flowers and animals in stylized form (de Beauclair, 205). Such a distinction would be difficult to make in the work of the Hmong of Thailand and Laos, however, since even flower and animal motifs, insofar as they exist, are usually "geometrized" almost out of recognition. In his study in the 1930s, Bernatzik (124) established that there were no figurative representations in the Hmong textile arts in Thailand. More recently, realistic figurative representations appeared on the commercialized textiles of Hmong refugees in camps in Thailand; these, however, are recent innovations in Hmong culture (Cohen, in press).

Within the geometric style, de Beauclair (205) distinguishes several "ground forms," such as triangles, rhombs, crosses, and meandering lines. These ground forms appear in many variations: "The variations consist of the changing filling of interstices and in the coloration" (ibid: 205, author's translation). These same "ground forms" are also found among the Hmong of Thailand and Laos; however, while de Beauclair mentions the cross just as one ground form among others, and interprets neither, at least some of those she mentions can be reduced to the symbol of the cross or to one of its permutations.

The cross, in its various permutations, is not only the most frequently used, but also the most distinguishing of the Hmong designs. The high prominence of the cross in Hmong design is attested to by the fact that the Yao, who also use it, refer to it as the "White Meo design" (Butler-Diaz, 37, ill. 58). Butler-Diaz herself calls the design "Meo Forks," a designation that is also used by others. This "Meo Forks" design is also frequently used by the Hmong (Meo) (fig. 2), and occupies a central position in their own ornamental repertoire. It is significant that two other Yao designs that are named after the White Meo also embody the ground form of the cross (ibid: 37, ill. 55 and 56).

The cross and its permutations appear particularly frequently on one of the most prominent and distinctive components of the Hmong costume: the "sailor's collar" of the Hmong woman's jacket (Lewis and Lewis, 111). It is also found on many other parts of the Hmong costume, for example, on the coin bags of the Hmong festive attire (fig. 4; Lewis and Lewis, 110, lower right figure), on the ornamental bands of the Hmong woman's "apron," on the Hmong baby hat (Lewis and Lewis, 125, upper left figure), and, significantly, on the upper part of the Hmong baby carrier (Lewis and Lewis, 107, upper left and middle ills.). On both the sailor's collar and the baby carrier the cross occupies a similar position: it is located on the back of the woman, or of the baby as it is carried on the woman's back. Significantly, this location is similar to that occupied by the cross on the jacket of the shaman or the recently healed person. The cross is not as prominent on any part of the Hmong male's costume. Since women and babies are more vulnerable than adult males, it can again be inferred that the cross on the former's costume plays a protective role.

Authorities agree on the prominence of the "sailor's collar" on the Hmong woman's costume. Thus, Bernatzik (320) states that this is the most remarkable component of the woman's attire, and Lemoine (1972b: 116) reports that the most exquisite decorations are found on that collar. This richly embroidered or appliquéd rectangular ornament is frequently worn on the inside of the neck, so that its design cannot be seen without turning it over, a habit that is apparently intended to preserve it (Bernatzik, 320; Lemoine, 1972b: 116). The variety of the collars is enormous, as can be seen from the rich sample of collars in the Lewises' book (Lewis and Lewis, 112–113), but most (about two-thirds) are based on the Hmong cross in one permutation or another. The great frequency with which the Hmong use the cross in their ornamentation of textiles—especially on the woman's sailor's collar— may have escaped the attention of the students of Hmong art because it appears in a large number of permutations and variations that in turn are frequently multiplied over the face of the cloth several times, creating distinctive patterns. Only careful analysis,

Figure 4. Hmong traditional coin bags (author's collection).

therefore, can show that apparently diverse designs are structurally related to the basic prototypes of the Hmong cross.

The permutations and variations of the cross on Hmong costume and especially on the sailor's collars are much greater than those found on the crosses in ritual use. This state of affairs confirms the observation made by Campbell et al. (43) that "most of [the] religious articles [made by the hill tribes, including the Hmong] are simple in design and involve none of the skill devoted to secular crafts." Indeed, Hmong women vie with each other to evolve and execute the most original and complex ornamental designs; their inventiveness is widely appreciated in Hmong society (Bernatzik, 125–126). It is therefore the more remarkable that, despite innovations and outside influences, the basic ground form of the Hmong cross should be so frequently reproduced in their designs.

On the Hmong coin bags a single Hmong cross ordinarily constitutes the center of the design (cf. fig. 4). On the sailor's collars, this is generally not the case; rather, in the simplest designs, a series of two, three, or more +-formed, ×-formed, or double crosses appears horizontally arranged, sometimes resembling their layout on the papercuts on the house altar. Thus, in figure 5a, a row of three thin, green, embroidered, ×-like crosses, separated by small white diamonds, forms the basic design of the collar. The design on figure 5b is based on three +-like crosses. The most common design on the collars, however, is based on a pair of ×-formed crosses (figs. 2, 5c). While on some collars these ×-formed crosses are separated and hence clearly recognizable, on others they merge into one another and create a zigzag pattern, in which the individuality of the constituent crosses gets lost (fig. 5d). On some collars the two simple prototypes of the cross (the + and ×) merge into a double cross, as in figure 6, where the white lines form two +-formed crosses, while the broad dark bands form a pair of ×-formed crosses. In the center of that collar, a third +-formed cross can be seen, resembling that in figure 1; it is surrounded by an octagon of broad red bands that also constitute the inner arms of the two ×'s flanking it. Here we have an instance of a multistable design on a collar, closely resembling that on the altar papercuts.

Some other designs based on a pair of double crosses are also multistable. The multistability is sometimes produced by the combined effect of line and color, and therefore is not wholly discernible in black-and-white reproductions. Thus, the design in figure 7a can be seen as two double crosses, the arms of which are formed by the alternative red and green coloration of the little triangles of the design, which surround the

Figure 6. Sailor's collar of White Hmong woman's jacket (author's collection).

crosses' centers (represented in black-and-white in diagram 3a). However, if one concentrates merely on the horizontal and vertical lines defining the edges of the more saliently colored red triangles (the dark ones in diagram 3a), each cross becomes a swastika (diagram 3b).

The swastika and the sauvastika (reverse swastika; see Williams, 377–378) are, of course, widely disseminated Indian and Buddhist symbols, commonly found throughout the area. Williams (378), in fact, argues that the swastika, the Latin cross (i.e., the +-formed cross) and St. Andrew's cross (i.e., the ×-formed cross) are all derived from the same ancient source, the Aryan or Vedic sun and fire worship. The design of the collar in figure 7a in fact provides an unexpected corroboration of this argument, since it conjoins all three of these forms: the swastika emerges from the double cross (i.e., from the combination of a + and an ×) and thus in fact becomes one of its permutations.[5] The swastika, however, appears also independently on other Hmong collars, either simply, as in figure 7b, or in more complex, meandering permutations,[6] as in figure 8. The commercialized version of the latter design will be discussed below.

The analysis so far, however, does not exhaust the possible ways in which the design on figure 7a may be

5. This should not be construed to mean that the + or the × in any sense *precede* the emergence of the swastika; mine is a purely synchronic analysis and has no bearing on the process of development of Hmong symbolism.

6. The design on figure 8 strikingly resembles, but is not identical with, the Chinese meander pattern (Williams, 120, pattern no. 11). This similarity is further evidence of the close relationship between Chinese and Hmong designs.

Figure 5. Sailor's collars of White Hmong woman's jacket (author's collection). 5a. Upper left. 5b. Lower left. 5c. Upper right. 5d. Lower right.

seen. Thus, if one concentrates on the red triangles as a configuration, one gets two red ×-formed crosses with triangular arms resembling those of a windmill (the dark triangles in diagram 3c); this form of the cross is very common in Hmong textile ornamentation (e.g., Lewis and Lewis, 115, lower right ill. of Hmong man's jacket). Finally, if one concentrates on the center of the design, one gets a zigzag pattern of light lines, with a +-formed cross surrounded by a diamond-shaped blue in the middle, flanked by six half-diamonds (diagram 3d).

We have seen above that from one perspective, the Hmong altar papercuts can be seen as rows of simple ×-formed crosses, while from another they appear as double crosses surrounded by diamond-shaped squares (diagrams 2a, 2b). These possibilities are also inherent in the design on the collar on figure 9a, which reproduces most features of the papercuts—omitting, however, the +-formed crosses. It can be seen as consisting of two rows of four small ×-formed crosses, or as three large interlinking ×'s, each surrounded by three diamond-shaped squares. This latter design serves, in turn, as a point of departure for a large number of further permutations, successively ever more remote from the basic prototypes of the Hmong cross, as illustrated in diagram 1.a1–3. Here only some of these permutations will be shown, by way of example, but the presentation is by no means exhaustive. We begin with the triple ×'s surrounded by diamond-shaped squares (diagram 4a). This design is varied on the collar in figure 9b in that there appear only two diamond-shaped squares, which intersect in the middle of the collar. The small diamond formed by their intersection is rendered in a different color, as if to stress the intersection, while the center of each of the two ×'s is emphasized by a rosette (diagram 4b).

In a further permutation, the diamond-shaped square is emphasized at the expense of the cross. Thus, on the collar in figure 9c, the two blue, diamond-shaped squares are flanked by the remnants of the arms of two ×-formed crosses (diagram 4c). In a more complex

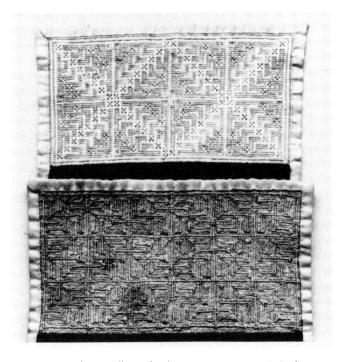

Figure 7. Sailor's collars of White Hmong woman's jacket (author's collection). a. Above. b. Below.

permutation (fig. 9d), the diamond-shaped square contains a smaller, regular square from the corners of which protrude the arms of the ×'s (diagram 4d); the ×'s are also inscribed inside each of the smaller squares. When the square inscribed in each diamond is enlarged and made to intersect with it, as on the collar in figure 10a, the arms of the ×'s disappear and the Hmong double cross is indicated only by the corners of the eight-cornered star so created (diagram 4e).

While in the above series of permutations the point of departure was the ×-formed cross, designs based on the +-formed cross manifest similar permutations. We start with the double cross on the collar in figure 6. As indicated above, the center of the design can be seen as a + surrounded by an octagon, formed of the inner

DIAGRAM 3 : ANALYSIS OF MULTISTABLE DESIGN ON ILL.(14)

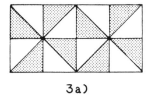

3a)

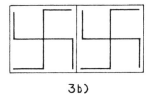

3b)

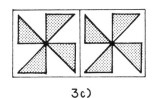

3c)

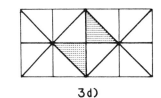

3d)

Figure 8. Sailor's collar of White Hmong woman's jacket (private collection).

arms of the two broad dark ×'s (diagram 5a). This way of seeing the design may, in turn, serve as a point of departure for the interpretation of permutations. Thus, the design on the collar in figure 10b can be seen as

two white crosses surrounded by two red octagons; a further, thin white cross can be seen in the middle of the collar (diagram 5b). The dark components of the octagons are decorated by S-formed "snails" (Dewhurst and MacDowell [eds.], 71). Snails or coils in various forms are an extremely common Hmong motif (Campbell et al., 127). Significantly, however, they appear on many collars around a central +-formed cross, in the same place as the dark bands on the collars in figures 6 and 10b. Thus, in figure 10c four snails surround a pair of pointed crosses (diagram 5c); and in figure 10d the +-formed crosses are created by four heartlike shapes with coils at their ends (diagram 5d). It thus appears that the very common Hmong "elephant foot" design (Dewhurst and MacDowell [eds], 70) is a remote permutation of the Hmong cross, with snails taking the place of the octagon surrounding the central +-formed cross.

Another line of permutations of the Hmong cross can be seen as starting with an arrangement of five small ×'s or +'s that merge into a big × (or +) with crossed arms (figs. 11a, 5a, and diagrams 6a, b). The same design is also frequently appliquéd on the batiked Hmong baby carriers (Lewis and Lewis, 107, upper left

DIAGRAM 4 : THE PERMUTATIONS OF THE X-FORMED CROSS
SURROUNDED BY A DIAMOND-SHAPED SQUARE

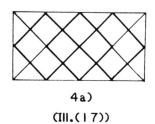

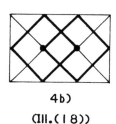

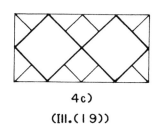

4a)
(III.(17))

4b)
(III.(18))

4c)
(III.(19))

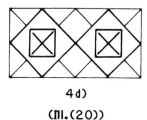

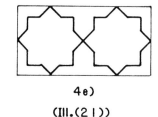

4d)
(III.(20))

4e)
(III.(21))

DIAGRAM 5 : THE PERMUTATIONS OF THE + −FORMED CROSS SURROUNDED BY
AN OCTAGON

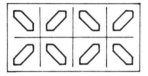

5a)
(III.(13),below)

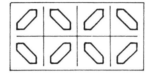

5b)
(III.(22))

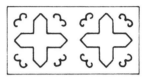

5c)
(III.(23))

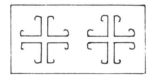

5d)
(III.(24))

Figure 9. Sailor's collars of White Hmong woman's jacket.
a. Upper left. b. Upper right. c. Lower left. d. Lower right.

Figure 10. Sailor's collars of White Hmong woman's jacket
(author's collection). a. Upper left. b. Upper right. c. Lower
left. d. Lower right.

Figure 11. Sailor's collars of White Hmong woman's jacket (private collection). a. Upper left. b. Upper right. c. Lower left. d. Lower right.

and middle ills.). If the arms of the four smaller crosses on diagram 6b are extended until they meet (diagram 6c), the emerging design (diagram 6d) becomes an ×-formed cross surrounded by a diamond-shaped square, identical in form with those found in diagram 4a (fig. 9a). This example indicates that there are complex structural affinities between the various lines of permutation of the Hmong cross.

Until now I have argued that many concrete Hmong textile designs on sailor's collars can be interpreted as permutations of the basic prototypes of the Hmong cross. The last and most speculative topic to be discussed here is the relationship between the ground form of the Hmong cross and some other ground forms of Hmong textile design. I do not have a complete inventory of such ground forms, but at least two kinds of design in addition to the cross are distinctive enough

and frequent enough to merit this designation, particularly an inverted V design commonly found on sailor's collars (figs. 11b, c) (compare to the lower half of the design on the collar in fig. 6), and a mazelike design, which has been variously called "reverie" (*bouw chua*, Campbell et al., 128–129), or in another variation "worm track" (*cua nab*, Dewhurst and MacDowell [eds.], 70). Both of these ground forms can be in some way related to the Hmong cross.

The inverted V design can be interpreted simply as a bisected ×. It should be noted, however, that the V is always inverted, that is, it reproduces the lower, rather than the upper, half of the ×. I was unable to detect the symbolic significance of this particular ground form, however.

The ground form of the maze lends itself more easily to interpretation. Symbolically, the maze appears to be a polar opposite of the cross: if the latter is a cosmic symbol, that is, the basic structure of the ordered world, the former symbolizes chaos. Its "unordered," unstructured, or "liminal" (Turner 1977) character is indicated by the above-quoted name "reverie." It is interesting, therefore, that the maze pattern is often developed from the cross, or is intertwined with it in a complex ornament. The maze design often starts with a +-formed cross as illustrated by the pattern on the illustration in Campbell et al. (128–129) and on the collar in figure 11d. On some collars, the maze pattern appears as a filling between the familiar ×-formed crosses. An even more complex intertwining between the two contrasting ground forms obtains on the collar in figure 9c. Here the dark-colored elements of a maze pattern in fact create the outlines of meandering

DIAGRAM 6 : THE TRANSFORMATION OF THE DESIGN ON III.(26) INTO THE DESIGN ON III.(17)

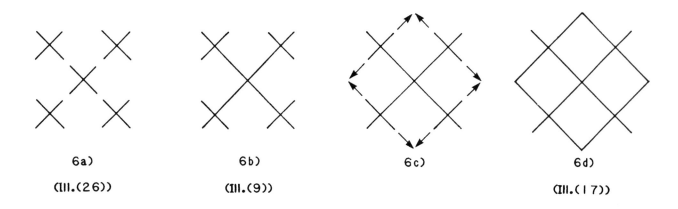

6a)   6b)   6c)   6d)

(III.(26))   (III.(9))   (III.(17))

sauvastikas, but they also form dark, diamond-shaped squares that fill up the larger, light-colored diamonds. These, in turn, with their protruding arms, form a variation of the Hmong cross (diagram 4c). In a variety of ways, then, the ground forms of the cross and of the maze intertwine with one another in complex designs, which could well be interpreted as attempts at integrating the opposites of cosmos and chaos, or of structure and flow.

The Hmong cross on commercialized Hmong textile products

Following the Hmong insurgence in northern Thailand in the mid-1960s (Abrams), many Hmong villages were resettled in the lowlands. Among the steps taken to rehabilitate these resettled Hmongs (Hearn), various Thai and foreign relief organizations and individual local middlemen initiated the commercialization of Hmong textile products (Cohen 1983: 8). In the mid-1970s, tens of thousands of Hmong refugees from Laos, many of whom had for years fought the Pathet Lao, fled into Thailand after the communist takeover of that country. Following this influx and internment in refugee camps, the production of the Hmong commercialized textiles was vastly expanded. This expansion engendered a veritable explosion of forms, variations, colors, and color combination on Hmong products that flourished for a number of years; only in the 1980s did it begin to undergo increasing standardization and routinization (Cohen, 1982, 1983, and in press). Although remuneration was low, the refugee women—with ample time on their hands and their basic needs supplied by the UN commissioner for refugees— applied themselves to an imaginative development and embellishment of their traditional ornamental designs with new materials, and on new products.

Despite the apparent proliferation of new designs on the commercialized textiles, in virtually all of them the ground form of the cross can be discovered, as, for example, on almost all of the twelve designs of figure 12, taken from the catalogue of one of the relief organizations marketing the refugee crafts, Camacrafts.

In the simplest cases, the design of the cross was reproduced on a commercialized product in one of its traditional permutations. In some such instances, the basic prototype of the Hmong cross appears in high relief without further elaboration, as, for example, the ×-formed cross in figure 13, where it is worked out in

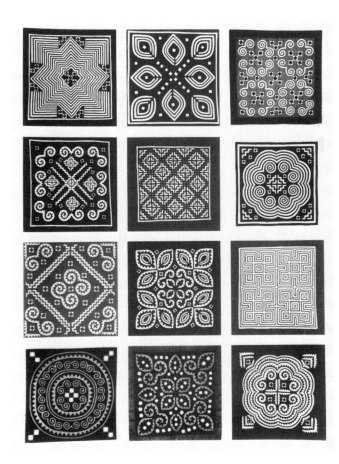

Figure 12. Samples of Hmong commercialized "squares" (from Camacrafts 1984: 13).

broad, parallel appliquéd bands of green and white. In other instances, the cross design is merely indicated by the coloration of an underlying pattern, as in figure 14, where the image of an × emerges from the contrasting white and red coloration of the small +-formed crosses of the underlying pattern. Finally, there are instances in which the prototype of the Hmong cross is barely recognizable without careful inspection of the design, that is, the double cross formed by the leaflike shapes in figure 15.

Even more complicated are some of the designs on commercialized products derived from the various permutations of the ground form of the Hmong cross that were discussed above. The ×-like cross surrounded by a diamond-shaped square (sailor's collar on figs. 9a, b and diagrams 4a, 6d) serves as the basis of a wide variety of designs on such products (cf., for example, the illustrations in Dewhurst and MacDowell [ed.], 29). A variation of that design appears on the

Figure 13. Hmong commercialized "patch," probably from Ban Vinai Refugee Camp (author's collection).

Figure 14. Hmong commercialized "patch," probably from Ban Vinai Refugee Camp (author's collection).

"square" in figure 16, where the ×-formed cross is contained *within* the diamond, so that its arms do not protrude from it as in figure 15. Other permutations of that same design, presented in diagram 4, also appear in different variations on some commercialized articles. Thus, on the pillow cover in figure 17, the permutation of diagram 4c appears in a heavily embellished variation: in place of each single line, there appear several alternating appliquéd brown and white lines, but the basic form is that of a diamond with the protruding arms of an ×-formed cross. The design also appears in Dewhurst and MacDowell ([eds.], 70) under the name "spider web"; since such a "web" is found only on commercialized products, this name is probably a mere designation without symbolic significance.

Other permutations of the Hmong cross underwent a similar process of embellishment in their commercialized variations. Thus, the starlike permutation on the collar of figure 10a and diagram 4d is in its commercialized variation developed into a more complex design through the multiplication of parallel appliquéd lines.

While in all these examples the basic "traditional" designs are easily discerned, in some of the more extreme commercialized variations they are barely recognizable. Thus, the design on the appliquéd pillow cover in figure 18 is a variation of the diamond with protruding arms, the coils forming the diamond, and the small ×'s the protruding arms of a large ×.

The swastika-formed permutation of the Hmong cross has also been used as the basis of interesting commercialized variations: thus, the design on the collar in figure 8 is quadrupled on the appliquéd "square" in figure 19. The four identical designs form a weakly emphasized +-formed central cross. Each quarter reproduces the basic design of figure 8, embellished by alternately colored lines, which fill out the whole surface of the square. The design on the quarters has also been used on other commercialized Hmong products, as, for example, on the "square" illustrated in Dewhurst and MacDowell ([eds], 48–49).

Figure 15. Hmong commercialized "square," Ockenden House, Nam Yao Refugee Camp Project (private collection).

Figure 16. Hmong commercialized "square," probably from Nam Yao Refugee Camp (author's collection).

A particularly high degree of complexity is achieved on the appliquéd "square" in figure 20. The multistable design on this square integrates two permutations of the Hmong cross—the swastika and the diamond with protruding arms—all through a sophisticated use of alternating colored lines. At the center of the design is a sauvastika (diagram 7a) inside which nestle four crosses, as on the collar in figure 11d; however, they are surrounded by alternating colored lines, which fill out the whole surface of the square. These lines give rise to a pattern that forms a central diamond with protruding arms (diagram 7b); within that central diamond the lines create a swastika (diagram 7c), whose arms fill out the whole area of the diamond.

Many other designs on commercialized Hmong textiles could be similarly analyzed as variations of one or another of the traditional permutations of the ground form of the Hmong cross. Catalogues such as that of Camacrafts (1984) or Dewhurst and MacDowell (eds.) show this clearly. Enough has been said, however, to show that the apparent explosion of new and varied

ornamental forms characteristic of the recent "baroque" of commercialized Hmong textiles is deceptive. The Hmong have embellished and elaborated their traditional designs, but on the whole they have preserved their ground forms; their nonrepresentational commercialized designs hence have remained essentially orthogenetic (Redfield and Singer), despite external influences and the pressures of the market.[7] And among the traditional designs on commercialized Hmong products, no ground form is more frequently and consistently encountered than the Hmong cross.

Conclusion

In this paper, a symbolic interpretation of the wide variety of the apparently merely decorative designs on Hmong costumes has been presented. For that purpose, the most common ground form underlying these

7. The only completely new development in commercialized Hmong textiles is the emergence of figurative representations. This is dealt with in Cohen, in press.

Figure 17. Hmong commercialized "square," probably from Nam Yao Refugee Camp (author's collection).

Figure 18. Hmong commercialized pillow cover, probably from Nam Yao Refugee Camp (author's collection).

designs, that of the Hmong cross, has been singled out for analysis. As it is in other regions and cultures, the ground form of the cross in Hmong culture is basically a microcosmic symbol—it symbolizes the basic structure of the universe, as conceived in Hmong mythology (Chindarsi, 19). However, it appears in several permutations and many variations that are specific to Hmong culture. It seems, indeed, that the Hmong proclivity to innovate and vary the presentations of their symbols helped to conceal the underlying symbols on their ornaments from students of their culture.

I have shown that the microcosmic symbol of the cross serves in Hmong ritual a protective magic function; I have argued by extension that it performs the same function when used in the designs on Hmong costumes. This argument is supported by the following facts: (1) the cross is placed on a similar spot when tacked ritually onto people's clothes and when used as ornament on their costume; (2) it is oriented in a direction from which a place may be most threatened or a person most vulnerable: opposite the entrance of a

house, or on the back of a person; (3) it is used by people most in need of protection: the shaman when performing, the sick or recently healed person, and on the clothes of women and babies (but *not* of Hmong men).

No relationship was discovered between the ground form of the Hmong cross, or its permutations and variations, and Hmong social organization; in this respect, the Hmong differ from other, more isolated ethnic groups, whose designs reflect basic structural features of their society (e.g., Adams). I speculate that the reason for this discrepancy can be found in the exogenous origin of Hmong cosmic symbolism and of the Hmong cross, which may well have been adopted from the Chinese, under whose influence the Hmong lived for hundreds of years (e.g., Geddes, 9–12). This explanation is supported by the close resemblance between some Chinese and Hmong ornamental designs, but needs further investigation.

Finally, in this paper only one—albeit the most widespread—ground form of Hmong design has been explored. While the existence of several others has been noted, and the links between them and the Hmong cross indicated, no systematic ''vocabulary'' of such ground forms and their interconnections has been proposed. The preparation of such a vocabulary may well yield deeper insights into the connections between Hmong cosmology, mythology, magic, and design.

Figure 19. Hmong commercialized ''square,'' Thai Tribal Crafts, Chiang Mai.

Figure 20. Hmong commercialized ''square,'' Ban Vinai Refugee Camp (author's collection).

DIAGRAM 7 : ANALYSIS OF THE MULTISTABLE DESIGN OF III.(40)

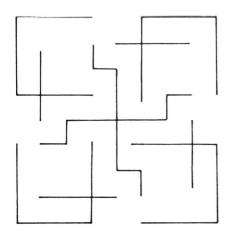

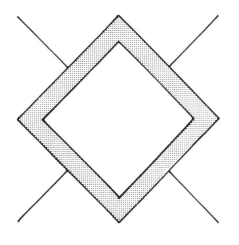

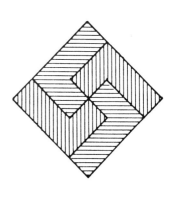

7a)
Central sauvastika
(also III.(16))

7b)
Central diamond with protruding
x-formed arms

7c)
Swastika within
central diamond

This paper is based on data of a study of the commercialization of the arts of the hill tribes in northern Thailand, collected during several field trips between 1977 and 1984. The study was part of a larger project supported by grants from the Harry S. Truman Research Institute for the Advancement of Peace at the Hebrew University of Jerusalem and, for 1979, by a grant from Stiftung Volkswagenwerk. Their support is hereby gratefully acknowledged. Thanks are due to U. Almagor for his comments on an earlier draft of this paper. For complementary publications, see Cohen 1982, 1983, and in press. All diagrams are by Tamar Soffer, Department of Geography, the Hebrew University of Jerusalem.

REFERENCES

Abrams, A.
1970. "With the White Meo Tribesmen in Thailand," *The New Leader* 6.7.1970: 8–11.

Adams, M. J.
1980. "Structural Aspects of East Sumbanese Art," in J. J. Fox (ed.), *The Flow of Life: Essays on Eastern Indonesia*. Cambridge, Mass.: Harvard University Press, pp. 208–220.

Bernatzik, H. A.
1947. *Akha und Meau: Probleme der angewandten Völkerkunde in Hinterindien*. Innsbruck: Wagner'sche Univ.-Buchdruckerei.

Bewig, J.
1978. *Chinesische Papierschnitte*. Hamburg: Museum für Völkerkunde.

Binney, G. A.
1968. *The Social and Economic Organization of Two White Meo Communities in Northern Thailand*. Washington, D.C.: Advanced Research Projects Agency (mimeo).

Butler-Diaz, J.
1981. *Yao Design in Northern Thailand*, rev. ed. Bangkok: Siam Society.

Camacrafts.
1984. *Camacrafts: Handicrafts from Northern Thailand* (catalogue). Bangkok: CAMA.

Campbell, M. et al.
1978. *From the Hands of the Hills*. Hong Kong: Media Transasia.

Chindarsi, N.
1976. *The Religion of the Hmong Njua*. Bangkok: Siam Society.

Cohen, E.
1982. "Refugee Art in Thailand," *Cultural Survival Quarterly* 6(4): 40–42.

———.
1983. "The Dynamics of Commercialized Arts: The Meo and Yao of Northern Thailand," *J. of the National Research Council of Thailand* 15(1): part II, 1–34.

———.
(In press). "Hmong (Meo) Commercialized Refugee Art: From Ornament to Picture."

Comber, L.
1969. *Chinese Magic and Superstitions in Malaya*, 4th (rev.) ed. Singapore: Eastern University Press.

Cooper, R. G.
1975. "Resource Scarcity and the Hmong Response: A Study of Settlement and Economy in Northern Thailand," Ph.D. diss., Univ. of Hull.

———.
1978. "Dynamic Tension: Symbiosis and Contradiction in Hmong Social Relations," in J. Clammer (ed.), *The New Economic Anthropology*. London: Macmillan, pp. 138–175.

de Beauclair, I.
1970. *Tribal Cultures of Southwest China*. Taipei: Oriental Cultural Service.

Dennys, N. B.
1968. *The Folklore of China*. Amsterdam: Oriental Pr. [1876].

Dewhurst, C. K., and M. MacDowell (eds.).
1983. *Michigan Hmong Arts: Textiles in Transition*, Michigan State Univ., Publications of the Museum, Folk Cultural Series, vol. 3, no. 2.
——— et al.
1983. "Michigan Hmong Textiles," in Dewhurst and MacDowell (eds.), 1983, pp. 15–25.

Eliade, M.
1971. *The Myth of the Eternal Return*. Princeton, N.J.: Princeton Univ. Pr.

Geddes, W. R.
1976. *Migrants of the Mountains*. Oxford: Clarendon Pr.

Graham, D. C.
1961. *Folk Religion in Southwest China*. Smithsonian Miscellaneous Coll., vol. 142(2). Washington, D.C.: Smithsonian Pr.

Hearn, R. M.
1974. *Thai Government Programs in Refugee Relocation and Resettlement in Northern Thailand*. Auburn, N.Y.: Thailand Books.

Ihde, D.
1979. *Experimental Phenomenology*. New York: Putnam & Sons.

Kasemani, Ch. [B.E.]
2527. *Ban Meo* [The Hmong House]. Chiang Mai: Tribal Research Center (in Thai).

Lemoine, J.
1972a. "L'initiation du mont chez les Hmong, I," *L'Homme*, 12: 105–143.

———.
1972b. *Un Village Hmong Vert du Haut Laos*, Paris C.N.R.S.

Lewis, P., and E. Lewis.
1984. *Völker im Goldenen Dreieck* (People of the Golden Triangle). Stuttgart: Ed. Hansjörg Meyer.

Meo Handbook.
1969. *Meo Handbook*. Bangkok: Joined Thai-U.S. Military Research and Development Center.

Morechand, G.
1968. "Le chamanisme Hmong," *Bull. de l'Ecole Francaise d'Extreme-Orient*, 64.

Mottin, J.
1979. *Fête du Nouvel An chez les Hmong Blanc de Thaïlande*. Bangkok: Don Bosco.

———.
1981. *Allons faire le tour du ciel et de la terre: le chamanisme des Hmong vu dans les texts*. Bangkok: Don Bosco.

Redfield, R., and M. Singer.
1969. "The Cultural Role of Cities," in R. Sennett (ed.), *Classic Essays in the Culture of Cities*. New York: Appleton-Century-Crofts, pp. 206–233.

Savina, F. M.
1930. *Histoire de Miao*. Hong Kong: Impr. de la Société de Missions-Ètrangeres.

Schrock, L., et al.
1970. *Minority Groups in Thailand*. Washington, D.C.: Dept. of the Army, pamphlet no. 550-107.

Tapp, N.
1982. "The Relevance of Telephone Directories to a Lineage-Based Society: A Consideration of Some Messianic Myths among the Hmong," *J. of the Siam Society*, 70(1–2): 114–127.

Turner, V.
1977. "Process, System and Symbol: A New Anthropological Synthesis," *Daedalus* 106: 61–79.

Williams, C. A. S.
1960. *Encyclopedia of Chinese Symbolism and Art Motives*. New York: Julian Pr.

Yang Dao
1982. "Why Did the Hmong Leave Laos?" in B. T. Dowring and D. P. Olney (eds.), *The Hmong in the West*. Minneapolis: Refugee Study Project, Center of Urban and Regional Affairs, Univ. of Minnesota, pp. 3–18.

Figure 17. Seibal Stelae 7. Eighth century. Stelae 5 and 7 at Seibal are in fact wall panels that were set to frame the staircase of Structure A-10, a building on one of the main plazas. Both feature ballplayers, and together the two panels suggest that ball was played on the A-10 stairs.

The classic Maya ballgame and its architectural setting

A study of relations between text and image

MARY ELLEN MILLER and STEPHEN D. HOUSTON

The Mesoamerican ballgame has long been a subject of fascination for the European and modern viewer.[1] At the time of the Conquest, Spanish conquistadors admired the skill and stamina of the Aztec athletes who played the vigorous game. Even the rubber ball, with its greater ability to bounce than any other material then known to man, was a wonder to a world that had never before known this material. European games played with a ball were greatly transformed by the incorporation of the rubber ball. (How different tennis would be today were it played with a *leather* ball, as it was before the discovery of the New World!) Many new games were invented, and eventually they superseded the old sport in Mesoamerica.

Associated with human sacrifice and religious practices that the Spanish deemed idolatrous, the playing of the ballgame eventually vanished from much of Mexico. The Prehispanic game, however, continues to intrigue the modern world—perhaps in part because of the human sacrifice known to occur in certain Aztec games. Many modern sports breed violence among players and even spectators, but we tell ourselves that injury and death are not condoned, only accidental. Yet the recurrence of violence in these sports leads us to consider whether they are inherently violent, as well as their resemblance to ritualized warfare. Although we do not expect football players to die on the field, we take sport very seriously, and in moments of intense conflict, fans, coach, and players alike use words such as *killing* and *death*. A ballgame played for life and death stakes appeals to mankind's darkest side, and thus only whets our thirst to know more about the ancient game, where violence and death were sanctioned.

As played by the Aztecs in sixteenth-century Mexico, the ballgame was enacted and understood on several levels: as a sandlot sport, indulged in by most adolescent boys; as a public game, eagerly gambled on by avid spectators; as a sort of gladiatorial ritual, in which captives might be killed; as a reenactment of cosmic conflict between Venus and the sun; and as a game that the gods themselves might play. The game

itself may have taken many forms. Among most Mesoamerican peoples, formal games were played in a special kind of building, the ballcourt, generally formed by two parallel structures, often with supplementary walls or structures that demarcated an end zone. The playing surfaces encompassed a ground surface in the shape of an open or closed letter *I* as well as the vertical or sloping side walls. Points were scored either by driving the ball into an end zone or other designated area or by hurtling the ball through a high, relatively small ring placed in a side wall.

According to sixteenth-century chronicles, the Aztecs built two ballcourts within the limits of the sacred precinct of Tenochtitlan. One was reserved for play by the gods, the other for humans. A surviving illustration of the precinct shows only one court (and only seven of the seventy-eight temples reputedly within the compound as well), which adjoins the skull rack, suggesting some sort of relationship between the game and human sacrifice, particularly decapitation. In one late manuscript in Prehispanic style, the ballcourt itself was seen as a place of grisly skulls, reinforcing the notion of sacrifice in ballgame (fig. 1); in other records, skulls are shown as balls, as if to suggest that the heads and skulls of those sacrificed in the aftermath of the

Figure 1. Page 68, Codex Magliabecchiano. Postconquest manuscript. Two ballplayers in an I-shaped court face each other across rows of skulls. Rings flank the sides. Drawing by Mary Ellen Miller.

1. We dedicate this paper to Floyd Lounsbury. We gratefully acknowledge the help of Michael Coe, John Graham, Ian Graham, Nicholas Hellmuth, Justin Kerr, George Kubler, Peter Mathews, and Berthold Riese.

ballgame might return as balls in another game. Human sacrifice itself was also portrayed in the ballcourt (fig. 2).

Given the powerful associations of the ballgame with human sacrificial rituals, the Mesoamerican ballgame could not survive in its Prehispanic form after the Spanish conquest. In fact, by the end of the sixteenth century, the Spanish had razed all masonry courts in Central Mexico that had been in use at the time of the conquest. The game did survive as a sort of sandlot sport, though, and the direct descendant of the Precolumbian game is still played today, throughout Mexico.[2]

* * *

The Maya ballgame is known largely through archaeological evidence. Like the ballgame of Central Mexico, it was probably played on many levels, from sport to ritual of kings. It is in this latter regard that we wish to consider the game most closely, particularly during the Late Classic (A.D. 600–900) period. By this time, the ritual had become formalized, obscuring its origins.[3] At many cities across the Classic lowlands, Maya lords played ball in courts constructed at the hearts of ceremonial centers. From their central location, it would seem that ballcourts were one of the foci of elite life.

2. Particularly as documented for the state of Sinaloa. See Leyenaar (1978). The paraphernalia of the game as well as large photographs of its play today were featured in an exhibition at the Museo Nacional de Antropología, Mexico City, timed to accompany the World Cup soccer championships in 1986. In Mexico today, national success in soccer is often linked to prowess in the Prehispanic game (Castro-Leal 1986).

3. The origins of the Mesoamerican — and particularly Maya — game remain obscure. Although the game was long thought to be a ritual designed to replicate the movement of heavenly bodies, its actual play may have been invented first, through experimentation with nodules of rubber. Rubber itself comes from the tropical rain forest, suggesting a lowland origin for the game. From recent archaeological evidence, it can be deduced that by very early times, the game was played in a court, or so the appearance by 1000 B.C. of two parallel structures — like later ballcourts — on the site plan of the Olmec site of San Lorenzo would appear to indicate.

Theodore Stern has made the most extensive study of the indigenous, New World ballgame (Stern 1950); he includes a summary of all known theories about the origin of the game up to its date of publication. Stern's treatment of the Maya game, however, is largely ethnographic, with less attention to archaeological materials. The symbolism of the ballgame is considered in some detail by Walter Krickeberg (1966), but he finds the archaeological materials of the Maya of little use in understanding the meaning of the game (p. 274). Architecture and artifacts of the Maya ballgame have been documented recently by Eric Taladoire (1981) and Nicholas M. Hellmuth (1975).

Despite the wealth of evidence for the Maya ballgame, relatively little is known of its character. Many cylindrical pots from royal tombs show the game being played, and ballplayers adorn markers and panels set in ballcourts. But what is puzzling is that the majority of sculptured images associated with ballplaying occur not in ballcourts but rather on stairways; these stairways are frequently carved with scenes and hieroglyphic inscriptions explicitly recording the ballgame. Furthermore, stairs are featured on a large number of images of the ballgame. To elucidate this intriguing problem of ballplaying imagery and its architectural setting, we may consider, on the one hand, the evidence from specific illustrations of play, all the way to the great amphitheatres created by the Maya where enactment of the ballgame may have been commemorated, and, on the other hand, the hyieroglyphic evidence. The latter is limited to the two basic ballgame glyphs that have been identified, and the nature and placement of their occurrences. For historical reasons, such materials have surfaced slowly for the Maya, and before one attempts to use such materials to understand Classic Maya life, data of this sort demand scrutiny. Are they meant to be taken at face value, that so-and-so played the ballgame on a given date, attired in a certain fashion, in a given architectural setting? A brief consideration of, first, the nature of Maya art, and second, the historical understanding of the Maya ballgame, is necessary to interpreting the works of art and writings that appear to describe the game.

The nature of Maya art

Maya art is often thought to be realistic, perhaps because of its apparent naturalism and its attention to human body proportions that roughly coincide with western canons. It *is* realistic in the sense that it portrays real, historical individuals in roles that they may have performed. It may also look more realistic because of the relationship of image to frame: like modern photographs and modern painting, the art of the Maya is often cut and framed in a self-conscious fashion similar to Western art. This characteristic may encourage an exaggerated notion of the closeness of Maya art to twentieth-century sensibilities. In the view presented here of Maya art and its use of both text and image, however, Maya art is not realistic in the sense often used in European art, nor is it realistic in the way that a news report and a wire service photo might be.

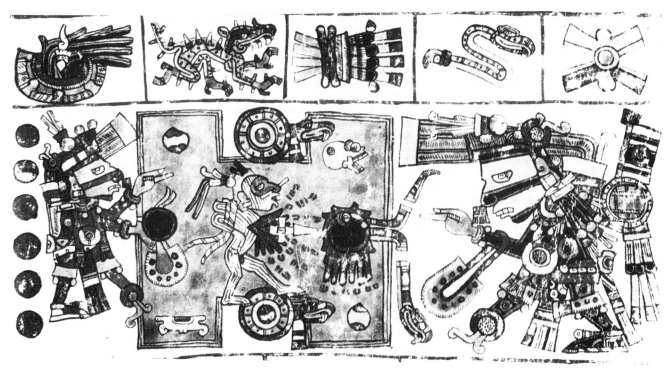

Figure 2. Page 21, Codex Borgia. Preconquest manuscript. A candy-cane-striped captive is sacrificed in the center of a ballcourt. After *Codex Borgia* 1963.

The text is indeed anchored to the image, but the text and image are often not identities.[4] Both can function independently.

In Maya hieroglyphic writing, text is usually specific and linear, linked to a particular chronological frame. This linear quality stems in large part from the fact that Maya hieroglyphs represent language, which communicates information in a syntactically ordered and consecutive fashion.[5] In contrast, images, although

shaped by a particular event and reined to a textual statement, are free to make reference to many events, and often do. This can be a source of ambiguity. The accession of a lord to high office, for example, manifests itself in many ways on Classic monuments. At Palenque, such a text is accompanied by the acceptance of a headdress by the new king; at Piedras Negras, by the seating of the new king in a niche. As we see, there is not just one way to represent accession. Occasionally, texts appear without imagery or have survived without imagery: in the case of a statement of accession, for example, the meaning is nevertheless clear. More rarely, images occur without texts. Generally, however, the text and image work as a unit, and from all evidence were conceived as a whole. Text is not a secondary consideration, nor is it a gloss; images are not specific illustrations of a narrowly construed verbal construction.

Just how text and image relate in Maya art, however, can be complex. For example, one of the most common events recorded in Late Classic Maya texts is "capture"—as in the famous capture of Jeweled Skull

4. The question of the relationship between image and text in Maya art was first addressed by George Kubler, who recognized that texts could both identify pictorial elements and complement them (1969: 3–5). Flora Clancy subsequently (1983) described the same two possible relationships between text and image in terms established by Roland Barthes (1964): *anchorage* and *relay*. Barthes developed his terminology to handle advertising and cartoons; Clancy wanted to deal with frustrating and ambiguous Maya texts. Since then, Clancy has identified the relationship between text and image in the Palenque Group of the Cross as one of "simultaneity and equivalence." Text and picture "meet like caption to illustration" (1986: 26). Marshall Durbin has proposed that Classic texts are merely symbols and signs, not language, thereby implying their subsidiary nature (1980: 103–121). Arthur Miller has also recently considered the problem and suggests that "visual images are the opposite of writing," since images expand the message and writing contracts it (1983).

5. In fact, from a linguistic point of view, the text

underrepresents language in that features obligatory in speech are often not present in script.

by Bird Jaguar of Yaxchilán (fig. 3). Phonetically, the glyph can now be read *chucah*, "is captured." The presence of the glyph and the illustration of Bird Jaguar taking an unfortunate captive with his name impressed on his body probably helped Tatiana Proskouriakoff originally to discern the identity between both glyph and scene (1963). A survey, however, of Maya art and texts produces many instances of the glyph for the verb *chucah* and few artistic depictions of it. Capture itself is rarely illustrated; the scene that occurs with a text recording capture is usually of the display of a captive by a victorious lord, *after* the capture (fig. 4).

Such images often seem to be conflated in Maya art. For example, in figure 4, the text relates a capture at A2, and indeed the victorious lord does hold his prey by the hair, as is typical of Mesoamerican depictions of capture. But in fact, the event is not just "capture" but also "display of the vanquished lords": these captives have been stripped and bound; they have adopted the shredded and punctured costume of the defeated; from ear to brow, their hair has been trimmed.[6] We know from the Bonampak paintings and elsewhere that such events follow the actual taking of captives. Lintel 3 from Bonampak is another example (fig. 5). The event recorded is capture, and at first the representation of a Bonampak lord pressing his foe to the ground appears to be a simple illustration of that verbal glyph. But the captive has already been taken: he is bound around the neck and he has already had blood taken from his tongue, as the stream of bloody dots from his mouth would indicate. So the scene is of more than capture: it is also of display, and the two have been conflated into a single image.

The representation of Maya—and in general, Mesoamerican—rituals often encompassed a broad range of events. The great battle scene at Bonampak, for example, includes many stages of the conflict— from preparation to confrontation to the capture and disarming of captives. Some scenes in the Bonampak murals depict events just as they are beginning: musicians and other performers appear in preparation for rituals and individuals are just getting dressed. Other scenes show events as they happen: related sequentially, the battle takes place, and subsequently captives have their fingernails torn out. Usually, however, there is simply not enough space on a Maya monument to relate such a sequence. More characteristically, Maya art depicts one of the events— or a combination thereof—from the end of a string of

6. Compare, for example, plate 100 in Schele and Miller (1986).

Figure 3. Lintel 8, Yaxchilán. Mid-eighth century. Captives (center) being taken by Bird Jaguar (right) and one of his cahals, or regional governors. Although the capture would appear to be just taking place, the captives are already shown naked and bound. Drawing by Ian Graham.

related activities: hence the illustration of the display of a captive in association with a text that records capture. The accession scenes at Piedras Negras, in like manner, show the new king on his throne, in his royal garb, the sacrificial victim dead at the base of the ladder leading to his niche. Such representations appear to be conflations, with references to the earlier events made through costume, pose, or subsidiary figures.

It is also evident that fewer events were recorded in the Early Classic; thus, the level of conflation is even more dense. Because conflation in formal portraiture was the standard, it was probably not perceived as such. Early Classic scenes of warfare, for example, are very rare, but the presence of captives on many monuments would seem to imply that warfare occurred more commonly. The Leiden Plaque, for example, shows the lord standing over a captive. The text records accession, and, like the Piedras Negras niche figure, presumably includes the human sacrifice of a victim previously taken in war.

These Early Classic representations, rich in polyvalent imagery, established a precedent and tradition in Maya art. Most lack narrative, in the sense that they do not "tell" a story; they do, however, refer to various moments of a single ritual as well as to many other events. The extended sequential imagery such as

Figure 4. Panel from Salinas/Usumacinta Area, now in Australian National Gallery, Canberra. Eighth century. Here the victorious lord subjugates two captives. The event, "chucah," or "is captured," is recorded at A2. Drawing by Stephen D. Houston.

is seen in the murals of Bonampak develops only in the Late Classic, and then, particularly in the most plastic art—painting—and at cities along the Usumacinta drainage.[7] Even when such narrative art emerged, it remained encumbered by conflations and multivalent imagery. A pictorial, narrative record such as that of the

7. The now-lost paintings at Uaxactún may indicate that narrative began to emerge at the end of the Early Classic. Throughout the seventh and eighth centuries, narrative painting develops on slip-painted pottery.

Bonampak paintings remains a carefully constructed universe, designed to evoke a rich world of symbols, events, and eras.

In order to describe the interaction between text and image, we would like to introduce a term from music, *resonance*.[8] Unlike mere conflation, the overlapping of images or glyphs, resonance implies temporal duration. If we return to the example of display of captives as the depiction usually represented in association with the glyph for capture and consider its resonance, it is possible to see that display is related to capture—and

8. *Resonance* refers to the "reinforcement or prolongation of sound by reflection" (*OED*: 2511). We have chosen this term because the musical metaphor seems appropriate: like two musical effects reinforcing one another, Maya text and image reinforce and prolong the overall effect, creating a whole greater than the sum of the two parts.

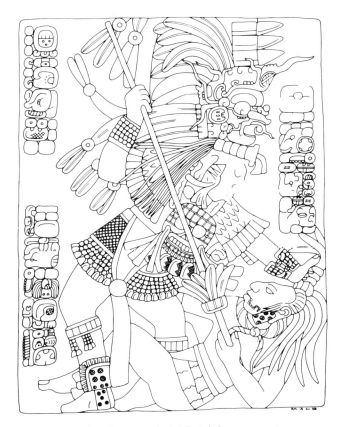

Figure 5. Lintel 3, Bonampak. Mid-eighth century. A Bonampak lord takes his captive; "chucah" is written at A3. Although presumably just fallen, the captive has already been stripped and bound; blood runs from his mouth. Appropriately enough, the victorious lord wears a headdress of Chac-xib-chac; it is this god who frequently is depicted carrying out sacrifice. Drawing by Peter Mathews.

that, perhaps, for the Maya, it was the chosen point of emphasis, even though it occurred later. Display automatically connoted the necessary capture beforehand; it was, perhaps, the most important element of the process of taking captives. The choice of depictions was a resonant one for the Maya: it both implied the textual record and amplified it, without, of course, contradicting it.

The relationship between text and image is one we must bear in mind when considering depictions and texts of the Maya ballgame. Like other events, the ballgame encompassed many sequential elements, from initiation of the game to its final resolution. The images of the ritual can be descriptive, resonant, or conflated —or all three. The evidence for the nature of the Maya ritual of the ballgame—both figural art and inscriptions —is not specifically documentary: both art and text must be considered in light of their resonant qualities, which allow us to see the moments and events as conceived by the Maya.

Maya ballcourts and ballgame art

From relatively early times on, archaeologists and explorers knew of Maya ballcourts in northern Yucatan. Their discovery was generally associated, however, with the rise to power of Central Mexican Toltecs in Yucatan, and ballcourt architecture was long thought to be evidence of such foreign contact. Because of its associations with human sacrifice and the knowledge that such practices occurred in Postclassic Central Mexico, nineteenth-century scholars assumed that the game, too, was a Postclassic, Central Mexican phenomenon. The ballgame imagery of Chichen Itzá, for example, portrays a particularly blunt brutality, one usually associated, until recently, with Toltec domination. At Chichen Itzá, six panels set into the Great Ballcourt show teams of Maya ballplayers, and at the center of each scene, a defeated player is having his head cut off (fig. 6). On each panel, a great skull is carved on the surface of the ball, as if to suggest the metaphorical or actual use of desiccated skulls of previous losers, either as the ball or embedded in it. Similar imagery at El Tajín was also thought to derive from the violent, sacrificial tradition of Central Mexico.

From the Quiche Maya epic tale, the Popol Vuh, the ballgame was also understood to be crucial to the Maya of highland Guatemala at the time of the conquest.[9] In

Figure 6. Chichen Itzá, Great Ballcourt talus. Central motif of one of the six carved panels. Early Postclassic. Here, at left, a winning ballplayer has decapitated his defeated, kneeling opponent (right). Blood scrolls surround both players; six snakes and a tree sprout from the severed neck of the victim. The ball itself is shown as a great stench-belching skull; the heads of the decapitated victims may have been used to form hollow cores of rubber balls. Drawing by Linda Schele.

the Popol Vuh, two pairs of brothers play the ballgame against the lords of the underworld. The elder pair, Hun Hunahpu and Vuqub Hunahpu, are defeated and sacrificed in the game; the underworld gods hang Hun Hunahpu's severed head in a calabash tree nearby. A daughter of an underworld lord sits under the tree and receives spittle from the desiccated head, which impregnates her. She flees to the surface of the earth, where she is delivered of twins, Hunahpu and Xbalanque, the Hero Twins of Maya legend. Like Hercules, they are demigods, and like Hercules, they overcome the nether regions. As adolescents, they discover their father's ballplaying gear and cause such a ruckus that the underworld deities command them to their court. Ultimately, through a series of wily tricks, the Hero Twins outsmart the underworld lords, not only defeating but also dismembering them. The Twins then leave the underworld to take their places as heavenly bodies.

For the Quiche Maya, the role of the ballgame was central to their cultural epic. Until ballcourts came to be recognized on Classic Maya site plans during the 1920s, however, the ballgame—whether played at Chichen Itzá or described by the Quiche Maya—was considered a late phenomenon in Maya culture. Not until 1932, when Frans Blom completed his initial study of Maya ballcourts, was there sufficient evidence for recognition of a native Maya ballgame of Classic

9. The Popol Vuh was written down in Roman script in the Quiche language at the middle of the sixteenth century. Of the many

translations from the Quiche, the most recent one by Dennis Tedlock is the most informative (1985).

date (Blom 1932). Blom was able to show that ballcourts were present at many Maya sites, including Uaxactun, Piedras Negras, and Palenque. Because of the perceived absence of foreign influences at those sites, the ballgame, it was then assumed, must have been a native Maya form. Reliefs of ballplayers were discovered at Piedras Negras, and the game was also seen to share the courtly elegance characteristic of Classic Maya art in general.

The sacrificial aspect of the Maya ballgame was less readily accessible: the Classic Maya game was assumed to be fundamentally different from the one played at Chichen Itzá, El Tajín, or Tenochtitlan. In discussions of the Classic Maya game, human sacrifice was never considered. Little was known of the game or the use of the ballcourts themselves.[10] Despite how little was known, interpretations of the ballgame tended to assume that the Classic game differed greatly from the Postclassic one, particularly as illustrated at Chichen Itzá. In the courtly world of Classic art, no brutality was recognized, and in fact, many of the illustrations known at the time tended to convey the notion of a much simpler game. The carving found at Piedras Negras, for example, shows eager youths at sport—a notion far more palatable to Anglo-American archaeologists than the cruel scenes at Chichen Itzá. Pre—World War II archaeologists of the Classic Maya made little attempt to disguise their desire to identify themselves with the ancient Maya. One need only read the general works of J. E. S. Thompson to sense the belief that white Anglo-Saxon Protestants were the spiritual heirs of the Maya.

Even the recent revolution in our historical understanding of the Maya touched the ballgame very little.[11] The ballgame was seen as play, not a subject for historical record, and it received relatively little consideration as history, even though many Aztec ballgames had been considered noteworthy historical events in their own time. More recently, however, new discoveries of Maya ballgame art—both through archaeological excavations and the random digging of looters in the 1960s and 1970s—have prompted a new consideration of the meaning and nature of the Maya game and associated ritual (Hellmuth 1975; Schele and

Miller 1986). The most important new discovery was of a carved stair at the threshold of the doorways of Structure 33, Yaxchilán, the building that commemorates the accession of one of that city's greatest kings, Bird Jaguar, who came to power in 752. Worked onto each riser of the stair is a ballgame scene, and the three central ones feature nobles who strike a ball that is shown as a bound, trussed captive. From these newly discovered works, it is now clear that, particularly as recorded by Maya kings and their close associates, the game being commemorated was a prominent ritual of the royal house. The art suggests that the game could be played for the highest stakes of all: one's life. As a life and death ritual, it replicated man-to-man combat, albeit in a public arena.

* * *

Located at the hearts of ceremonial precincts, ballcourts were the settings for public playing of the game, much like their later Central Mexican counterparts or the Maya courts described in the Popol Vuh. The typical Classic Maya ballcourt had a vertical-sloping-vertical profile, rather than the straight vertical profile found in Central Mexico. The single long sloping surface would seem to have been designed to keep the ball in play in the central alley. The sloping talus is usually about twice as long as any other surface except for the ground floor of the ballcourt.[12]

The appearance of the profile of the court is intriguing: it is *not* the profile against which most Maya ballplayers strike the ball. Only one Maya monument, Stela 6 from Edzna, shows play against what is indisputably the sloping talus of a Classic Maya ballcourt. A panel at the Art Institute of Chicago is more ambiguous (fig. 7), as an individual on the left of the panel blocks the view of the rest of the structure. In this representation, however, a ballcourt does appear to have been intended, since no flight of stairs with sloping risers is known at any Maya site. Aside from these two exceptions, however, all depictions of Maya ballgame show the game in play against a flight of stairs.

The best—and most chilling—examples of ball being played on stairs come from Yaxchilán, where Roberto García Moll uncovered the top tier of steps on Structure 33 and found it to consist of thirteen uneven

10. Function of Maya architecture was, in general, not a subject of discussion, and ballcourts fared little differently from temples or palaces.

11. The "revolution" in the historical understanding of the Maya began with the articles of Heinrich Berlin (1958) and Tatiana Proskouriakoff (1960). For a consideration of the impact that this "revolution" has had on Maya studies, see Schele and Miller (1986).

12. At Lubaantún, Belize, there is evidence of stepped side walls to a ballcourt, but this stepped effect may be only the "stepped-perpendicular" architectural facing typical of architecture throughout the site (cf. Hammond 1975, figs. 30, 54).

Figure 7. Ballgame panel, Art Institute of Chicago. Eighth century. Flapped cutouts and twisted legs of the player at right probably indicate that he will lose the game in play, perhaps by taking the oncoming ball on the chin. Although damaged, the player at left will probably win. Tlaloc ornaments and skull pectoral such as he wears generally characterize victorious warriors. Drawing by Linda Schele.

blocks, all of which had carved risers—eleven featuring ballplaying scenes—and which are now collectively known as Hieroglyphic Stairway 2. The most interesting scene and text occur on the central block, itself the largest stone of the entire tier (fig. 8). On it, the Maya artist configured a complicated image: Bird Jaguar the Great, king of Yaxchilán, dressed in ballplayer garb, adopts the pose of a ballplayer and prepares to strike the massive ball that hurtles down the stairs toward him. The ball, however, is shown as a trussed individual, upside-down, bound, tied, and apparently with his neck snapped back; his caption identifies him as a captive of Bird Jaguar. Two dwarves with star signs attend the king, perhaps indicating the cosmic setting of the event. The architectural form of the stairs frames the hieroglyphic text, in a configuration suggestive of other monuments at Yaxchilán and Piedras Negras, where hieroglyphic texts create architectural space for a scene.[13] Had the Maya artist wished to show Bird Jaguar within the symmetrical frame of the ballcourt, he could easily have worked the text of the right-hand side of the monument into such a configuration. In the upper left-hand corner of the scene, directly above the rendering of the stairway, is a miniature version of Step VII in place on Structure 33's stairway, implying that the ballgame not only corresponds to an actual event but also takes place on Structure 33. As will be discussed

below, a glyph for ballgame occurs three times in the text on the step.

Ten other blocks of the riser feature scenes of the ballgame. In addition to the central panel, two other blocks show a human figure within the ball. On Step VI, the bound captive is shown frontally and upside-down (fig. 9); the accompanying phrase would appear to name him as Jeweled Skull, the famous captive of Lintel 8.[14] On Step VIII, Bird Jaguar's dorsal view is presented to the viewer so that we see his elaborate backrack; in this case, the backrack shows the same opening to the underworld that is represented beneath a bound captive on the central step of Hieroglyphic Stairs 3 at the same site. On four other risers, the ballplayers—identified as either the king or one of his *cahals*, that is, regional governors[15]—play ball in a strange long-snouted, floppy mask that presumably would have made such sport difficult. What is most interesting about this mask is that it is the same one worn by the ballplayers who wait on the sidelines in Room 1 of the Bonampak murals. On two other risers, women sit cross-legged in front of the bouncing ball. On a total of ten of the risers, the ball bounces down a flight of from three to six stairs. The scheme of the panels is repetitive, like an extended screenfold manuscript.

What are we to make of this representation on stairs? Are we to believe that the Maya ballgame was played against staircases in preference to playing in ballcourts? Or are we dealing again with a resonant image, one like the images associated with warfare, that is not an illustration of the stage of the ritual that we expect, particularly given the textual statement? Ballcourts were undoubtedly used for play of the ballgame, as the presence of sculptures in ballcourts featuring ballgame imagery would attest.[16] Rather than propose that the preponderance of Classic Maya representations

13. See, for example, the rear of Yaxchilán Stela 11, where glyphs form the stepped interior of a corbelled arch, or Piedras Negras Lintel 3, where glyphs indicate an interior chamber.

14. This badly eroded text is problematic. The phrase on the ball would seem to begin with "captor of Jeweled Skull," then followed by two other glyphs, but the Jeweled Skull name is prefixed by a bar indicating five, and thus possibly referring to some other individual. The longer text does not name Bird Jaguar directly, but only by inference: his parents are named E2-F6 (in this context, the text names Shield Jaguar at E4). In other words, it is possible that Bird Jaguar and Jeweled Skull are not the protagonists of this block.

15. David Stuart has worked out the phonetic value of this title and some of its political implications (1983). Working independently, Peter Mathews arrived at the same conclusions (Mathews and Justeson 1984).

16. Many ballcourt markers have been located in situ; most, such as all three sets recovered from the Copán court, feature ballplayers. Only the markers found at Lubaantún, however, show architecture. Featured is a stepped background, probably stairs, or perhaps the unusual architectural batter of that site (see n. 12).

Figure 8. Step VII, Hieroglyphic Stairs 2, Yaxchilán. Mid-eighth century. Accompanied by two dwarfs with star signs, King Bird Jaguar of Yaxchilán prepares to strike the bound captive hurtling down the stairs. Ballcourt glyphs appear at F5 and Q2. Drawing by Ian Graham.

document the play of a sort of ballgame that took place outside the confines of the court, we suggest that the images are not identities with text. The image that most frequently accompanies the textual statement of ballgame is the play on stairs. That image holds a relationship to the ballgame like that of display to capture: as resonant qualities, text and image amplify and reinforce one another. At the same time, emphasis is given to the event on stairs, as if to imply the most important part of the ritual.[17] The event represented on

17. In his book on the ballgame in Mesoamerica and the United States Southwest, Eric Taladoire argues that the stepped structures shown on the Yaxchilán risers do not refer to particular architectural forms; rather, he believes, they are general conventions for architecture (1981: 360). Nevertheless, most Maya representations of architecture can be identified with actual structures or their types, and it seems unlikely that ballcourts would be reduced to architectural generalizations.

the Yaxchilán carved risers comes from the end of the ritual cycle; following play in a ballcourt, the sacrifice of the captive opponent on a flight of stairs would appear to be one of the last possible events.

Prior to the discovery of the Yaxchilán stairs, this aspect of ballgame art was not clear, but as we hope to show, a large proportion of other known ballgame imagery is consistent with this emphasis. Carved on stairs from throughout the Maya region are images that are associated with the final act of the ballgame, the sacrifice on stairs. Other loose stones, often without architectural context, can be understood as blocks associated with stairs or ballcourts. Enigmatic ballgame images on Maya pottery, too, can be linked to the ballgame. In large part, these representations of the ballgame are resonant ones, citing not the play in ballcourts but the sacrificial dénouement of the cycle.

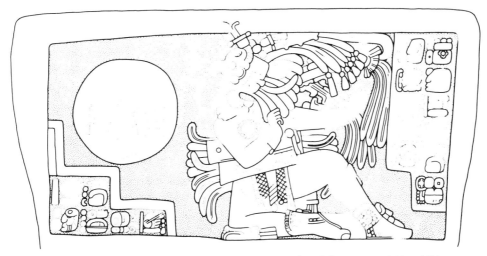

Figure 9. Step VI, Hieroglyphic Stairs 2, Yaxchilán. Mid-eighth century. A Yaxchilán king receives a bound, upside-down captive as the ball. The ballplaying glyph at E1 is followed by a ballcourt sign at F1. Drawing by Ian Graham.

Several other balls are worth examining in light of
the provocative image of the Yaxchilán balls. All three
ballcourt markers at Copán show a ball between two
players (fig. 10).[18] On the middle marker, the ball is in
play, but on the two end markers, the ball is suspended
by a thick, twisted rope. By comparison with the
markers, Copán Altar 4, a large sphere of volcanic tuff,
can be seen to be a ball (fig. 11). Like the ball shown
in play on the markers, the circumference of the altar is
bound with a thick rope. A spiral has been dug from
the top of the stone to the rope, possibly to receive
blood offerings following play of the ballgame.

As Flora Clancy has pointed out, Altar 8 from Tikal
shares a similar composition with this altar and with the
two end ballcourt markers (fig. 12a; Clancy 1976). Like
them, the upper surface of Altar 8 is a circular scene
divided into two sections; the upper two-thirds is
divided by a thick rope. A single bound captive (the
upper portion) lies supine atop a skeletal personified
Tikal emblem glyph, the lower third. The captive wears
an elaborate headdress and necklace, suggesting high
rank prior to capture. He is named in the caption,
which flanks the rope, and the glyph at the top of the
second column includes the same elements as his
headdress. The captive's arms are bound in back, and
the single, thick rope runs from his arms to the edge,
where the rope then encircles the periphery. The entire
stone is thus bound like the enormous rubber ball of
the Copán scenes, and Altar 8 itself represents a ball. If
rotated and viewed from another angle (fig. 12b), Altar
8 can be seen to show the captive in the same manner
as the captive of Yaxchilán Step VII (fig. 8). Most altars
at Tikal refer to sacrifice of one sort or another; here,
the bound suspended representation of the captive on
Altar 8 indicates that he met his death in ballgame.

The discovery of the Yaxchilán steps has provided
not only new imagery of the ballgame but also new
archaeological information. The stairs themselves form
part of a program celebrating the first few years of Bird
Jaguar's reign as king of Yaxchilán. Set at the top of
Structure 33, the stairs would also seem to be in perfect
position for just such a sacrificial ritual as the one
represented on the risers. The size and nature of the
thirteen Yaxchilán steps can also be used now to
suggest a possible architectural placement for the
corpus of small ballgame panels without known
provenience.[19]

Figure 10. Copán ballcourt markers. Mid-eighth century. Top,
north marker; center, center marker; bottom, south marker.
Set in the alley of the Copán ballcourt, these markers are a
window into the underworld. Better preserved than either the
earlier or later set, these markers probably date to the first half
of the eighth century. Drawings by Barbara Fash.

In the 1960s, a number of small panels, some
bearing fragments of a longer text and others showing
ballplayers engaged in play, turned up on the world art
markets (figs. 7, 13).[20] Since their first appearance,

18. For an interpretation of the meaning of the Copán markers,
see Claude Baudez (1984: 139–154), Schele and Miller (1986:
251–252), and Jeff Karl Kowalski (1987).

19. Grouped by Peter Mathews with other unprovenienced

materials and considered by him to come from an unknown Maya,
referred to by him as Site Q and thought perhaps to be El Peru, a site
along in the San Pedro Martir drainage (1979).

20. At the time it was thought that they formed a group, although
only a few have been published (Coe 1973; Mayer 1978, 1980)

Figure 11. Copán Altar 4. Late Classic. A great hunk of rock has been bound to form Altar 4, as if it were a ball of the sort described in figure 12. Its carved surface would guide a liquid flow, perhaps of human blood. Photograph by Mary Ellen Miller.

these panels have been dispersed among private collections and museums around the world. Most of the panels do not fit easily into a sequence, although at least two can be reconstructed as having adjoined one another (fig. 13).[21] An anomalous feature of the panels is their varying size: among them, they vary by 19.5 cm—a number that seems at first too large for a unified, extended composition.[22] Yet the Yaxchilán steps vary just as much: the panels of unknown provenience probably once composed one or more staircases, not a ballcourt wall, just like the Yaxchilán blocks.[23] At some unknown site in Campeche or the

and they may come from different structures, if not different sites. Through Mathews's data, we have been able to identify eighteen of these panels.

21. For an interpretation of these two panels, see Schele and Miller (1986: 258).

22. The height of the figural panels ranges from 25 cm (Art Institute of Chicago panel) to 43 cm (a panel in Paris). Mathews notes that three other panels are 37, 38, and 39 cm high. Purely glyphic panels measure 39, 39.5, 42, and 44.5 cm. Four other measured panels have been sawed or trimmed at the lower edge.

23. The Yaxchilán steps vary from 34 to 53 cm in height, with an average between 39 and 40 cm, and they vary even more greatly in depth. Excluding members of the Site Q corpus which have been trimmed at the bottom, the panels average 36 cm in height. Except for one panel, all the Site Q panels were sawed to a thickness of only 3 to 4 cm thick. Piedras Negras has one of the few Classic lowland Maya ballcourts with carved panels. Dos Pilas's ballcourt contains two panels, but we suspect these panels were freestanding stelae set later in the ballcourt. The Piedras Negras panel, much larger (1.43 × 70 cm) than any step from Yaxchilán or panel from Site Q, was centrally placed on the sloping talus of ballcourt K-6 (Satterthwaite 1944: 35–36). The Site Q panels are essentially different; they are small, separate panels, like those of the Yaxchilán steps.

Petén, perhaps the sawed and discarded remains of these risers will be found.

The names of the bound victims on Yaxchilán Steps VI and VII suggest that they are captives taken earlier in warfare. Because of their upended postures, and in the case of Step VII, snapped neck, the captives appear to have met their deaths in the play of ballgame. It may have been the manner in which kings publicly polished off their noble enemies. The imagery of the Site Q panels also implies the notion of noble opponents. In figure 7, for example, both players bear noble titles and wear ballgame equipment over their war attire. The fallen posture of the player at right, however, as well as his costume, would seem to indicate that he is the defeated one. The punched flaps of his loincloth, the cut of his hair along his brow, even his earflare, are all typical of the defeated captive (cf. fig. 4). The defeated ballplayer, in this instance, would appear to be a king. Opponents in the deadly game might have been the

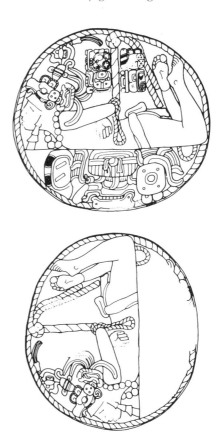

Figure 12. a. Altar 8, Tikal. Drawing by William R. Coe. b. Altar 8, Tikal. Redrawn by Linda Schele. Eighth century. When viewed from its side (b), Altar 8 is almost identical to the bound ball on Yaxchilán Step VII (fig. 8), suggesting that the bound captive on the altar is also a ballgame sacrifice.

Figure 13. Reconstruction drawing of Museum of the American Indian panel (left) with other panel in private collection. Eighth century. At left, the Maya lord is dressed as the Jaguar God of the underworld; his opponent at right appears as God L. Drawing by Linda Schele.

most important lords of the land. These are, however, resonant images, perhaps conflating the separate events of battle, ballgame, and sacrifice.

Both the Yaxchilán stairs and the Site Q panels relate vignettes that do not seem to compose a single, coherent narrative. Set one over another, three carved risers of the Hieroglyphic Stairs at Dos Pilas also feature ballplayers (figs. 14a and b); like a three-lintel composition at Yaxchilán or the three-room configuration of the Bonampak paintings, they seem to relate a sequence of events. The uppermost riser is too eroded to allow us to consider the imagery, but the middle panel shows three individuals in active play with a ball against a flight of stairs. Although the latest

in its associated dates, the lowermost panel (fig. 14b) may show the prelude to the game. Draped in hides (like those of fig. 18) and wearing enormous deflectors, what appear to be two teams face one another across two large, tied bundles, perhaps containing balls. Staircases in general served as the loci for sacrifice and torture, and many were public galleries for the reenactment of the defeat and humiliation of particular enemies (Miller 1983, 1986). This very staircase at Dos Pilas was in all likelihood the setting for a sacrifice linked to the ballgame.

In light of the scenes of ballplayers associated with stairs, it is instructive to reexamine other small panels with illustrations of the ballgame. When Sylvanus G.

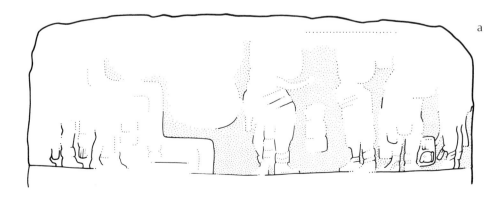

a

Morley published a small panel (44 cm) from Laguna Perdido, he labeled it a ballcourt marker because of its figural representation (fig. 15). Like the Yaxchilán steps, this panel shows individuals at play against a flight of stairs, and there is no doubt of their tangibility: the third step supports the ball. In all likelihood, this panel was a staircase riser itself, indicating the locus of the final sacrifice of the game. During their travels in southern Campeche, Karl Ruppert and John Denison explored the little-known site of Uxul (1943: 74–77). Associated with Structure VI was Altar 2 (fig. 16), a large block measuring 34 cm × 66 cm × 107 cm deep. One hundred fifty-one glyphs are inscribed on the top of the monument, and the unusual but unfortunately eroded text includes three initial series. The front of the effaced panel shows a rising profile of four tiers of steps with a large ball on the third riser, flanked by two pairs of ballplayers. Both the scene and the size of the block argue that this so-called altar also once formed part of a staircase.

Other configurations of sculpture and stairs confirm the importance of stairs in the ballgame ritual. At both Seibal and La Amelia, wall panels (misnamed stelae) flank staircases, creating a sort of amphitheatre of the ballgame. Seibal Stelae 5 and 7 both depict ballplayers (fig. 17), and, set on opposite sides of the stairs of Structure A-10, they appear to be in dialogue, as if using the stairs between them for the play of the ball.[24] La Amelia Stelae 1 and 2, like the Seibal stelae, are set at the sides of stairs. Although they have been identified as dancers, their postures and kneepads suggest instead that they are ballplayers (Greene, Rands, and Graham

1972: plates 82, 83). Not only do the two La Amelia figures thus engage in play, but the staircase between them includes six known carved risers, three glyphic and three figural. Morley's drawings of the steps are poor, but the three figural ones show reclining personages in relation to the main figures (Morley 1937–1938, III: 303–304).

At Copan, poised jaguars flank the Jaguar Staircase in the same manner as the players at La Amelia and Seibal. Three carved stones in front of the stairs create the illusion of a ballcourt alley, and again the reference is probably to the ballgame. The architectural arrangement is repeated at the Reviewing Stand, and the three "alley" markers there show fresh young maize foliage, fertility generated through sacrifice.[25]

Although not associated with stairs, paintings from within the Maya cave at Naj Tunich also provide evidence of the preferred resonant image of the ballgame on stairs (Stuart 1981). Two separate cave paintings depict a ballplayer, each of whom stands in front of a flight of stairs. Both are simple black line drawings, almost sketchlike, but neither *is* a sketch; both are resonant images rather than direct illustrations of the game in the ballcourt.

Maya ceramics also frequently depict the ballgame. Many make no reference to any architectural frame, but those that do show any form of architecture generally show stairs.[26] Despite the wealth of sacrificial scenes on polychrome ceramics, the ballplayer vessels avoid any depiction of sacrifice. A particularly handsome example of Maya ballplayers can be seen on a vessel in the Dallas Museum of Fine Art (fig. 18). On this pot, two

24. John Graham kindly pointed out the Seibal configuration to us. See the map of Seibal in Willey et al. (1975) for the placement of this architectural arrangement on the plaza.

25. See the reconstructions in Tatiana Proskouriakoff (1946).

26. A search of Nicholas Hellmuth's photographic archive has produced only one pot that shows architecture other than stairs.

Figure 14. Carved risers, Hieroglyphic Stairs, Dos Pilas. a. Middle riser. b. Lower riser. Eighth century. In *a*, two apparent teams of ballplayers face each other across two large, bound balls. The long flaring skirts are probably deerhides similar to those worn by the players in figure 18. Below, in *b*, a game is in play against a flight of stairs. Drawings by Stephen D. Houston.

b

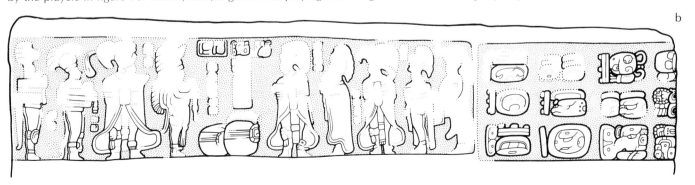

Figure 15. Laguna Perdida panel. Late Classic. Seen by
Morley at the *chiclero* camp at Laguna Perdida, this panel
shows two players engaged in play against stairs. After
Morley 1937–1938, vol. 3, plate facing p. 325.

pairs of players face each other across three steps. The
ball has the same glyphic expression as have many
balls carved on sculpture.[27] On a vessel of dramatically
different style in the St. Louis Art Museum, five
ballplayers engage in play at the base of a flight of
stairs. Three other individuals, two of whom are
singing, stand on the upper levels, again showing these
steps to be functional. On a third pot (fig. 19), two
Maya lords in ballplayer gear meet each other across a
diminutive pyramid.

The Classic ballgame, then, was no mere sport, but
often a ritual of kingship, engaged in by noble

opponents. In their art related to the game, the Maya
emphasized not the play of the ballgame in their many
courts, but its sacrificial dénouement. The scenes of
sacrifice may only recall the game; perhaps the
sacrifice did not actually involve the death of an
opponent in which he took the form of the ball, but the
Maya nevertheless chose to carve this particular image
in stone. It is a resonant image, one that brings to mind
the game as well as the death of the defeated
opponent.

Maya ballgame texts

As we have seen, Classic Maya art contains much
evidence of the ballgame and the places where it was
played. The hieroglyphic writing that accompanies the
art is no less informative: glyphic texts refer directly to
ballplaying, occurring in contexts suggesting both the
ritual framework of the Classic game and the
conceptual link between stairways and ballcourts. Maya
glyphs also document the historical and legendary
figures who participated in the sporting rituals of the
Classic era. Such historical references make it possible
to connect the ballgame to dynastic politics (especially
where these resulted in martial conflict), as well as to
the activities of the particularly energetic rulers.

There are now only two sets of glyphs known that
refer to the ballgame. One glyph is architectonic and
depicts a section through a ballcourt, with a ball
nestled in between (fig. 20a). In a number of instances
the full section is reduced to a single structure
(fig. 20b), a variant form more common on stairway
texts than on those found in ballcourts themselves. It is
possible that the two forms are functionally distinct,
with the full section referring to the structure itself and
the other to the act of ballplaying.[28] With few
exceptions, the full form appears in ballcourts.

The other ballgame glyph was identified by David
Stuart, who noticed a correspondence between the sign
illustrated in figure 20c and a rendering of a ballcourt
in the Dresden Codex. Stuart further suggested, on
convincing epigraphic grounds, that this glyph was read
pitz, or "to play ball" (Barrera Vásquez 1980: 657).
Much evidence can be marshaled in support of this
identification and reading, but suffice it here to say that

27. On both pots and sculpture, balls are commonly inscribed
with the numbers 9, 12, 13, or 14 and a glyph to be read *nab* or
na:ab. *Na:ab* is generally understood to mean "water lily" or
"standing water," but to date no sense can be made of the glyph in
the context of the ballgame.

28. The identification of this glyph was made jointly in a seminar
at Yale University and subsequently published by one of us (Houston
1983). It later came to our attention that Peter Mathews had already
made the same identification (Schele 1982: 108).

Figure 16. Uxul panel. Eighth century. Two teams of ballplayers again play in front of a flight of stairs. After Ruppert and Denison 1943.

the glyph often serves as a caption to ballplaying scenes, such as that illustrated in figure 7. The sign also functions as a title employed by Classic lords. Important individuals presumably earned the title because they had participated in such events, or because they were of a rank suitable for ballplaying.

Many examples of the ballgame glyphs occur in ballcourts, as might be expected. These include a recently discovered example from the Belizean site of Caracol (fig. 20d) and another from a ballcourt at Naranjo (fig. 20e). But these are a relatively small number of the set. Many more can be found in contexts not apparently related to the ballgame, namely on hieroglyphic stairways. Examples of the ballcourt sign occur on stairways at Copán, El Peru, and Yaxchilán. At Copán the glyph occurs on a riser of the Reviewing Stand, a stairway that faces a pavement with three regularly spaced blocks, arguably the simulacra of

Figure 18. Ballplayer pot, Dallas Museum of Fine Arts. Late Classic. Dressed in long, draping hides, ballplayers engage in play against a flight of stairs. Rollout photograph copyright Justin Kerr 1985.

Figure 19. Pearlman 11. Late Classic. Here two men play the ballgame against a diminutive pyramid. The large fan at left is probably a portable marker. Rollout photograph copyright Justin Kerr 1982.

ballcourt markers. As for the "ballplaying" glyph, it too is found on a large number of stairs, the most notable coming from La Amelia, Caracol, Dos Pilas, and Seibal.

The context of the Maya ballgame inscriptions helps reveal their larger implications. Especially clear evidence of the character of Maya ballplaying comes from Yaxchilán, specifically from the steps of Hieroglyphic Stairway 2. Both kinds of ballgame glyph occur on the blocks, with the *pitz* sign appearing more frequently (fig. 20f, g, h, i). The syntax of several glyphic passages indicates that the sign refers to the accompanying scenes, which show kneeling players poised to strike balls containing the images of captives (figs. 8, 9). Step VII (fig. 8) bears an inscription that begins with mythological events, apparently in reference to successive decapitations, and continues with an account of ballplaying in contemporary time. The form of the final phrase resembles an inscription from a hieroglyphic stairway at El Peru, which corresponds to the Yaxchilán text in at least two of its signs (fig. 20j). In addition, a *pitz* glyph on the Naranjo Hieroglyphic Stairway appears in the same glyphic context as the well-known record of war that took place between Naranjo and Caracol.

Another example of the ballcourt sign appears not on a stairway, but on a probable tomb sculpture from

Tortuguero. The pieces of this carving, known prosaically as Monument 6, now reside in several collections, but a good deal can still be made of their calendrical and dynastic content (fig. 20k; Riese 1978: 187). The ballcourt glyph on Monument 6 occurs after a war verb, and in association with a skull. The latter is a feature suggesting decapitation, as portrayed explicitly in the ballcourts of Chichen Itzá and El Tajín. Moreover, a ballcourt sign from Caracol figures importantly in a text relating to war. Caracol Altar 21 concerns, among other things, an apparent war against the massive site of Tikal, after which Caracol emerged as the possible victor and, for a time, monuments ceased to be erected in Tikal.

The conjunction of war and the ballgame is thus well documented. That such events are also found on stairways is consistent with other characteristics of glyphic staircases. To a large degree staircases record war and the capture of persons intended for sacrifice, although the most spectacular of all, the Copán Hieroglyphic Stairs, stresses instead the succession of rulers at that site. On occasion, stairways seem even to have served as "victory" monuments, the tangible expressions of control by foreign groups (Baudez and Mathews 1979). Yet, in more concrete terms, stairways offered a place to display, torture, and sacrifice captives

(Miller 1986: 114–115). The location of stairways on plazas ensured a good view for assembled observers, and the platform located above many stairways helped support individuals attending the bloody display of captives (Miller 1986: plate 2). This function is further illustrated by the images of bound captives carved on stairways; in climbing these risers, rulers reenacted vividly the humiliations of the defeated that occasioned the carving (Marcus 1974; Miller 1983). Possibly, then, glyphic stairways possessed multiple functions: the kinetic involvement of the viewer in reenacting the torture of captives, the recounting of martial events leading to the display of hapless sacrifices, and, by semantic extension, the fusion of a related activity, in this instance the ballgame, with the humiliation of rival groups.

The relationship between architectural function and imagery finds an intriguing parallel in Maya script. It is by now well attested that in writing their script, Maya scribes practiced the conflation of signs, presumably for aesthetic reasons but perhaps also to save space (Thompson 1950: 41). As a result, a string of consecutive signs often appears as a cluster of overlapping or infixed glyphs, usually with some collective phonetic or semantic relation. It is also widely accepted, if somewhat more controversial, that the visually dense iconography of the Classic Maya has an underlying metalinguistic structure, and that the line of division between glyphs and iconographic images is at times difficult to perceive. Against this background, it seems plausible that the Maya treated architecture in the same fashion: related and consecutive events, each taking place in a distinct architectural setting, might have been conflated into the imagery embellishing a single structure. Such a building would then have become *resonant* with several functions, in this case with the ballgame and the display and sacrifice of captives, for the Classic Maya resonance — insofar as we know — was rarely so pronounced or made so explicit as it was in images of the ballgame.

The Classic Maya ballgame was far more than frivolous sport: it was, rather, a ritual correlate of war and human sacrifice. This was true in later times also. The scene of decapitation at Chichen Itzá, like the scene of the trussed captive at Yaxchilán, is a resonant image, citing the echoes of the aftermath rather than the direct play for which the participants are dressed. Even in the Popol Vuh, the play of the game is directly linked to the trials that the Hero Twins undergo each

night. The Hero Twins withstand each trial in a "house," presumably a chamber on a platform. In Classic times, that "house" might have been a pyramidal platform or a flight of stairs, the focus of so much sacrifice. The Classic Maya confirm the nature of the ballgame by the emphasis chosen in their ballgame art and inscriptions: in that art, they saw the ballgame as part of a larger ritual cycle, with a focus on human sacrifice. In this regard, the Classic Maya can now join the rest of Mesoamerican peoples, for whom such associations have long been clear.

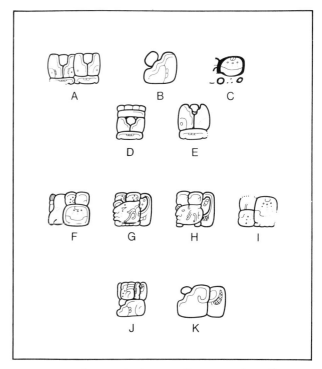

Figure 20. Ballgame glyphs. a. Ball in court. b. Ball on stairs. c. "Pitz" glyph. d. Ballgame glyph from new ballcourt marker, Caracol. e. Ballgame glyph from fragmentary ballcourt ring, Naranjo. f–i. Ballgame glyphs from Hieroglyphic Stairs 2, Yaxchilán. j. Ballplaying glyph, Hieroglyphic Stairs, El Perú. k. Ballcourt glyph, Tortuguero Monument 6. Drawings by Stephen D. Houston.

BIBLIOGRAPHY

Barrera Vásquez, Alfredo, et al.
1980 *Diccionario Maya Cordemex: Maya-Español/Español-Maya*. Ediciones Cordemex, Merida.

Barthes, Roland
1964 "Rhetoric of the Image." In *Image, Music, Text*. Stephan Heath, trans., pp. 32–51. Hill and Wang, New York.

Baudez, Claude
1984 "Le roi, la balle, et le maïs: Images du jeu de balle Maya." In *Journal de la Société des Américanistes*, n.s. vol. 62, pp. 139–154.

Berlin, Heinrich
1958 "El glifo 'emblema' en las inscripciones mayas." In *Journal de la Société des Américanistes*, n.s. vol. 47, pp. 111–119.

Blom, Frans
1932 "The Maya Ball-Game Pok-ta-Pok." In *Middle American Research Series Pub. No. 4*, pp. 485–530.

Castro-Leal, Marcia
1986 *El juego de pelota: una tradición prehispánica viva*. Instituto Nacional de Antropología e Historia, Mexico City.

Clancy, Flora
1976 "Maya Pedestal Stones." In *New Mexico Studies in the Fine Arts*, vol. 1, pp. 10–19.
1983 "A Comparison of Zapotec and Maya Glyphic Styles." In *Highland-Lowland Interaction in Mesoamerica: Interdisciplinary Approaches*, Arthur Miller, ed., pp. 223–240. Dumbarton Oaks, Washington, D.C.
1986 "Text and Image in the Tablets of the Cross Group at Palenque." In *Res 11*, pp. 17–32.

Codex Borgia
1963 Fondo de Cultura Económica, Mexico City.

Coe, Michael D.
1973 *The Maya Scribe and His World*. The Grolier Club, New York.

Corpus of Maya Hieroglyphic Writing
1978– Volumes 2 and 3. Peabody Museum, Harvard present University, Cambridge.

Durbin, Marshall
1980 "Some Aspects of Symbolism in Classic Maya Stelae Texts." In *Symbol as Sense: New Approaches to the Analysis of Meaning*, Mary L. Foster and Stanley H. Brandes, eds. Academic Press, New York.

Greene, Merle, Robert Rands, and John Graham
1972 *Maya Sculpture from the Southern Lowlands, the Highlands, and Pacific Piedmont, Guatemala, Mexico, and Honduras*. Lederer, Street, and Zeus, Berkeley.

Hammond, Norman
1975 *Lubaantún: A Classic Maya Realm*. Peabody Museum Monographs, no. 2. Harvard University, Cambridge.

Hellmuth, Nicholas M.
1975 "Pre-Columbian Ballgame: Archaeology and Architecture." *FLAAR Progress Reports*, vol. 1, no. 1.

Houston, Stephen D.
1983 "Ballgame Glyphs in Classic Maya Texts." In *Contributions to Maya Hieroglyphic Decipherment*, vol. 1, pp. 26–30. Stephen D. Houston, ed. HRAFlex Books, New Haven.

Kowalski, Jeff Karl
1987 "Copán Ballcourt Sculpture in the Context of Mesoamerican Ballgame Symbolism." Unpublished ms.

Krickeberg, Walter
1966 "El juego de pelota mesoamericano y su simbolismo religioso." Juan Brom, trans. In *Traducciones mesoamericanistas*, Sociedad Mexicana de Antropología, vol. 1, pp. 191–313. Mexico City.

Kubler, George
1969 *Studies in Classic Maya Iconography*. Memoirs of the Connecticut Academy of Arts and Sciences, vol 18. New Haven.

Leyenaar, Ted J. J.
1978 *Ulama: The Perpetuation in Mexico of the Pre-Spanish Ball Game Ullamaliztli*. Inez Seeger, trans. E. J. Brill, Leiden.

Marcus, Joyce
1974 "The Iconography of Power Among the Classic Maya." In *World Archaeology*, vol. 6, no. 1, pp. 83–94.

Mathews, Peter
  1979 "The Monuments of Site Q," unpublished ms.

Mathews, Peter, and John S. Justeson
  1984 "Patterns of Sign Substitution in Mayan Hieroglyphic
       Writing: 'The Affix Cluster.' " In *Phoneticism in
       Mayan Hieroglyphic Writing*, John S. Justeson and
       Lyle Campbell, eds. Institute for Mesoamerican
       Studies, pub. 9, State University of New York,
       Albany.

Mayer, Karl
  1978 *Maya Monuments: Sculptures of Unknown
       Provenance in Europe*. Acoma Books, Ramona,
       California.
  1980 *Maya Monuments: Sculptures of Unknown
       Provenance in the United States*. Acoma Books,
       Ramona, California.

Miller, Arthur
  1983 "The Communication of Power Among the Lowland
       Maya: Images and Texts." Paper read at the
       American Anthropological Association meeting,
       Chicago, November 19, 1983.

Miller, Mary Ellen
  1983 "Some Observations on Structure 44, Yaxchilán." In
       Contributions to Maya Hieroglyphic Decipherment,
       vol. 1, pp. 62–79, Stephen D. Houston, ed.
       HRAFlex Books, New Haven.
  1986 *The Murals of Bonampak*. Princeton University Press,
       Princeton.

Morley, Sylvanus G.
  1937– *The Inscriptions of Petén*. 5 vols. Carnegie Institute
  1938   of Washington Pub. 437. Washington, D.C.

Oxford English Dictionary
  1971 Compact shorter edition. Oxford University Press,
       New York.

Proskouriakoff, Tatiana
  1946 *An Album of Maya Architecture*. Carnegie Institution
       of Washington Pub. 558, Washington, D.C.
  1960 "Historical Implications of a Pattern of Dates at
       Piedras Negras, Guatemala." In *American Antiquity*,
       vol. 25, no. 4, pp. 454–475.
  1963 "Historical Data in the Inscriptions of Yaxchilán, Part
       I." In *Estudios de Cultura Maya*, vol. 3, pp. 149–
       167.

Riese, Berthold
  1978 "La inscripción del monumento 6 de Tortuguero." In
       Estudios de Cultura Maya, vol. 9, pp. 187–198.

Ruppert, Karl, and John Denison, Jr.
  1943 *Archaeological Reconnaissance in Campeche,
       Quintana Roo, and Petén*. Carnegie Institution of
       Washington Pub. 543, Washington, D.C.

Satterthwaite, Linton, Jr.
  1944 *Piedras Negras Archaeology: Architecture, Part 4:
       Ball Courts*. University Museum of the University of
       Pennsylvania, Philadelphia.

Schele, Linda
  1982 *Maya Glyphs: The Verbs*. University of Texas Press,
       Austin.

Schele, Linda, and Mary Ellen Miller
  1986 *The Blood of Kings: Dynasty and Ritual in Maya Art*.
       Kimbell Art Museum and George Braziller, Fort
       Worth and New York.

Stern, Theodore
  1950 *The Rubber-Ball Games of the Americas*. American
       Ethnological Society Monograph 17 New York.

Stuart, David
  1983 "The Epigraphic Evidence of Political Organization
       in the Usumacinta Drainage." Unpublished ms.

Stuart, George E.
  1981 "Maya Art Treasures Discovered in Cave." *National
       Geographic Magazine*, vol. 160, no. 2 (August),
       pp. 220–235.

Taladoire, Eric
  1981 *Les terrains de jeu de balle: Mesoamériquc et Sud-
       ouest des Etats-Unis*. Mission Archéologique et
       Ethnologique Française au Méxique, Mexico City.

Tedlock, Dennis
  1985 *Popol Vuh: The Definitive Edition of the Mayan
       Book of the Dawn of Life and the Glories of Gods
       and Kings*. Simon and Schuster, New York.

Thompson, J. Eric S.
  1950 *Maya Hieroglyphic Writing: An Introduction*.
       Carnegie Institution of Washington Pub. 589,
       Washington, D.C.

Willey, Gordon, et al.
  1975 *Introduction: The Site and Its Setting: Excavations at
       Seibal, Department of Petén, Guatemala*. Peabody
       Museum of Archaeology and Ethnology Memoirs,
       vol. 13, no. 1. Harvard University, Cambridge.

A Cuna shaman's box of wooden carved figurines representing auxiliary spirits. (Photograph by A. Parker, from Parker and Neal 1977)

The invisible path

Ritual representation of suffering in Cuna traditional thought

CARLO SEVERI

The representation of suffering is a crucial issue in Cuna traditional thought.[1] In a previous study of a Cuna therapeutic chant devoted to the therapy of mental illnesses (the *nia-ikala kalu*: "Villages by the Wayside of Madness" [Gomez and Severi 1983]), I described the characteristic Cuna cosmological framework for the interpretation of sickness. In that study, based on both the verbal and the pictographic versions of the *nia ikala*, I showed how in Cuna tradition the classical shamanistic explanation of evil and pain as the result of a voyage of a human "soul" in a mythical world is associated with a more specific theory of soul exchange between animal spirits and human beings. The memorized chant of the Cuna medicine man, while narrating the adventurous voyage of a "lost soul," gradually describes a process of invisible metamorphosis of the "inner body" of the sick man. This transformation explains, in traditional terms, the symptoms of mental illnesses (Severi 1982).

That analysis of *nia ikala* also showed that Cuna picture-writing technique plays an essential role in the transmission of this esoteric interpretation of illness. Cuna pictography is not to be viewed as a primitive stage of an evolution toward the phonetic notation of

1. Fieldwork among the Cuna has been supported in 1979 by a Grant of Collège de France (Paris) and, in 1982, by the Fondation Fyssen (Paris). Gabriella Airenti, Bruno Pedretti, Pascal Boyer, and Michael Houseman read an original draft of this paper, and reacted with thoughtful remarks. K. Jarrat helped me in translating this paper into English. I wish to thank them here. Today, most Cuna live in the San Blas Archipelago of Panama. Cunaland (Tule Neka) numbers from 27,000 to 30,000 persons, who speak a language traditionally associated with the Chibcha family (Holmer 1947, 1952). A small Cuna group, which still rejects all contact with the white man, lives in the Chucunaque region of the Darien forest, near the Colombian border. Essentially, the Cuna are tropical farmers. In his brief historical survey, Stout (1948) speculates that Cuna society, one of the first to come into contact with white men after the discovery of the American continent, was "heavily stratified, and divided into four classes: leaders, nobles, citizens and slaves." Political power today is held by the *onmakket*, an assembly of all the adult males in the village, supported by a varying number of elected leaders (*sailakan*). The Cuna kinship system is bilineal, uxorilocal, and founded on strict group endogamy (Howe 1976).

language, but as a refined art of memory, which helps the shaman in preserving, interpreting, and teaching the traditional texts (Severi 1985).

In this paper, which represents an attempt to introduce the basic features of Cuna traditional representation of suffering, I shall focus on the ritual conditions of the application of *nia ikala*.

At first glance, very few gestures accompany a Cuna healing chant. Before singing, the shaman sits for a few minutes in silence, his face expressionless as he burns cacao grains or crushes acrid-smelling red pepper pods in a small ceremonial brazier. Then the chant begins. The ritual may be performed by day or by night, but it must always occur in a separate, semidarkened corner of the hut. A monotonous musical refrain, the chant is pronounced before two rows of statuettes that face each other around the hammock where the ill person lies. These figurines represent auxiliary spirits.

When the shaman creates smoke by burning the grains and pods, he is performing perhaps the only metaphorical gesture that accompanies the chant. To the shaman, the word itself is like smoke. This visualization of the word attracts the spirits, establishing the first, and decisive, sacrificial contact with the statues that witness the ritual.

The spirits drink up the smoke, whose intoxicating effect opens their minds to the invisible aspect of reality, and gives them the power to heal. In his chant, the shaman addresses long invocations to the spirits, telling a story in which neither he nor the sick person's body play a dominant role. The true protagonists of the chant are the army of watchful spirits, themselves seers or *nelekan*, who live in the crudely sculpted wooden statuettes arranged near the chanter's brazier. Their task is to find the human soul, wandering lost through the invisible world inhabited by evil spirits, the soul whose absence has brought pain and physical disorder to the Indian lying in the hammock. The *nelekan* will face the dangers and adventures of the voyage; they will duel with the spirits of evil. Thus an *ikala*, the Cuna word for "path" and "route," as well as for "healing chant," is the story of a voyage through the invisible. Each

From the pictographic version of the Cuna therapeutic chant for mental illnesses (*nia ikala*): The shaman-chanter sits near his ritual brazier.

known illness corresponds to a different *ikala*, but the voyage, the duel, the search for the soul, are present throughout all the native tradition. Each time, the smoke is offered to the warrior spirits; each time, the shaman asks them to return "beyond the horizon" (Holmer and Wassén 1953) to seek out and challenge the enemy spirits.

When the shaman is seated before his brazier, both exhorting and impersonating his *nelekan*, he addresses the evil spirits in a language incomprehensible to the uninitiated Indians. The *ikala* are sung in a ritual language unknown to the profane and understood only by seers, healers, and leaders (Sherzer 1983). The uninitiated call this language *purpa namakke*, a term that means both "speaking obscurely" and "speaking of souls." To them (as well as to many scholars of shamanism), the concept of relationship between visible and invisible, soul and body, which in the esoteric Cuna shamanistic tradition is extraordinarily refined, appears to be reduced to a sort of familiar, fairy-tale simplicity. Illness is the pure absence of soul, whereas the cure comes by reestablishing the soul's presence. In this perspective, pathology and therapy are simply the reversal of each other. The shaman is an ideal intermediary, to whom the community entrusts its relations with the invisible. The contact between two conflicting corporeal states (and, as we shall see, between differing states of the entire world) is illustrated in the shaman's "speaking of souls." Much anthropological commentary on the shamanistic healing of so-called "primitive" societies (Eliade, Métraux, Lewis, are but a few examples) revolves around this mirrorlike relation between pathology and therapy — often simplified in the idealized representation of good

spirits challenging the evil sickness-bearers to a verbal duel. This outlook coincides with the beliefs of the uninitiated Cuna, and provided the initial, spontaneous response to our first questions about traditional healing practices, after we witnessed the rituals for the first time. During the first stages of fieldwork, the uninitiated Indian's naive functionalism ("the shaman chants for such-and-such reason") coincides perfectly with the anthropologist's educated functionalism ("the ritual arbitrates a conflict, tending to re-establish order in the world of symbols and relations").

For our interpretation of the Cuna chants, we shall adopt an entirely different procedure. Since, as we shall see, the Cuna idea of the body and the world cannot be completely encompassed in the concept of the soul's voyage, we shall choose not to discuss Cuna traditional knowledge of illnesses in the framework of a general typology of shamanism. In reality, we may call the Cuna rite "shamanistic" only as long as we bypass the outdated problem of formulating a general definition for shamanism, and only because of the preeminent role of several concepts (soul, spirit, voyage, duel) traditionally considered "shamanistic" in anthropological literature. The study of Cuna healing chants makes it clear, however, that if we insist on applying these worn-out descriptive clichés to the Amerindian area today, the result we get may be likened to a long-neglected puppet theater, whose principal characters remain always missing, or whose backdrops are too often the wrong color.

By way of introduction, let it be said only that shamanism is understood here as a certain way of conceiving the invisible aspect of reality, and as a particular *style* of worldview related to it. I am

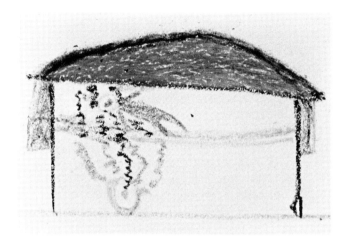

Nia ikala, pictographic version: The smoke exuding from the ritual brazier fills the shaman's hut, where the sick person lies.

convinced that the iconological study of the ritual scene can provide insight into this style of thinking. In this perspective, shamanistic chants[2] can be interpreted only if we also analyze the conditions required for their performance in Cuna culture: semidarkness in the ritual hut, alert silence preceding the chant, the smoking brazier. To examine these conditions I shall attempt to find the common logic underlying two perceptions of the rite: the chanter's sapient, dogmatic exegesis, and the more vague, but not less decisive view of the uninitiated. The study of these two perceptions will entail a discussion of the three problems posed by the ritual scene: the soul (*purpa*), the spirit (*nele*), and the setting (gestures and words, rite and chant) in which the soul and the spirit are evoked.

The soul and the secret

> The human body is the best image of the human soul.
> *Wittgenstein*, Philosophical Investigations, II, IV

According to popular Cuna belief, which may give us a first, rudimentary explanation of the chant's meaning, the shaman knows the secrets of the soul and how to follow its travels through the world of the spirits. Traditional exegesis is inseparable from the learning of the chants. This learning is based upon three different spiritual principles that preside over the perceivable existence of every living body: *nika*, *purpa*, and *kurkin*.

2. I shall refer here to *Mu ikala* (Holmer and Wassén 1953), devoted to difficult childbirth, and *nia ikala*, dedicated to the therapy of mental illnesses (Holmer and Wassén 1958; Gomez and Severi 1983).

In his classic description, long accepted by most scholars, Erland Nordenskiold (1938), the pioneer of Cuna ethnology, noted that this triad was made up of univocal concepts: *nika* relates to the idea of physical force, *purpa* to the immaterial double or replica, *kurkin* to the more abstract idea of "character," "talent," and "personality."

A few of Nordenskiold's early examples show the meaning of *purpa* for the noninitiated Cuna: it is an object's shadow, a man's mirror-image, an animal's cry resounding in the forest. Like *nika*, *purpa* is closely associated with the idea of life: a body without *nika* is weak; a body without *purpa* is lifeless. *Purpa* is as present in stones as it is in living animals, trees, or men; only a corpse is devoid of *purpa*.

In Cuna traditional thought, life springs from the contrast between visible and invisible. Every living thing (and rocks, clouds, stars, and the depths of the sea are as alive as humans) owes its own perceivable appearance (*wakar*: "face," to the Cuna) to the invisible presence of *purpa*. A shadow, a faraway cry, even the reflection of one's image are feeble traces of an invisible presence whence life flows. However, unlike the Judeo-Christian idea of the soul, which is often portrayed as an image of the body, in the shaman's view *purpa* has no image. Rather, the Cuna traditional concept describes the combination of invisible properties inherent in every living body:

> The sun's heat is *purpa*. Seated by the fire, you can feel its *purpa*. If you hear an unseen hunter shoot his gun in the forest, you have heard *purpa*. The sound of thunder is *malpurpa*. The notes of a flute are its *purpa*. The gurgle of a stream is *purpa*. The hiss of the wind is *purpa*. Even a

man's voice is called *purpa*. When you hear an animal cry far off in the forest, that is its *purpa*.

Nordenskiold 1938

These examples illustrate the shaman's view of *purpa*. From his esoteric point of view, one can never see *purpa*, as the noninitiated Indians naively believe. One can only hear, feel, or perceive it other than by sight. The visible world seems to issue from the invisible according to a generative model: one meaning of the word *nikapurpalele*, which combines the ideas of physical strength (*nika*) and invisible double (*purpa*) is "fetus." Before acquiring the "face" (*wakar*) of a human being, the living body inside the mother's womb, perceivable only by the sense of touch, is the most precise incarnation of the concept of *purpa*.

The idea that the body can be duplicated as immaterial presence (shadow, reflection) is common amongst noninitiated Cuna. Shamanistic tradition adds to it the concept that animate objects contain an inherent duality. Thus the body is not purified of its matter and then duplicated in some faraway invisible world, as in Western tradition. Rather, Cuna traditional thought focuses on the inherent invisible properties of the living body: like Janus (and as the seat of events and conflicts: illnesses), the human body is intrinsically double, *because* it is a living thing.

Nonetheless, the concept of *purpa* is not extensive enough to encompass the human body as a whole. *Purpa* can be applied only to separate organs recognized by Indian anatomy. When the Cuna shaman speaks of the human body, he does not mention "organs," but *nikapurpalele*: entities that describe, from the outlook of a world metaphysics, not only an "invisible body" but the very life that throbs through that body.

As we have said, *nika* means physical strength. But how does traditional shamanistic thinking represent this elementary force, and what role does it play in the organism's life? Rubén Pérez Kantule, one of Nordenskiold's Cuna collaborators and coauthor of one of his most important books (1938), made a drawing of *nika*. His picture says more than any verbal description can.

The concept that ordinarily relates to simple physical strength (a good hunter's skill, a warrior's valor) is pictured here as a cloud hovering around the Indian's face. Rubén tells us that this cloud makes the Indian's face invisible to the evil spirits who unleash illnesses. Like *purpa*, this vision of *nika* as a shield that deflects the spirit's gaze is based upon the contrast between

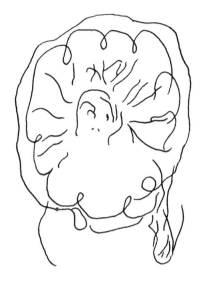

visible and invisible. The two concepts are joined in the idea of *nikapurpalele*, which applies to each organ of the human body, whose spiritual double is the organized combination of the separate organs' *nikapurpalelekan*. This spiritual double possesses a third property: *kurkin*. Nordenskiold is partly correct when he contrasts *kurkin* to *purpa* and *nika*, translating the former as "intelligence" or "talent." *Kurkin* does more than contrast with *purpa* and *nika*, however. It actually represents a complex combination of the two. *Kurkin* (literally, "hat") is the principle of the invisible strength that makes the human body resplendent and powerful, as opposed to *nika*, which hides its face from the spirits. When the shaman in *The Way of Mu* prepares for his duel with the spirits of illnesses, he "makes his hat [*kurkin*] grow" before the spirits that are the lords of the trees (Holmer and Wassén 1953).

Kurkin nikka (to have *kurkin*) means to have "invisible spiritual strength"—the gift of vision—as opposed to *nika*, the physical strength of the hunter and the warrior. Both spirits and shamans share the privilege of possessing powerful *kurkin*. *The Way of Mu* gives an example of the aggressive connotation of this notion when it describes the "great duel with the headdress" (*kurkin* in the text). During this duel, the *nelekan*, the shaman's auxiliary spirits, challenge the "animals of Mu," meaning the spirits of illness (ibid., v. 383 ff.), and claim that they have "more powerful hats."

We find another interesting interpretation of *kurkin* in *Villages by the Wayside of Madness* (Severi 1982, vv. 374–378), where "shaking one's hat in front of someone" means to seduce him or her and arouse love. Finally, some species of mushrooms (presumably hallucinogenic, although, unfortunately, we still know nothing about their shamanistic use) are called the evil spirits' "hats" or "mental strength": *nia-kurkin*. In the shamanistic vocabulary this is one definition for hallucination.

We may now return to the popular belief that plainly describes the contrast between illness and healing, and try to reformulate it in the shaman's perspective.[3] In this outlook, the idea of impaired equilibrium is always at the origin of the illness. The "main body" (*sailapurpa*), which is the *purpa* of the visible body, or the invisible part of the real body, is, in the shaman's words, "wounded by a double wound": both visible and invisible. The ritual formula for designating the first signs of pain, caused by the soul's flight, is *purpa nai*, which we can translate as "There is something invisible (though not a replica, or image) hanging around the Indian's neck" (the verb *nai* is usually applied to necklaces, and here *purpa* takes its general meaning of *purpalet*, "the invisible").

The common Indian belief will be that a "soul" (a *nikapurpalele*) has fled the body. But the shaman uses those same words to indicate the breaking of the primary relationship between the body and its invisible aspect.

Kurkin's energy, on which is based the shaman's healing power, is activated through the eyes. Literally, *kurkin* is the "strength of the eyes." Thus "seeing the invisible" is the Cuna shaman's first healing act. Likewise, no cure can be found if the shaman has not first "seen the direction" taken by the illness-bearing spirits. There are two possible ways to achieve this result: some people are gifted with innate wisdom acquired at the moment of their conception in the mother's uterus. Others may serve a lengthy apprenticeship with a teacher of healing chants. Shamans who possess innate wisdom are called *nele* (seers). The *nelekan* act daily upon illnesses, but they are also able to foresee the community's future. Those who have no innate gift but acquire their learning during an apprenticeship spent studying the healing texts (passed on by oral tradition) are called *inatuleti*, or "medicine men." These two categories are not equal. A Cuna with innate gifts can always become an *inatuleti*, by following a teacher. But the medicine man can acquire the *nele*'s vision only rarely, and under exceptional circumstances (Nordenskiold 1938).

3. I have discussed this topic in a previous study, devoted to the Cuna theory of souls (Severi 1981).

The *nele*'s wisdom, which the community is asked to acknowledge from birth onward, comes from the child's innate knowledge of the sexual act whereby he was conceived. His vision springs from the knowledge of this secret, which confers upon the newborn's body an extraordinary spiritual strength. *Mimmi kurkin nikka kwalulesa*: "the baby was born with a caul" (*kurkin*), the midwives declare when a child's head is almost entirely covered with the placenta as it leaves the mother's womb. This condition, essential but insufficient, allows the Indians to recognize a real *nele*. The child's "hat" is the sign of an exceptional form of conception: during coitus the parents' sexual *purpakan*, in the form of sperm and menstrual flow (both called *nikapurpalele* by the Cuna), have "slipped" into the child's body. This supplement of soul, or abnormal concentration of sexual *purpa* in the *nele*'s body, gives the child a power over his parents' lives, and also an awareness of the mysteries of sexuality, something that is rigorously hidden from his peers. It is this knowledge that supplies the *nele*'s particular *kurkin*. The "hat" placed on his head by his mother's placenta symbolizes his vision, which is invariably conceived as a legacy of spontaneous and complete knowledge that can never be achieved through apprenticeship alone.

This unique, rare gift of vision (which Cuna attribute also to rock crystals) can in a human mind only grow, just as the child's body goes from the fragility of infancy to the vigor of adulthood. All it needs is *nika*, physical strength. As a consequence, a *nele*'s initiation calls not for the study of the chants, but for a series of ritual baths called *nika okannoket* ("make strength grow") and *ipia okannoket* ("give the eyes strength"). These baths are strictly regulated according to the young boy or girl's age. Once again, we can see the characteristic interdependence of the two basic principles of the Cuna theory of souls: *nika* and *purpa*. Here, the *purpa* are the invisible properties of the medicinal plants contained in the baths the young *nele* undergoes. They expand around the seer's body (almost as a sort of invisible fumigation), forming the cloud-shield of physical strength (*nika*) that protects the *nele*'s spiritual strength (*kurkin*) from the attacking spirits.

Just as the *inatuleti* and the *nele* undergo differing initiations, they also play two separate healing roles. Cuna shamanism makes a strict distinction between two stages of healing. The diagnosis includes identifying the nature of disease, of the attacking spirits, and of the stricken body sites. This role is always performed by the *nele*, with his divining techniques. The true healing cure, which calls for the application of medicinal plants or the ritual recitation of a chant, is always the duty of the *inatuleti* alone.

There is a further distinction between the role of the *nele* and the *inatuleti*, depending upon whether they are healing an individual illness or a collective disease. When a collective illness threatens the existence of an entire village, not even the most prestigious *inatuleti* can oppose it. In this case and in this case alone, the *nele* steps out of his role of seer and diagnostician to combat the pathogenic spirits directly. At such times, the *nele* falls into a deep, prolonged sleep, while the villagers observe a series of prescriptions, first and foremost of which is sexual abstinence. In his dreams, the *nele* travels to the world of the spirits, to whom he offers a handful of ashes taken from his ritual brazier. This offering inebriates the spirits, just as *chicha* (an alcoholic beverage distilled from corn) inebriates humans. In this state, the spirits are harmless and willing to accept a truce with human beings. To keep the *nele* from losing his way, one of the oldest and most experienced *inatuleti*, called the *apsoketi*, guides him by singing the *apsoketi-ikala*. This chant "clears the vision" and literally orients the *nele*, telling him about the places he travels through in his dreams and identifying the spirits to whom he will make his offering (Howe 1976). Clearly, in this case the two main categories of shamans exchange roles: the *apsoketi* shows the seer the "invisible way" to the illness, while the *nele* takes direct responsibility for the healing role. Here Cuna shamanistic tradition accumulates and hands down the knowledge of the spontaneous, almost "natural" source of innate wisdom: the birth of the newborn seer. The *apsoketi-ikala* (literally, the "chant of chanting," or "the chant of healing word") virtually contains that knowledge.

Thanks to his infallible vision, the *nele* is always considered superior to the *inatuleti*. But there is also a hierarchy within learned knowledge, as shown by the institutional organization of shamanistic learning. During the *inatuleti* apprenticeship, the teaching naturally begins with the study of relatively brief texts used for the healing of less serious illnesses. The young *inatuleti* will approach the great texts only later, and only if the teacher decides that his apprentice possesses the necessary skills. The only *inatuleti* who can become the *nele*'s teacher or guide is one who, through many years of apprenticeship, has acquired the knowledge of the *apsoketi-ikala*, one of the "higher chants" in the hierarchic order of shamanistic learning. By slowly ascending through the hierarchy of the healing chants, the *inatuleti* can thus establish a different relationship with the seer's innate knowledge and even hold some degree of control over it.

This complex set of relationships between role and knowledge can be understood only if we refer back to the key concept of Cuna soul theory, that is, *purpa*. It has already been said that the *inatuleti* has no innate gifts; he acquires his powers through the study of healing chants that, like the *nele*'s body, are exceptionally endowed with *purpa*. As we have seen, *purpa* is the basis of the Cuna idea of organic life. For the noninitiated Cuna, it is the mirror-image, a shadow, or an echo. For the shaman, it is the essential property of a living body, something that is never visible but can be felt or perceived like the heat of a fire, the voice of a man or the cry of an animal. When applied to shamanistic knowledge, *purpa* implies the idea of a secret.

Each healing chant generally tells of the shaman's travels with his spirits in search of the kidnapped *nikapurpalele*. But every chant is accompanied by a second text, which the young *inatuleti* learns only at the end of his apprenticeship. This text, which the Indians call *secreto* in Spanish and *ikala-purpa* in Cuna ("soul of the chant," but also "invisible part of the path"), is the only true source of the chant's effectiveness. A *secreto* generally narrates the origin of the illness, describing the mythical coitus that conceived the evil spirit that created the illness.[4]

Before ritually reciting the chant, the *inatuleti* must repeat the *secreto* silently, for his hearing alone. Were the *inatuleti* not to evoke in silence the secret origin of the illness, his chant would be ineffective. The *inatuleti*'s other source of power lies in his *nelekan*, the ritual statues arranged around the hammock. These spirits are also endowed with *purpa*, and the *inatuleti* always performs his ritual chants before them. Their power is linked to the idea of vision: as it says in *The Way of Mu*, the *nelekan* "bring things to life with their eyes" (Holmer and Wassén 1953). They do not derive their power from their likeness to certain supernatural beings. On the contrary, they are strong because their bodies, the very wood from which they are carved, are animated by *nika-purpa*. Once again, it is not their physical appearance (*wakar*) that counts. Only the *purpa* contained in their bodies allows them, as the

---

4. On this point, see also Sherzer (1983).

chants say, to "use their vision to penetrate" the world of the spirits. Thus the *inatuleti*, unlike the *nele*, has no direct access to the invisible. During his apprenticeship, he obtains only indirect access to *kurkin* — spiritual strength — by acquiring extra *purpa*, which is inherent to the chants and makes them effective.

All the complex Cuna conception of *purpa* is based upon this idea of the secret, which links the soul to the shaman's word, and that word to the knowledge of the invisible. But if we take the idea of *purpa* one step further, beyond the mere identification of the secret aspect of material things, and include all the corporeal perceptions other than vision, we will have a better understanding of the logic underlying shamanistic knowledge. In light of this interpretation, the soul's voyage becomes a metaphor for the experiences felt by the sick person. In other terms, the spirits' invisible world describes not only a separate realm of the universe, but also that state of *perceiving without seeing* which *is* the feeling of pain.

Expanding upon the traditional Cuna way of thinking, we may recall that because the *purpa* has been lost in an unknown place, *the illness is also a secret*. That invisible presence hanging around the neck of the sick person in which the shaman recognizes the first symptom of illness designates a perception that the common man cannot explain. During a second, parallel voyage, the shaman must uncover, but never publicly reveal, that secret, using his knowledge of the chant's hidden part. His prestige, along with that of the tradition itself, depends upon the ritual confrontation of these two secrets.

In other words, as long as we limit our analysis to the theory of souls, which the specialist sees as both the cause of illness and the source of his power to heal, we may think that Cuna traditional healing is based upon an orderly hierarchy between two categories of indigenous specialists — seers and medicine men — who share the same secret knowledge. But what kind of knowledge is this? From a theoretical point of view, the theory of *purpa* essentially reflects a traditional way of organizing the living body's *qualities*. As a theory regarding the properties of the world, it leaves the relationship between the visible and invisible largely unexplained. In exoteric Cuna terms, it appears to be a paradoxical confrontation between two secrets. To shed further light upon this problem, let us return to the legend of the Cuna soul and follow his meanderings along the *ikala*, that invisible path which leads from the Indian village to the mythical world.

The island and the spirits

Wherever our language leads us to believe there is a body, but no body exists, there is a spirit.
Wittgenstein, Philosophical Investigations, 1, 36

Seated near the sick Indian's hammock, the shaman silently recites the secret part of the chant (*ikala purpa*). Next he speaks aloud, to evoke a familiar landscape: the Indian village, the nearby river, the ocean, the forest. Progressively, and with ever greater visionary force, the chant will contrast the description of the Cuna territory with an imaginary geography that lies beyond the horizon. Before we proceed, it may be useful to reflect upon the thin line between visible and invisible that delineates the different spaces of the shaman's view of the world.

Today, most Cuna live on small islands of coral origin, located in the San Blas Archipelago along the Atlantic coast of Panama. These inhabited islands, often linked to the coast by a long log bridge, are usually flat and barren. The horizon is marked off on one side by the ocean and on the other by the Darien forest. Farming and hunting supply the Indians' main livelihood and are performed entirely in the forest on the mainland. Fishing has been practiced only recently, often in the area within the coral reef that protects the island from the Atlantic, and makes the shallow water around the island particularly calm and navigable. Often densely populated, the villages are made up of large reed huts built one next to the other, housing the extended Cuna uxorilocal family. As described by the Cuna, this spatial arrangement, typical of the entire archipelago, is rigidly divided among the Living, the Dead, the Animals, and the Great Trees. Thus the world appears to be apportioned horizontally (north to south and east to west) among these four groups.

The mainland is the site of agriculture, hunting, and fresh water; the islands, usually possessing no water sources, are the place where social life and rituals occur. This first impression, however, with its naive, dichotomous view of Cuna space, is immediately complicated by a paradox. On the mainland facing the island, at the mouth of the river that supplies fresh water, there is an unusual clearing in the forest. Here lies the village of the dead. Thus the dead inhabit the same territory as the animal spirits who are the constant source of illness and death. There is no place in Cuna thinking for the concept of natural death. Those who die have been attacked by a hostile spirit. They are always victims of revenge or a fatal error. The forest is a difficult, perilous place; it conceals the *kalukan*, the "villages" inhabited by spirits who attack men if they venture too close. These spirits kill such men, drive them mad, or make them ill. A *kalu* can materialize on a rocky cliff overhanging the ocean, under a thornbush, or in a swamp (Prestan 1976). Paradoxically, the land of the dead is also fertile; here the living find their nourishment. When it is time to observe the great funerary rites, the entire population of the village moves to this spot. Let us briefly describe two such rites, which will lead us to a more accurate vision of their symbolic organization of space.

In Cuna society, when an adult or elderly person dies, the whole community moves to the village of the dead, at the first light of dawn. After the procession has reached the mouth of the river, the corpse is laid out in a wall-less hut. The dead person's head "faces toward dawn," and the whole body is covered by a white cloth. In the symbolic language of *Mu Ikala*, this metaphor always designates the vagina: "From the midst of the woman's white cloth a human being descends," "Her secret white cloth blossoms like a flower" (Holmer and Wassén 1953, vv. 90, 432). Next, the corpse is covered with dirt, which is beaten with shovels and baked by the flame of a brazier until it forms a smooth, compact layer. The brazier will remain at the burial place, where relatives will keep it burning constantly. We are reminded of the observation of Wittgenstein (1967): "The destruction of fire is *total*, unlike that caused by laceration, beating and so on. It must have been this that impressed the human being." The brazier is surrounded by two woven-reed stars, designating the passage into the realm of the dead; the skull of a dog ("to keep the animals away," says Paolino, one of the chiefs of the village whom I knew best); several stones; a cup; and red pepper seeds. Bunches of multicolored feathers and flutes hang from the balsawood poles that hold up the roof. At times, during the funeral chants, these feathers are threaded into the flutes, almost as if to represent sound; they accompany the Chant of the Dead (*masar ikala*) that leads the corpse on its perilous voyage to the realm of the dead. To facilitate this voyage, the living build a small boat, which contains the hunting weapons the dead man will need to defend himself. Like the village that represents it, the realm of the dead is an exact replica of the world of the living, with one exception. There everything is golden. The Cuna say that the gold is the *color* of the realm of the dead. At sunset, the whole community goes back to its island, where

everyone shares a meal and then has a communal bath of purification. This rite is repeated for three consecutive days after the death, plus the ninth day of the first month and the thirtieth day of the next six months.

When a child dies, the ritual aspect decreases considerably. The body is buried in inhabited earth, inside the family hut, beneath the hammock where the living child slept. The Cuna believe that this type of burial will help the family have another child. The dead child's body still bears the male seed, which will make it germinate like a plant. Thus, whereas proximity with an adult corpse is strongly precluded, close contact with the child inseminates the barren land inhabited by the living.

In loco burial is one way to introduce a second repartition of Cuna space along vertical lines: from the top of the sky to the depths of the underworld. Here the world of the dead is an underground place, the "pure golden layer of the earth" mentioned in *The Way of Mu* (v. 183 ff.).

This underground world is made of eight layers. The four upper layers are the birthplace and hideout of the evil illness-bearing spirits. At the very bottom of the fourth layer lies the source of the "golden river" that leads to the lower layers of the earth. It is through these regions that a dead Indian's *purpa* must travel to reach the eighth and lowest layer, home of the spirit of the balsa tree (*nele ukkurwar*). Considered a powerful seer, this spirit is the shaman's main helper and leader of all healing spirits.

By burying the child beneath the hammock in which he always slept, the Indians hope to keep his *purpa* from having to enter the perilous world of the spirits, through which the sick Indian's soul must always travel. Indeed, even though the first underground layer may be potentially hostile, it is thought to be as fertile and populated as the mainland across from the island. Moreover, it transforms the child's body into a forest plant that can reproduce and return to a woman's womb as a "bleeding fruit" (Holmer and Wassén 1953, v. 165). This is why, in one memorable passage from *The Way of Mu*, the mother is described as a "well-rooted tree-woman":

> In the pure golden layer of the earth the root holds up its trunk: as deep as the golden layer your root is planted solidly [in the earth]; . . . as far as the golden layer [of the earth] it transforms [everything] in pure gold. . . . One by one, the animals climb your spotted limbs dripping with blood. . . . Your limbs curve and bend in the wind; beaten

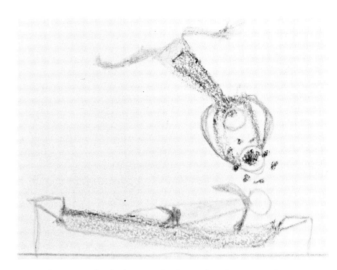

Nia ikala, pictographic version: Here the auxiliary spirits of the trees come down to drink the smoke from the shaman's brazier. The traditional belief is that smoke is an inebriating beverage for them.

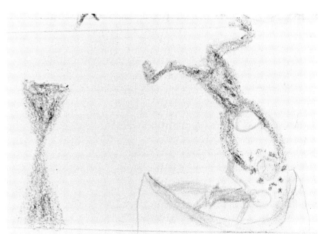

by the wind your limbs send forth a piercing sound like ropes on the foreigner's silver boat.

Ibid. vv. 183–187

In this dramatic description, where birth is likened to a tree bearing fruits in the forest, it should not surprise us to find an allusion to the white man's world, such as the one Lévi-Strauss (1949) has called an example of the "myth's plasticity." Both the horizontal and vertical limits of the world designate a confused space in which spirits, illnesses, natural disasters, and foreigners may cohabit. We shall consider later this aspect of Cuna cosmology. For the moment, let us point out the interchangeability of the earth/sky and island/forest axes. In *The Way of Mu*, the spirits live both "underground" and "beyond the horizon." In *Villages by the Wayside of Madness* (Gomez and Severi 1983),

when the shaman's spirits are preparing themselves for their search of the lost soul, they peer "beyond the cardinal points," *thereby seeing* the underground world of the spirits. The two images, horizontal and vertical, live side by side and complement each other in Cuna thinking. The result is a world full of dangers, where enigmatic "fractures" in visible reality give hostile force a hiding place.

To this we should add a Cuna tradition according to which the universe is made of an endless cloth woven with infinitesimal threads. In *Villages by the Wayside of Madness* there is a description of the "innumerable threads that weave the ocean spray" (ibid., vv. 137 ff.). Thus the traditional Cuna idea of the "village of the spirits" is conceived as a tear in the invisible cloth of which the world is made. In *The Way of Mu*, this idea of the world's invisible pattern is expressed through the image of an enormous net held up at the horizon by the seer spirits. The chant says that this net is invisible not because it is hidden in the underground world, but on the contrary because it "has assumed the color of gold" (ibid., v. 486), by reflecting extremely intense sunlight.

Thus an invisible village, a *kalu* can be concealed anywhere in the world: not only underground or at the edge of the horizon, but also beyond the heavenly vault, which a chant recorded by Densmore (1924–1926) describes as a gigantic mirror of the world. "When I look into the distance, I see clouds like big trees / clouds like boulders, made of tall, grey rocks / I see the clouds like men moving and bending forward / The clouds move nearer / there are clouds that look like a crowd of men advancing. . . ."

For the Cuna, the universe is a dense mosaic of differing, antagonistic territories. Both the horizontal and vertical axes emphasize the *defensive, temporary* character of the earth's upper layer, home of the living. Thus the island, a spot of barren earth emerging from the ocean, resembles the smooth, baked layer of dirt that covers the corpse in the village of the dead. Both places are littered with signs and symbolic objects, threatened on all sides and defended by ritual weapons.

In this ceaseless conflict between the Indians and their enemies, even the spirits are weapons. In this perspective, the double row of statues that witness the shaman's chant, to whom he gives both the word and the power to heal, becomes a decisive element in Indian healing. As the only one able to travel through the world of the invisible, the category of "seer spirit" is crucial to shamanistic theory of souls.

Nevertheless, spirits always maintain an ambiguous character: caught in the eternal conflict between good and evil, they dwell in the no-man's-land between the everyday and the unknown. Obviously spirits are enlarged projections, a hypertrophy of the ideal Cuna identity, which includes the splendor of physical strength as well as the idea of mental prowess. But this identity also refers to an outside world, unknown and perhaps hostile, which includes the animal and the foreigner (Severi 1981). The clear-cut distinction between good and evil spirits—the vegetable spirit *nele* is a "friend" and resembles us, whereas the animal spirit *nia* is an "enemy" and unlike us—is only an apparent one, for the realm of the spirits has a negative definition only ("their world is *not* like ours"). Thus it is a place of constant ambiguity, of torturous uncertainty, of a disorder that not even the seer can always predict.

No one can ever guarantee that the forest hides no animal seers, or that a tree or medicinal plant conceals no poison. Above all, as elsewhere in America, the spirit is not an ancestral presence for the Indians. The statues do not commemorate the past of the Cuna; rather, they represent a need to understand the present-day world, to interpret the worries and conflicts weighing upon the Indian village *today*.

Although the personage of the foreigner may appear to be absent from shamanistic tradition, the ambiguity of the healing chant's negative character, the hostile spirit, forces us to reconsider this impression. Paradoxically, it may be precisely the outsider who actually commands the rite's most secret transformations. Let us contemplate the most banal example: the white man. The defensive nature of the inhabited island, with its correlate of a symbolic universe divided into antagonistic territories, as described above, is not simply the result of some "primordial fear" of nature and of its forces (although from a realistic point of view this element does exist). Its configuration derives from Cuna history, marked by tenacious resistance to European and American colonization. It is only relatively recently that the great majority of Indians have migrated to the San Blas Archipelago. The Cuna of the islands are the only ones who have accepted living in relative, albeit wary, proximity to the white man. Indeed, if the historical surveys of Nordenskiold (1938) and Stout are correct (1947), these islands are the very refuge to which the Cuna have been banished by colonization.

Farther away, in Chucunaque, the Darien forest touches the Colombian border. The Indians who have refused to accept any external change in their lifestyle still live there. A busy exchange of messengers keeps the two groups connected, but the strict rule is that the Chucunaque Cuna will "speak" only to the island Indians. Even today, the mainland Cuna will not accept any relations with the Panamanian descendants of Latin, Eastern, and Afro-American invaders.

Naturally, one admires the Cuna's constant struggle to maintain their tradition and identity. Still, it would be unfair to them to limit ourselves to a superficial representation of the facts. Certainly, pride and anxiety have played an equally important part in keeping both mainland and island Cuna isolated. Competition, fear, and attraction seem to combine in the Cuna general attitude toward all strangers.

The Indians call the white man *waka* ("evil spirit"), not *tule* ("man"); *merki*, the other term reserved for *gringos*, is anything but complimentary. But although he may often be despised as a nonhuman being, the white man remains a carrier of power. If he is deprived of his strength and sufficiently controlled, he may even become a kind of trophy. In this case, the white man's much-flaunted power can become the symbolic booty in a conflict between rival villages. Thus, for instance, one of the two communities of the island I came to know best "possesses" a Protestant mission. In response, the other community has allowed a few Catholic missionaries to start a settlement and found a small hospital near the village. Colonization has introduced the white man into the Cuna's conflictual context, touching off a kind of competition between intracultural and intercultural strife.[5]

Certainly, the present dynamics of Cuna competitiveness are not unrelated to their forced restriction in space. Consequently, the illusory possession of a white hostage seems to be a reward, albeit bitter, for these people, who find themselves cut off from the world, while tragically locked in the conflicts generated by this isolation. Ironically, it is this situation that today enables the white man, temporarily low economically and militarily, to effectively overcome the strenuous resistance raised against him for centuries by the Cuna.

It should never be forgotten that the American Indians, particularly those of Central America, have been living side by side with the white man for several centuries. Even when, as in the case of the Cuna, they have been able to combat effectively a generally destructive physical contact, the Indians have still maintained that this now inevitable presence has irreparably lacerated their world, upsetting once and for all the balance of forces regulating it. Transformations not directly produced by the repeated military expeditions, Spanish and other, are now linked to this deeply rooted and obsessive certainty that something has been torn apart. The ultimate crisis that the Golden Men (Olotule, as the Cuna call themselves) have always managed to repel from their world now insinuates itself surreptitiously, threatening the very transmission of traditional knowledge. The result is a struggle that pits elders who feel betrayed against youths trapped between dissatisfaction with their own world and attraction to, but fear of, a world of which they have little understanding. Today white penetration is more subtle and widespread than it once was. Despite their

stubborn heroism, the old men have been unable to fence it off completely.

The healing chants are also rooted in this crisis, as we have indicated elsewhere in our discussion of the madness-chant's image of the foreigner as illness (Severi 1982). But it is in the ambiguous definition of the evil spirit that the crisis most thoroughly unfolds. The relationship between the white man and the spirit that delineates the Cuna theory of madness is still alive and clearly defined. Not all evil spirits are subject to summary association with the foreigner, but there is no doubt that all foreigners are spirits. This explains how the "invisible village of the white man," the big-city kalu, has become a legitimate part of the language used to narrate Cuna history and politics, and how it is that the spirits of the forest are traditionally believed to have participated in the Spanish-Indian world. Indian accounts portray the animal spirits as enigmatic tricksters consistently present in the countless clashes and ambushes that for centuries have pitted the Indians against the whites. The Indians know perfectly well that it was men, and not mysterious animal spirits, who fought those battles. Still, they also think that war produces spirits and that a conflict cannot take place without their help. For analogous reasons, these same spirits show up in descriptions of illnesses.

This aspect of the conception of the spirit leads us to recognize one of the basic functions of Cuna shamanism: to represent, in a symbolism only partially dependent upon mythology, the ambiguous and anxiogenic dimension of the unknown. In terms of Cuna cosmology, this dimension is described as an unknown, yet possible space, a terra incognita, in which traditional thought represents the foreign, the new, and the incomprehensible. As we shall see later, the description of these ambiguous, ever-changing aspects of the world is always linked to the representation of pain.

Let us return to the spirits, to examine their positive incarnations. The ritual representation of the land of the spirits, as minutely described in the shaman's travels, reveals what we would call a reverse function of the representation of the unknown. By this we mean the image of the auxiliary spirit of an ideal Indian identity, which is in turn built up as a striking reversal of the afterworld. This work of legitimation of identity is certainly the most spectacular and public of the shaman's functions, although its foundations are kept well hidden from the ordinary Indian.

We shall come back to this identity-building aspect of the shaman's discourse. First, however, it should

5. Such a situation is analogous to the one described, from the viewpoint of analytical therapy, by H. Searles (1979), especially in the essay "The effort to drive the other mad."

be remarked that this new image of the shaman's activity will not fit easily into the orderly hierarchy of shamanistic roles that a simple analysis of the traditional theory of souls would lead to. The ambiguity of the spirit can be understood only by recognizing the unstable balance that exists between the ever-changing everyday world and the fixed categories of the mythical world. If even the seer spirit of balsa wood, the shaman's chief helper — whose job it is to restore the lost soul to the sick person's body — is itself fraught with the ambiguity between good and evil (and resemblance and dissemblance to the human form), we cannot simply claim that "using some spirits to protect man from some other spirits" reflects the traditional thought of a small group of shamans, themselves the product of a society seeking a way of settling its conflicts. We cannot just say that the shaman evokes evil merely in order to exorcise it by traveling through the unknown territory of the stranger and bringing back its tamed image.

Only by seeing the complex symbolism of the shaman through the restrictive lens of soul theory can we uphold an image of the healer as intermediary between the spiritual world and the community. If we concentrate instead on the idea of the spirit itself, with its ritual manipulation and its predominance in the chants, it will lead us to a different view of the intricate web of social relations expressed in the ritual recitation of shamanistic chants.

In reality, the traditional image of the spirit, the tale of its voyage (mirroring the travels of the lost soul and foretelling its "return"), the chant's repeated comments about the spirit's personality, hesitations, angers, and so on, all define the perspective from which Cuna thinking approaches the general problem of the *relationship with the invisible*. This is the very dimension that the theory of souls leaves unresolved. At first, Indian tradition seems quite clear about this. The spirits live in an invisible society where, as in human society, one may run into leaders and subjects, the brave and the cowardly, and, as in *The Way of Mu*, even drunkard and temperate beings, wise seers and mindless thugs. Too often, the anthropological interpretation has been that these symbolic relations are simply "replicas" of the real relations that exist in society. But this approach is merely a transcription of the exoteric Indian conception itself, which postulates a fundamental specularity between this world and the other, tending to explain real relations on the basis of symbolic ones.

Actually, the true nature of the relationship between the spirits and Indian society emerges only if we acknowledge that relations "among spirits" are not a "reflection" of relations among Indians, except as a gross caricature. Rather, the analysis of the relations among spirits reveals the set of *relations among relations*, which constitute the deeper dynamics of all shamanistic tradition. Two groups of relations are the foundation for the shaman's chant, as well as for the healer's public image and even for the very idea of his voyage. The first group defines the shaman's relations with the spirits during the rite; the second includes his relations, after the long process of initiation, with the Indian community. If we want to understand the dynamics of the shaman's activity, we must study the nature of relationships established between these two sets of relations that crystallize in the representation of the spirit's world. From this point of view, the spirit becomes *the key to conceiving any relation in traditional thought*. In other words, to understand the relations among the spirits who people the chants, we must take a closer look at the society surrounding the shaman, comparing the relations *among Indians* with the relations *between spirits and Indians*.

This more complex outlook leads us to Bateson's crucial observations on ritual symbolism, and to his concept of "progressive differentiation" or schismogenesis: "Schismogenesis," Bateson wrote in 1936, in his all-too-neglected classic, *Naven*, "is a process of differentiation in the rules of individual behaviour, which results from a combination of cumulative interactions among individuals" (Bateson 1958: 175). In this perspective, the study of an individual figure's roles in a set of relations — which we now intend to apply to the social image of the Cuna shaman — must consider the "reactions of individuals to the *reactions* of other individuals" (ibid.).

This crucial remark takes us away from vague considerations on individual personality, which may or may not be compatible with the group's cultural imprint. What we have now is an abstract and purposely formal outlook concerning a combination of relations and the dynamic behind their evolution. Bateson theorized two fundamental types of schismogenetic relationship: complementary and symmetrical:

> Many systems of relationship, either between individuals or groups of individuals, contain a tendency towards progressive change. If, for example, one of the patterns of cultural behaviour, considered appropriate in individual A, is culturally labeled as an assertive pattern, while B is expected to reply to this with what is culturally regarded as submission, it is likely that this submission will encourage

Some auxiliary spirits perched in a Cuna hut. These spirits are supposed to witness the ritual recitation and help the shaman in his therapy. (Photograph by A. Parker, from Parker and Neal 1977)

further assertion, and that this assertion will demand still further submission. We have thus a potentially progressive state of affairs, and unless other factors are present to restrain the excesses of assertive and submissive behaviour, A must necessarily become more and more assertive, while B become more and more submissive. . . . Progressive changes of this sort we may describe as *complementary* schismogenesis.

There is another type of relation, however, that in Bateson's words "equally contains the germs of progressive change. If, for example, we find boasting as the cultural pattern of behavior in one group, and that the other group replies to this with boasting, a competitive situation may develop in which boasting leads to more boasting, and so on. This type of progressive change we may call *symmetrical* schismogenesis."

Later (1972), Bateson expanded on this formulation. More generally, we can say that symmetrical schismogenesis is the "progressive separation" that occurs when competition is based upon the accentuation of a single relational response, whereas complementary schismogenesis is founded upon the progressive exaggeration of different types of relational behavior. Following these ideas, it can be argued that the process of schismogenesis, be it complementary or symmetrical, is not only a way for individuals or groups

(not necessarily only *real* ones) to differentiate themselves from each other, but also an essential means of coexisting, establishing unstable relations, and sending messages (Houseman and Severi 1986). Thus the ultimate separation of individuals and groups should be understood as the final *degeneration* of the schismogenetic process, which actually points to the conditions of an unstable relationship. In this perspective, Bateson's proposal of a theoretically endless series of cumulative interactions provides us with a model for the transient relationships that link sets of relations.

Armed with these new ideas, we may break away from the static concept of hierarchical relations between seer and healer, which had developed out of our analysis of soul theory. We can now go on to examine the specific way in which the shaman *builds meanings* by manipulating spirits. The preservation, representation, and administration of his secret knowledge—chanted in a language the profane cannot decipher—is certainly his way of differentiating himself from the other Cuna, after his lengthy initiation. On the other hand, the community's very identity is deeply rooted in the shaman's secret and in the tradition whence he derives his authority. To the "golden men" (as the Cuna call themselves), the shaman's knowledge is the summit of their history and culture. Thus when the shaman—who knows not only the secrets of the invisible souls, but also the *lingua franca* that enables him to make pacts with the animal and vegetable spirits —shows himself to be as different as possible from the others, he is confirming the group's shared rules of behavior. The case of healing epidemics, in which the seer's sleep requires the entire village to observe a series of rigorous prohibitions (related to food and sex), is the clearest example of this complementarity between the shaman and the group (Howe 1976).

We have here the prerequisites for describing these dynamics as *complementary schismogenesis*, in Bateson's terms. The more unique the shaman declares himself to be, the more exceptional and rare his qualities and powers, the more the group will reiterate his conformity to an all-inclusive, single model for collective identity. Furthermore, we can now discard the idea that relations among spirits are a reflection of real relations among men, and thus explain the community's relations with the spirits. Precisely because it concentrates only on defining relations among relations, the theory of schismogenesis *does not distinguish* between symbolic and real relations. Indeed, from this point of view, such a distinction may even seem meaningless: not only do symbolic relations fail to represent social relations, but all relations are *both* real and symbolic, albeit at different logical levels. Thus visible and invisible cease to appear as two fixed poles, or two distinct cosmological regions. Rather, they become two qualities of everyday experience, continually intertwined in the most varied relations. As a consequence, the relationship with the spirits, as described in the ritual recitation of a therapeutic chant, *competes* with real relations, rather than reflecting them. Contrary to a persistent anthropological belief, the shaman is certainly not the only person able to contact the spirits. In Cuna society, quite literally, *anyone* can do it. It might even be said that communicating with the spirits is not the exception, but the rule. The forest is teeming with invisible presences and almost every Indian knows short formulas, invocations, or magic spells with which to address them.

We must add, however, that the very initiation process whereby the shaman becomes a "seer" *like* the spirits (and learns to speak *their* language) sets off a parallel process of differentiation *between the shaman and the spirit*. To avoid losing his identity and thereby forfeiting his healing powers, the shaman must ritually negotiate contracts that will *control* both his own

auxiliary spirits and the rival pathogenic spirits. Thus the chanter's invocation of the spirit's help necessarily implies two contradictory schismogenetic processes. On the one hand, the shaman strives to preserve the *difference* between himself and the group, to maintain a distinction between his own behavior, which is ostensibly transgressive, and that of the community, which conforms to pre-established rules. On the other hand, when he relates to the spirits he must act on the basis of a conventional but precarious bond with them. This does not mean that the shaman "identifies" with the spirits. On the contrary, performing a symmetrical behavior, he *competes* with them. It is clear that, in differentiating himself from the human condition he is *moving closer* to the world of the spirits, along the lines of a *symmetrical schismogenesis*: the stronger the auxiliary spirit, the more powerful the shaman must be. And as the pathological spirit grows more threatening, so must the shaman be able to respond accordingly. The shaman's ritual recitation is completely immersed in these unstable dynamics. The chant is both invocation and duel. When the shaman silently repeats the chant's secret and then feeds the inebriating beverage to his own auxiliary spirits, thereby reinforcing their "headdresses" (i.e., their mental strength), he is walking a thin line between these two rival sets of relations: complementary to the other Indians and symmetrical to the spirits.

Thus the healer-chanter must always *remain different*, both from the other Indians in day-to-day life *and* from the spirits in the rite. This crucial position is the foundation of his power, as represented in his chant to the spirits and reconfirmed each time he pronounces it. Such a complex network of relations, with its abstract implications, is quite clear in Cuna society. The Cuna are extremely careful in scrutinizing and evaluating the healer's position as it continually changes in the vast range of relations between humans and spirits. And the shamans themselves, with their constant struggles for supremacy, always keep an eye on one another.

Unlike the knowledge handed down in myths, the power to heal is under constant exposure to the jealous and critical surveillance of the social group. If the personality of the shaman (the *nele* or the *inatuleti*) is not sufficiently differentiated from normal behavior, the power to heal can disappear. The reverse is also true: loss of power can become a threat to the shaman himself. If he seems unable to control his relations with the spirits, he will appear to resemble them too closely.

This behavior may be viewed as excessive symbolic transgression, leading him to social margination and even, in some extreme cases, to capital punishment. In many Amerindian societies (see, for instance, Devereux 1963 for the Mohave case) the shaman's chances of losing control of his own powers are foreseen and described in detail. Such a failure is felt to be a threat to the entire community. As a result, the shaman becomes a terrible danger, and often is killed.

·Thus, precisely because of the interconnection between the various differentiation processes, shamanism risks becoming (in societies other than the Cuna) what Bateson called a *degenerative system*, that is, one that eliminates itself through loss of meaning. This aspect of ceaseless danger, of borderline socialization, makes shamanistic tradition particularly sensitive to outside stimuli, and seems to characterize the social image of the Cuna shaman. Many ethnographers have pointed out that shamanistic symbolic systems (albeit acknowledged as such by intuitive methods) are extremely sensitive to anything new, foreign, or different. It appears that in many societies (certainly for the Cuna) shamanism is one of the most sensitive points of encounter with the outside world, the aspect of most rapid transformation in traditional knowledge. Yet because its renewed form dynamically adapts its basic coordinates to their new context, it is also one of the more durable.

Little is known about the history of Cuna shamanistic tradition, nor is this the place to dwell upon it in detail. There is almost general agreement on at least one point, however: the chants are relatively recent. As we will see, the Cuna themselves proudly recall the passage from ritual performances to the chanting. The available information is too scarce to permit any definitive conclusions, but we may reasonably suppose that if the chants existed in the rites described by sixteenth- and seventeenth-century observers, they probably were—as they still are in some Amazonian societies—a limited and minor part of a broader system of symbols and ritual gestures. It has only been in recent centuries, thanks to the Indians' contact, and especially to their direct or indirect *confrontation* with the white man, that the chants have grown to the unusual size and central importance recognized today. We may tentatively agree with those who have described the Cuna shamanistic tradition as the progressive transformation of a ritual system founded upon symbolic gestures (which still flourish in other societies neighboring to the Cuna), and we may support their claim that this evolution coincided with the "birth of an epic" founded upon texts and preserved in picture-writing, although still transmitted mainly by oral tradition (Kramer 1970).

Careful examination of the few great chants that have been published confirms this hypothesis, from the references to Spanish cannons to the spyglass of the seer spirits in *Villages by the Wayside of Madness*; from the foreigner's "silver boat" found in *The Way of Mu* to the modern chant "of the scissors" (*Tisla ikala*: Holmer and Wassén 1963). This evolution involves positive and resilient qualities, yet it is tormented by the presence (intermittent; not, as elsewhere, victorious and overwhelming) of a besieging civilization. With exceptional clarity, the traditional elaboration of this intermittent presence sheds light on the chant's hidden function: to construct a *terra incognita*, populated by symbols and continually redesigned, depending upon the disturbances imposed by history. We believe this to be an identifying trait of every traditional representation of suffering. If the Cuna shamanistic tradition strikingly reveals that function, it is because of the remarkably explicit way in which its discourse of the spirits and their ambiguities have provided a successful means of reacting to real and imagined encroachment by the white man. As a result, we can today recognize some of the traits of our own culture in the *terra incognita* of the Cuna healing chants.

Metamorphosis and pain

At first glance, the chants bear few traces of the elaborate mosaic of different symbolic spaces we have described above. The shaman's invocation almost neglects the mythical universe, dwelling upon the actual conditions of the rite. This leads us to the setting of the ritual scene, as reflected in the chants.

As we have seen, the etiological myth, relating the origin of evil and illness, is a secret in Cuna tradition. This unformulated text is the heart of the chant, and yet it is not entirely a part of it. The chant involves the idea that the unchanging partition into different worlds, which creates the permanent appearance of all beings in the universe, was never completed.[6] It is as if the static spatial order of the world had *already* been upset, merely by the appearance of illness. From the moment that this mythical universe, which can be orderly only inasmuch as it is abstract, is exposed to the

---

6. The reader will find a version of this myth in Severi (1982).

happenstance of daily life, and thus to the rhythm of time, the world is suddenly revealed to be the realm of disorder.

The healing chant must not only represent, but also explain—in its own perspective—pain. The mental model of the world it creates must withstand time and chance; suffering and mythical order must be able to coexist in it. From this dilemma arise the idea of metamorphosis—the ceaseless interpenetration of differing worlds, which is the true abstract horizon of the chants—and the narrative style of these texts, based predominantly upon formulaic enunciations, which are then varied almost imperceptibly (Severi 1985). Finally, apart from the mythical circuit to which the chants never stop alluding, the Cuna healer always describes a true *chain of transformations* in the *ikala*. This is the crux of the entire issue.

At the core of the chant, and of the entire ritual manipulation of illness, we find the Cuna idea of *binyemai*—the incessant changing appearance of men, animals, trees—everything in the world. Thus the jaguar in the *nia ikala* can soar through the sky, blazing like the sun, or sing in the night like an invisible bird in the forest (Severi 1982). Indeed, the jaguar *is* the sun, just as those sounds in the dark *are* the jaguar. This idea of a changing world, light-years away from the fixed consistency of the myth, allows the *Mu Ikala* woman in childbirth to become a tree whose leafless limbs are broken in the wind. Likewise, the fetus can become a bleeding fruit hidden among those limbs, or a log swept off by an impetuous river; and the shaman can transform that fetus into a bead or a cacao bean, perhaps even one of the same cacao beans burning at the foot of the sick Indian's hammock during the chant.

Thus is the shaman's voyage: not some simple fairy tale of the soul as many have believed, but the traditional form of describing the metamorphoses of a world immersed in time. Seen in this light, the Cuna shaman's voyage reminds us of Wittgenstein's definition of comprehension in a memorable passage of the *Philosophical Investigations* (Wittgenstein 1953). Wittgenstein remarks that the process of comprehension —defined by him as the logical movement of thought as unrelated to any kind of intentional psychology— objectively leads man to create *intermediary terms* to link different phenomena, while simultaneously "discovering pathways" through that "maze of streets" which is language. Such an elaboration of intermediate terms, here deriving both from cosmology and from the'

experience of pain, creates the impression that the shaman's chant is narrating nothing. Actually, the healer is minutely reclassifying a few fragments of his own reality into an entirely different framework: the world of the spirits. As we have said, the Cuna tradition defines "being sick" as "feeling without seeing." Thanks to the model of the soul's travels, Cuna traditional chants construct a net of intermediary terms around the experience of disorder and pain.

To pronounce the healing chants—in Cuna terms, "to follow the path"—is to use the word to explore the way leading to the many invisible replicas of the world, while creating a model for the experiential crisis that suffering always represents. The keywords in the Indians' commentary of the chants now acquire a deeper meaning: "to travel" means to attempt to understand the world's modifications, perceived through a model of physical pain, or the anguish that accompanies the delirium. "To establish a new pact with the spirits" means to weave this net of comprehension toward and beyond the limits of the known world, building a model for this *terra incognita* and simultaneously one for the experience of pain.

Thus although I have attempted to study the social dynamics of shaman activity from the double perspective of the soul and the spirit, and of the system of their relations, I would venture to say that shamanism is not to be considered *only as an institution*. Rather, its ultimate function appears here to be the construction, by way of traditional concepts, of a paradigm to balance the inner *terra incognita* revealed in suffering and the twin *terra incognita* situated at the limits of perception. The confrontation of these two aspects of experience—one situated *too far* and the other *too close* to everyday perception— reveals the fundamental features of the traditional representation of suffering.

Let us now recall again that the chants are probably the outcome of a recent evolution of an ancient ritual tradition. According to Kramer (1970), the "chant of chants" (*apsoket ikala*) records this most recent transformation of shamanistic tradition. It tells of a highly improbable, solemn, ecumenical assembly of chiefs and shamans from all the villages, in which it was decided that the chants, and the chants alone, would thenceforth narrate and preserve traditional knowledge. As a result, some therapeutic rituals disappeared, and the word became the sole, all-powerful instrument of the shaman.

Although it is formulated in the emblematic, sententious style of myth, this story can perhaps be taken literally. The origin of the shamanistic text is indeed the ritual gesture. Here the myth is so explicit that it almost acquires the character of a saga. It is as if one day a collective decision was made never to dance again, but to describe dances; to avoid masks and body paint, but to list them endlessly in minute detail; to stop mimicking the behavior of the animals, but to learn and speak their language.

Herein lies the essential paradox of this text: certainly the chants are descriptions of rites, just as the images of the spirits that populate the chants dance and perform symbolic gestures that the Indians may once have performed publicly in the middle of the Cuna villages. But today the chants are still very close to the ritual gesture itself: there is so little difference between the gesture and its description that the latter can almost be called a rite in itself. Emotions, images, ordinary objects, and rituals are brought forth in seemingly haphazard fashion, no longer arranged in any order of discourse. These fragments of reality appear together, both in the ritual scene and in the shaman's narration of his voyage. When ordinary objects are named in the ceremonial language, they are transformed, arranged in a different type of order, redimensioned to fit the theater of metamorphosis that is the rite.

We have spoken at length of the subtle relations between the soul, the secret, and the word. Almost as though confabulating to eliminate the superficial image of the world, in league with the spirits that redelineate the boundaries of visible and invisible, these relations turn the ritual into an incandescent crucible, where a world lying parallel to our own is evoked. From the esoteric viewpoint of shamanistic dogma, the paradox is explained in one word: *purpa*, the sonic dimension of the invisible. Thus the chant appears as a long sequence of pure sounds that keep the uninitiated from seeing the *Nia Ikala*'s world of invisible villages, or the *Mu Ikala*'s woman in childbirth, with her ''inner body'' torn asunder by the stormwinds of suffering. Once the ordinary objects (fruit, trees, beads, calabashes, brazier) have been minutely detailed in the *inatuleti*'s mystery language (which is also the language of the animals), they can no longer be seen with normal vision. To chant is to indicate the way — the *ikala* — to step out of the world. It is to remove evoked reality from the power of the eyes, just as physical or psychic pain appears to consciousness as an invisible internal

A one-legged spirit, with an impressive expression of pain on his face. (Photograph by A. Parker, from Parker and Neal 1977)

presence. It is as if the *ikala*, the path that dictates the logic of traditional chants, always beginning with a minute description of all that has preceded it, gave access to the invisible by using only sound.

Thus ''pathway of metamorphoses'' might be the best way to describe the shaman's own view of the spirit's voyage. This metaphor helps us to understand a crucial aspect of Cuna chants: the minutely detailed realism that always precedes the narration of the voyage. As the *Mu Ikala* makes perfectly clear, the rite — reduced to pure words — must always begin with the real world, as represented by the ordinary but authentic image of the person (a friend, a relative, an older woman) who has sought the shaman's help. The rite cannot proceed without first patiently recording these people's gestures, the tiniest modifications of their faces, the movements that express their anguish from the minute they sense that pain is felt by someone. Thus, setting in motion a sort of time reversal, the rite actually starts by returning to its antecedents: the entire beginning of the chant is a lengthy narration of the person (the old midwife in *The Way of Mu*, the wife of the madman in the *Nia Ikala*) who has asked the shaman to begin the rite. This realistic image reminds us, however, that the premise of any mythical voyage is real pain. Too many observers have considered the shaman to be a sort of bureaucrat of the soul, a peaceful negotiator of universal discord. In observing the shaman's actions, and especially his words, few have emphasized that they are always a complex representation of the *undecidable states* caused by uncertainty and conflict, both in the universe and in personal experience. Yet neither *The Way of Mu* nor *Villages by the Wayside of Madness* can be construed as mere accounts of a reestablishment of order, as a triumphant struggle against the forces of evil, illness, death.

In the chants the presentation of an interminable list of gestures, with its insistent repetition of objects and situations, is actually a continuous allusion to a tacit premise, the rigorously unspoken word that guards the secret. As in Amazonian cultures, in Cuna tradition power lies in knowledge and in the eloquence that knowledge bestows. Herein lies the power to transform and understand the inexpressible appearance of pain. The secret itself stands for the esoteric region of shamanistic tradition, that which describes the origin of the animals, the trees in the forest, the depths of the sea, the exploits of the stars. From the shaman's intimacy with this secret eloquence of the universe come the main rhetorical figures of the Cuna chant: the endless repetition, the continuous allusion to the gestures that accompany the shaman's words, the pungent smoke issuing from the brazier, the color of the cacao beans, the inebriating power of the ashes, the sufferings of the sick body lying in the hammock.

In chants, language is only one dimension in the production of meaning. The language of the chants is *fragile*; often, as in *Villages by the Wayside of Madness*, it borders on pure sound or onomatopeia. A perfect example is in the spirit village of metamorphoses (Severi 1982), where the echoes of animal cries accompany a complex classification of the

characteristic symptoms of madness. It is this fragility, reflection of a vision of the universe's complexity, that strikes us in conjunction with a powerful formulaic style. However, we do not intend to reduce the importance of these texts to the categories of the "birth of an epic" proposed by Kramer (1970). The very form of the chant—repeated pronunciation of formulas in varying tones—indicates that we are still far indeed from the creation of a literary genre. In the *ikala* the spoken word still serves as a ritual reconstruction of the experience of pain, delirium, or invasion by illness.

In this way we can understand the reason for the chants' obsessive realism, which always precedes and regularly intersperses the shaman's narration of his fantastic voyage. From this description of precisely defined bits of everyday life, we can clearly grasp the concrete connection of the chain of abstract concepts (soul, spirit, and path) implied by the ritual scene we have tried to analyze in this work. The suffering body stretched in the hammock, from which the soul is thought to have fled, the statues of spirits gathered around that body, the brazier with its dense cacao smoke: these symbols both materialize the text and indicate its ideal context. Almost by self-reference, the chant *contains* the ritual scene, just as the image of the ritual—deprived of gestures and reduced to the word alone—contains the chant. The ancient rite has disappeared, along with its symbolic gestures, but its style has been perfectly preserved in the intense traditional text, as still secretly intoned by the Cuna shaman.

REFERENCES

Bateson, G.
  1958 *Naven*, Stanford (1936).
  1972 *Steps toward an ecology of mind*, New York.

Densmore, F.
  1924– "Music of the Tule Indians of Panamà," Smithsonian
  1926   Miscellaneous Collection, vol. 77, no. 1, pp. 1–39, Washington.

Devereux, G.
  1963 *Mohave ethnopsychiatry and suicide*, Washington.

Eliade, M.
  1978 *Le chamanisme et les techniques de l'extase*, Paris.

Gomez, E., and C. Severi
1983   "Los pueblos del camino de la locura," *Amerindia*, 8.

Holmer, N.
1947   *Critical and comparative grammar of the Cuna language*, Etnografiska Museet, Goteborg.
1952   *Cuna ethno-linguistic dictionary*, Etnografiska Museet, Goteborg.

Holmer, N., and H. Wassén
1953   *The complete Mu-Igala*, Etnografiska Museet, Goteborg.
1958   *Nia-Ikala. Canto mágico para curar la locura*, Etnografiska Museet, Goteborg.
1963   *Serkan-Ikala y Tysla-Ikala*, Etnografiska Museet, Goteborg.

Houseman, M., and C. Severi
1986   "Bateson anthropologue." In G. Bateson, *La ceremonie du naven*, Paris.

Howe, J.
1976   "Smoking out the spirits: a Cuna exorcism." In Ph. Young, J. Howe (eds.), *Ritual and symbol in native Central America*, University of Oregon Anthropological Papers, 9.

Kramer, F.
1970   *Literature among Cuna Indians*, Etnografiska Museet, Goteborg.

Lévi-Strauss, Cl.
1958   "L'efficacité symbolique" (1949). In *Anthropologie structurale*, Paris.

Lewis, I. M.
1980   *Les religions de l'extase*, Paris.

Metraux, A.
1967   *Religions et magies Indiennes d'Amerique du Sud*, Paris.

Nordenskiold, E.
1938   *An historical and ethnological survey of the Cuna Indians*, Etnografiska Museet, Goteborg.

Parker, A., and A. Neal
1977   *Molas, Folk art of the Cuna Indians*, New York.

Prestan, A.
1976   *El uso de la chicha y la sociedad cuna*, Instituto Indigenista Interamericano, Mexico.

Searles, H.
1979   *L'effort pour rendre l'autre fou*, Paris.

Severi, C.
1981   "Le anime cuna," *La ricerca folklorica*.
1982   "Le chemin des métamorphoses," *Res 3*, Spring.
1985   "Penser par séquences, penser par territoires— cosmologie et art de la mémoire dans la pictographie cuna," *Communications*, 41.

Sherzer, J.
1983   *Cuna ways of speaking*, Austin.

Stout, D. B.
1947   *San Blas Cuna acculturation: an introduction*, Viking Fund Publications in Anthropology, New York.

Wittgenstein, L.
1953   *Philosophical investigations*, Oxford.
1967   *Notes on Frazer's Golden Bough*, Oxford.

Figure 1. Museo di Storia Naturale, Venezia, museum no. 403, coll: *Miani 1861*, h = 43.

Figure 2. *Idem*, back view.

Bari statuary

The influence exerted by European traders on the traditional production of figured objects

ENRICO CASTELLI

The present work aims at bringing together the various sources—archival, museum, and ethnographic—concerning the entire production of figured objects by the Bari, a Nilotic people of the present-day Republic of Sudan.[1] Among the many reasons for such an undertaking, my main purpose was to resolve the contradiction between the careful attention to form that is evident in the ancient Bari objects of everyday use—for example, spears, stools, female loincloths, and the statuettes, which are characterized by far less careful execution and a lack of accuracy (for example, rough surfaces, lack of attention to detail). Such a contradiction is extremely difficult to resolve if one relies on the point of view prevalent today, which thinks of these objects as belonging to the traditional ancestor cult.

The starting point for this research was the work done on the collection of Sudanese origin at the Musée de l'Homme. The Musée furnished both the place of origin and the date of acquisition of these objects, thus enhancing the importance of the relevant archival documents.[2] In reality, this collection (Castelli 1984) consists of a "fund" of objects from the Sudan, collected by the French consul in Cairo (Pacifique Henri Delaporte, 1815–1877), as well as many other people—including a traveler of great historical importance, Joseph Pons d'Arnaud (1812–1884). An engineer under the Egyptian Pasha Mohammed Ali, and author of an unpublished travel journal, d'Arnaud was appointed scientific leader of the second and third expeditions to the sources of the Nile, which expeditions reached Bari territory around 1840–1841. D'Arnaud collected numerous ethnographic objects destined both for the Pasha and as collections to be housed in the Museum d'Histoire Naturelle in Paris (Castelli 1983). On their arrival in Paris in 1843, the collections were exhibited in a so-called "ethnographic" room at the Louvre, which was later to become part of the Musée de la Marine. Over the years, other collections were added to the "fund," among them those of Delaporte and the traveler Lejean. The collection in its entirety is housed today in the Musée de l'Homme and constitutes without doubt the most important ethnographic testimony of the Sudanese Nilotic populations that we have.

D'Arnaud expresses himself as follows with regard to the Bari statuettes, in the manuscript diary-catalogue of ethnographic objects:

> Wood idols (or rather, *statues in wood*, because they seem to have no cult). One, of the male sex, and the other female, which show, better than any description can, the geometric tattooings among the women of these people, their attires, their colourings, their ornaments; it will be noted that the lower jaw has no teeth—as among the people; and the upper teeth of the statue are of human teeth pulled from young girls at the desired time. Circumcision is not practiced in the two sexes, which the statue also indicates. These two statues were offered to me by Queen Achouk, the King's favourite, who always accompanied him on his visits to us on board.
>
> N.B.: I regret that the male sex statuette, which had been destined for the viceroy, was lost in shipwreck during my return voyage (24-10-1841).[3]

Unfortunately, not one of the ten statuettes housed in the Musée de l'Homme coincides with this detailed description. The oldest registration documents currently filed at the Musée de la Marine date from 1856 and refer to eleven "fetiches des Barrys." All attempts made in Paris to trace this very first evidence of Bari sculpture have so far been unsuccessful. Even the collection

---

1. The Bari belong, linguistically speaking, to the eastern Nilotic family of languages; nomadic herdsmen, they migrated from east to west, settling in the area between the shores of Lake Turkana and the Nile itself, a settlement that was to become permanent long before the coming of European traders, thanks to the fertile lands to be found in the region. These had probably been cultivated by others in former times. In fact, ethnographic data regarding the presence of slaves, used exclusively to work the land, would seem to prove the existence of earlier populations in the area.

It is important to emphasize the presence among the Bari of the system of barter with other neighboring tribes, thanks to large iron deposits on their lands and of entire villages of blacksmiths, although nothing is known of their origin and role in Bari culture.

2. Archives of the Muséum d'Histoire filed in the Archives Nationales, those of the Société de Géographie, filed at the Bibliothèque Nationale, and those at the Musée de la Marine.

3. D'Arnaud, J. P. In the Archives Nationales, Paris Museum (A.N.P.M. AJ 45, colis 20).

belonging to Ferdinand Werne (a German traveler who accompanied d'Arnaud on the second expedition), which is housed in the Berlin Museum, lacks figured objects, nor does Werne himself mention any such objects in his catalogue. This collection—which is distinguished by the high quality of its exhibits and its relative completeness—demonstrates the uniqueness of d'Arnaud's two statuettes, which are so unfortunately lost to us. However, Werne's account of his journey, published in Berlin in 1848, contains an extremely significant passage: "They had brought along a crudely carved wooden doll which, contrary to our expectations, was just that. They thought it exceedingly funny when we inquired whether they revered it or prayed to it as a goddess" (Werne, pp. 316–317).

These few lines have helped me to resolve the contradiction contained in d'Arnaud's text, between "fetish" and "non-cult" objects. The first of these terms became indissolubly linked with the objects, while the second (the only true ethnographic data) was to disappear completely, buried because of innumerable factors, both cultural and economic: on the one hand, the preoccupations of a European nineteenth-century culture that saw in these objects confirmation of the primitive state of a people awaiting the word of God and economic "redemption" from their "savage" state; on the other, pure and simple economic interests, whereby a figured object, labeled as an object of cult, could be sold for more.

Given the importance of the two above-mentioned objects (which have unfortunately not come down to us), it is important to try tracing their origin more carefully. The king—by name Lokono—of whom d'Arnaud speaks, was in reality the "rain-maker" of the Bilinian Bari. Bilinian was the name given by the Bari to the mountains situated to the east of the Nile at about 10 km from the river itself; the surrounding villages were united under the military and political leadership of Lokono. One should keep in mind that the particular political structure of "age-classes" peculiar to the Bari, prevented any expansion of the rain-maker's predominance over all the Bari villages; cultural similarity was thus limited, leading to the supposition that the production of these figured objects was confined to the area of the Bilinian Bari.

As it happens, the descriptions mentioned coincide perfectly with the third and only example of Bari statuary that we have. The 43 cm high statuette is housed in the Museum of Natural History in Venice (figs. 1, 2). It is part of an ethnographic collection undertaken by Giovanni Miani (1810–1882), which he subsequently shipped to Venice for exhibition there.[4] The sculpture is in soft, light wood with a dark patina. The wealth of decoration—carried out with the aid of other materials (iron and leather)—consists of bracelets created by the spiral-winding of an iron band, thus confirming its Bari origin: this element, in fact, is to be found in all Bari objects of everyday use. The statuette is of a young woman dressed in a short chain-mail skirt attached by a leather belt—the typical loincloth used before the advent of colored glass beads. Of great interest is the scarification that decorates the ventral section and the forehead. It is carried out with a fine blade, by means of two very deep and closely set parallel incisions. Within the area delimited by these two lines, a series of smaller perpendicular incisions completes the motif, which opens out into an ample zigzag over the abdomen and a W on the forehead. A layer of what appears to be chalk has been made to penetrate the incisions with the purpose, probably, of highlighting the scarification designs against the blackish wood. The scarification line or cord is no longer than 5 mm, an extremely accurately done work, demonstrating a refined engraving technique together with a careful choice of both wood and colors.[5]

As regards the sculptural stance, it is rigid, with both arms and legs slightly apart, forming equal angles. The front view shows an upward-tapering bust supporting the head without any visible scansion. The side view is exactly the opposite: by exaggeratedly accentuating the nape of the neck and the chin, the artist has carried out a marked volumetric scansion of the head and neck.

4. The collection was brought to Italy in 1861; as regards the statuette (cat. 403), this was illustrated and described briefly in 1865: "model of a virgin in ebany [sic!] covered in iron . . ." (Miani, p. 99).

5. As regards the ventral scarifications: "Bari women have a large number of scarifications/incisions done, going from the navel to the breast, which resemble a corset decorated with geometrical designs" (Miani, op. cit., p. 28). Further, on the same page, the author informs us that the rain-maker's wives/women, and they alone, wear four ivory bracelets on their upper arms. The model for the statuette would therefore be a young unmarried Bari girl, and daughter to the rain-maker.

Regarding the abnormal enlargement of the knees, there is some precise information in the literature:

A remarkable deformity is frequently noticed in the Bari women, namely, the enormous enlargement of the *bursae patelae* of both knees, often to the size of an orange. This is probably caused by the fact that the women perform most of their duties kneeling and also by their being obliged to crawl into the huts on account of the low doorways (Emin 1888, pp. 5–6).

Such an expansion of the head is in fact fundamental to the cultural element that the artist was intent on showing, that is, the scarification on the forehead and the hairstyle. The extension of this motif over a horizontal surface, by providing sufficient engravable area, suggests a close-up view of the statue from above, a viewing position from which the distension of both frontal and upper surfaces of the face, scarification and hairstyle, can be fully appreciated and exploited.

It remains to be seen how Miani managed to acquire this piece for his exhibit. The answer may be found in his diary: he was in Gondokoro, the Bilinian landing place founded by traders in December 1860—in other words, at exactly the moment when the population, after suffering four years of drought, attacked the residence of Nygilö, the rain-maker of the Bilinian villages and the brother of the dead Lokono.[6] While the chief paid with his life for his inability to produce rain for the farming activities of his subjects, the members of his family took refuge on Miani's boats. Among them was Nygilö's son, who accompanied Miani during the following months. The information gleaned leads one to believe that it was during the sack of Nygilö's house that the last of the "original" statuettes left the Bilinian village, to be shipped to Europe later.

We will now turn to the other group of statuettes attributed to the Bari. While they differ in quality, they are far more numerous: there are about fifty objects, almost all of them reaching Europe between 1850 and the turn of the century.[7] In this study we will not

concentrate on the history of their acquisition. For this second lot, it will be more useful to study its propagation as so-called "Bari objects of cult" throughout European museums and ethnography.

At first sight, these objects show a remarkable diversity of formal solutions, although maintained within a rigid general approach. Elements in common are the rigidity of the trunk, the arms attached to the trunk, hands and feet expressed by mere parallel cuts, legs slightly apart or parallel, separated originally by a clean horizontal cut. The wood is hard and fibrous, the surfaces are never smooth and often apparently tinted with ochre. The eyes and ears, and at times the nostrils and mouth, are merely indicated by holes made with a red-hot iron. A leather thong passing around the neck and bust serves as a handle for carrying the object, as is usual with other Nilotic objects of everyday use. Worthy of note is the fact that, while there is representation of the male sex, in the entire collection there is no sign whatsoever of the female sex, although some of the statuettes are lacking in any sexual attributes altogether. Other than these general characteristics, specific elements make it sometimes possible to identify the hand of a particular sculptor or workshop and the sequence of production of several sculptures.

Two of the objects do differ from the rest in a series of details (figs. 3, 4). The statuette housed in the Musée de l'Homme (30.54.344) is 35 cm high; of the other (1382), all that remains is the photograph in the Photothèque of the Musée de l'Homme; this object, which was housed in the Musée de Douai, was burned during the war together with the rest of the ethnographic collections. It is quite clear that these objects are the work of the same artist. They are characterized by a large smiling mouth, superbly arched eyebrows, and an indentation along the neck. Although the arms adhere closely to the sides, two fissures between the arms themselves and the body allow for a leather thong to be passed through. The dentellation along the neck recalls the dentellated sticks

---

6. Brun Rollet (1855) is quite clear as to the kinship between Nygilö and Lakono. This information, also noted by Whitehead (1936), contrasts with Beaton's version, in which Nigila is portrayed solely as an adviser to the rain-maker Subek, Lokono's son, incapable of assuming the custom of generous offerings to propitiate rain, made previously by the crowd not far from Gondokoro, where he had taken refuge (Beaton, p. 188).

7. The statuettes comprising this group are housed in Musée de l'Homme (ten exhibits; donor Delaporte 1853: N° 30.54.335, 30.54 336, 30.54 337, 30.54.340, 30.54.342, 30.54.343, 30.54.344, 30.54.1846, 30.54.1847, 30.54.1848); Museum für Völkerkunde Berlin-Dahlem (five exhibits; donor Junker 1897: N° III A 784, III A 785, III A 786, III A 787, III A 4624); Musée d'Ethnographie Geneva (eight exhibits; donor Porte 1920: N° 8912, 8913, 8914 anonymous donor 1925: N° 8915, 10768, 10769, 10770, 10771); Museum für Völkerkunde Wien (ten exhibits; donors Buchta, Hansal, Emin 1880–1883: N° 10857, 12847, 12848, 12849, 14466, 14467, 16922, 16923, 16924, 16925); Merseyside County Museum—Liverpool (three exhibits; donor Melly 1854: N° R.1.20, R.1.21; donatore Parkyns 1850 (?) n.n.); Museo di antropologia e etnografia di Leningrado (five exhibits; donor Junker 1888: N° 5227.13, 5227.14, 5227.15, 5227.16, 5227.18); Staatl. Museum für

Völkerkunde München (one exhibit; donor Schweinfurth: N° 17.11.9); Linden Museum Stuttgart (one exhibit; donor Ketterer (?): N° 118718); Museo di storia naturale Venezia (two exhibits; donor Miani 1861: N° 403; s.n.).

To this list must be added the six exhibits housed in the 1800s in the Musée Berthoud in Douai and destroyed during the war.

I should like to take this opportunity to thank the curators of the above-mentioned museums for having so kindly put the information and the photographs published here at my disposal.

used generally (both for work purposes and in rituals) by the Nilotic tribes, and particularly by the Bari.[8]

What is surprising in these statuettes is the balance achieved between the volume of the head and legs and the torso itself, the upper part of which is hollowed out, differing distinctly from the lower part, which is trapezoidal. Worthy of note also is the large space between the legs at the point of attachment with the body. Such a clean cut and not very realistic incision is due to the carving tool used. Even today among the Lotuko, besides the axe (Lotuko-aloli), a wedge-shaped "percussion-knife" (Lotuko-atholu) is used to carve wood, with the width of the percussion plane affecting the minimum obtainable width of the cavity. An example of its use is the Bari stool, where the tool's largest dimensions are the basis for the lateral grilles that decorate these objects of everyday use. Undoubtedly, a tool of this kind is not well suited to all the requirements of a sculpture of the human figure; on the other hand, the object exhibited in Venice shows a careful and accurate execution with the use of this knife, an instrument that would be more apt for the cutting and finishing of surfaces. Yet another object, belonging to the Melly family[9] and housed in the Liverpool Museum since 1854 (fig. 5), has certain characteristics in common with the other two objects mentioned, that is, mainly the large smiling mouth and two underarm holes that suggest the possible presence of a leather thong long since lost. The bottle-shaped neck supports a head that is distinguished by its upward-tapering shape; a notched crest going from the

forehead to the nape of the neck suggests a hairstyle. Arms and legs are mere stumps so that the feet and hands are nonexistent.

The remaining sculptures have been divided on the basis of certain general formal characteristics. Often, such a division coincides with groups of objects belonging to a particular donor, a fact that is extremely significant. It leads one to suppose that these sculptures were destined for sale from the very beginning, and therefore made to order, each similar group being the work of the same artist or artisan "shop." The considerable diversity of approach between groups, on the other hand, would be due to the diverse dates of manufacture and the differences in the personalities of those who sculpted them.

The first group is characterized by the typical egg-shaped head where the carving of the eyebrows stands out above the face, the hollowed-out surface of which may be either oval or triangular, with the apex facing downward. The size of the surfaces seems to affect the degree of definition of the features: the mouth may disappear completely or be accentuated with a double prominence of the lips. This group contains objects from Berlin, Paris, Leningrad, Liverpool, Munich, and Vienna (figs. 6–24). Within the group, the similarity of the subgroup consisting of the objects housed in the Musée de l'Homme may be noted: the arms adhere to the trunk and end in projecting hands, which may be identified by horizontal cuts (figs. 9–15).

Yet another group may be identified by the characteristic mouth, in relief, which contrasts with the other facial features. This frequently leads to an amplifying of the facial dimensions at the expense of the total volume of the head, thus losing what is the most interesting aspect of these sculptures, that is, the ratio between the volume of the head and the surface of the face. The first series belonging to this group had a variety of donors: two objects belong to the Delaporte collection (figs. 25, 26); another two are from the Junker collection (figs. 27, 28). The characteristics of this series are the face, which one would define as almost monkeylike, framing prominent lips, and an enormous nose that totally obliterates the oval of the face, spreading out sideways and terminating in the accentuatedly protruding ears.

There is an even greater similarity among the Vienna statuettes. All have in common the conical-shaped head, its base, which is completely out of proportion, serving to house a vast oral cavity in which a few human teeth are still embedded in the upper jaw. Here

8. As regards the other three exhibits at the Douai Museum, there is little further to add, since the measurements are missing. From the photograph it would seem that in two of them, the eyes were created by embedding a seed or a bead in the wood, a rather unusual way, found only in one figure in Liverpool and in one in Vienna.

9. André Melly (1802–1851), a native of Genoa, was a rich cloth merchant in Liverpool. In 1850, together with his wife and his son Charles, he undertook a journey that eventually brought him to Khartoum, where he came in contact with all the most important members of the European community. He acquired various objects of Bari origin from Brun Rollet that are today housed in the Liverpool Museum. However, it was from a Tuscan merchant Nicola Ulivi (1792–1852) that he bought the Bari sculptures:

Later in the day Charles and his father went to see the collections of a certain monsieur Nicola, a tuscan naturalist, at that time absent on the White Nile. They found a number of horribly sculptured "fetiches". These were probably some of those Bari ancestor-figures which the Khartoum merchants used yearly to bring back from around Gondokoro under the impression that they were idols (Whitehead 1938, pp. 301–302).

again, one is aware of the hand of a particular artist, because of the unusual carving of the pelvis, which is thrown into relief. In two other objects the mouth is of exaggerated proportions (fig. 34a, b). Coming from different museums (Stuttgart, Berlin), these objects, despite their evident similarity in form, have been uniquely attributed to the Dinka—perhaps because the statues reached the above museums much later, at the end of the war against the Mahadias (1898).[10]

And finally, there is another group consisting of an internally similar series, characterized by the gradual disappearance of fundamental physical elements such as the genital organs, the navel, and the hands. What does remain of the human figure is the volumetric scansion between head, torso, and legs. The look of these objects appears to have been largely determined by the shape of the piece or branch of wood chosen for their manufacture. They are therefore thin and emaciated, or stocky and shapeless, according to the size of the wood from which fragments have been cut off with hasty inexperienced hands, to bring out the figure itself (figs. 35–48). The series that stands out from this group is that acquired in Paris in 1925 by the Genève Museum and is distinguished by its characteristic coloring. Against the body, usually tinted in red, the face—deprived of any artificial color and therefore of the natural yellowish color of the wood—stands out, accentuated by the arched monkey-black eyebrows (figs. 40–43).

If we now turn our attention to the means by which this large group of sculptures was obtained, we note, first, that only some of them were bought on the spot. One of the first direct testimonies informs us of their presence in merchant houses in Khartoum, together with other goods from the territories to the south. The existence in Cairo, during the last century, of a vast market in ethnographic goods coming from the African hinterland has been amply documented. It is interesting to note that an integral part of the buying campaigns for European museums were the visits of travelers and explorers to the houses of merchants (Arabs, Greeks, Jews, and so on) whose boats sailed the Nile. Romolo Gessi complains in a letter to one of his correspondents that W. Junker, who was visiting Cairo at the time,

10. C. F. Seligman, 1917. Confusion between carved Bari and Bongo objects has perhaps a precedent in the work of Rev. J. G. Wood, *The Natural History of Man*, London 1870, where one may note on page 500 an illustration of two objects side by side, one undoubtedly of Bari origin (Colonel Lane Fox's collection) but both attributed to the Bongo.

Figure 49. Museo di Storia Naturale, Venezia, without museum no., coll: *Miani 1861*, h = 53.

bought up everything of ethnographic value he could lay his hands on, thus causing the prices to rise. It is quite certain that Delaporte acquired the ten statuettes housed today in Paris on this market, and it was in this way that at least three of those in Vienna were bought, that is, in Cairo from the crew of the *Novara* on her return to Europe from an expedition in the Pacific.[11]

There are also fundamental differences in the manner of their registration in museums: from the "fetishes" of Delaporte to the "ancestor figures" of Junker, to the vaguer "human representations" (Emin), to the complete lack of any interpretation whatsoever of the objects in question, along with highly dubious attributions as to origin (White Nile, Dinka). There is no mention, one may note, of the presence of statues of the ancestors, either in the reports of missionaries such as Angelo Vinco or Antonio Kaufmann—whose care for precise observation in the sphere of religion and ritual was considerable—or by travelers such as Baker or Brun Rollet or Lejean. Yet all of these people spent long periods of time among the Bari (1850–1880).

It was during the period when waterway contacts with Bari territory were interrupted that the basis was laid for the development of a European "scholarly" tradition concerning the precise nature of the statuettes. It differed markedly, at least in part, from the original museum and ethnographic data, but it served well the image of Africa that Europe was gradually building up for itself: the image of a primitive world, a polytheistic world, tied to its unknown rites, of which the numerous human and animal representations—with what was emphasized as their deformed appearance—were the objective and undeniable manifestation.

The first eye-witness account of the ancestor cult among the Bari having wooden images as its object comes down to us from Mounteney-Jephson, a traveler and journalist sent by Stanley in 1888 to rescue the reluctant Emin Pasha. Mounteney-Jephson's stay among the Bari was short, and the result is a series of errors and stereotypes in the chapter dedicated to them (Mounteney-Jephson, pp. 140–141). This account regarding statuettes of the ancestors which would hang in Bari huts was taken up by Stigand Bey, an English official and commissioner or administrator of the Mongalla province at the turn of the century. His book, which appears to be posthumous, does mention the presence of statues of the ancestors among the Bari, but the information is confined to the introduction to the volume, and is not to be found in the chapters dedicated to Bari customs and ways (Stigand, p. 44). The credibility of such information was laid open to

discussion by Seligman, who, in a long and well-argued note, stresses the fact that the author, because of his early death, was unable to read the proofs before printing (Seligman, p. 412).

Seligman himself at first advanced the theory of cultural influence by Sudanese populations living on the west bank of the Nile, in order to explain both the presence of the Bari statuettes and their disappearance on the eve of the twentieth century. This theory, however, was repeatedly criticized, as, for example, in the stimulating review that Evans-Pritchard wrote in 1928 on the above article by Seligman, his preceptor. Evans-Pritchard asks whether perhaps many of the sculptures then in European museums were not in fact manufactured directly for such museums by craftsmen aware of possible economic gain, rather than being an integral part of local tradition. Although he was lacking in data relative to the Bari, the possibility of a production of statuettes for an overseas market was brought to mind by a similar case which he had himself observed among the Azande. In the following years, Seligman, given the impossibility of obtaining any on-the-spot information as to the use of wooden statuettes, decided to exclude these from the text of his work on the black populations of South Sudan; the only mention made of the statuettes is in the introduction to the volume itself. Here, his previously held theory of a cultural borrowing with the populations of the west bank of the Nile gives way to another, more prudently expressed, hypothesis: that of a remote influence from the regions of the interior of Zaire (Seligman 1932, p. 23).

After the Second World War, a growing interest in African art and a renewed attention to the different formal solutions to be found in primitive art—aided by the unprecedented possibilities offered by the development of graphic reproduction—began to appear in various studies on African sculpture. In some of these works, which were attempting to provide a complete panorama of black sculpture on a continental scale, the Bari objects were rediscovered; they were, after all, one of the very few examples of sculpture outside the regions of the rain forests (so much richer in such art forms). The inclusion of objects about which scientific knowledge was extremely limited, the sources contradictory and the aesthetic value almost unrecognized, led to the uncritical adoption of the interpretation—in reality a legend—which would have them objects of cult and statues of the ancestors, and

11. Concerns those from the collections previously housed at Castello di Miramare in Trieste (nos. 16922, 16923, 16924, 16925).

photographic reproduction compensated for the nonexistent ethnographic evidence.[12]

To further the study on the Bari statuettes, one should also mention certain wooden clubs with their handles carved in the shape of a human head. While there is very little information on these objects, what we do have is extremely valuable. One archival document, d'Arnaud's travel journal, in fact is quite explicit in its reference to the presence, among the gifts received from Lokono, of a wooden club with a carved human head: ". . . on leaving, they made me a gift of their ax, a club with the head of a man, and a seat which a slave always carries after them" (D'Arnaud, op. cit.).

It is worth noting here that the objects described, as part of the attributes of a chief, assume over and above their specific function the characteristic of insignia of rank: this is probably also the case of the club with carved human head which the Bari rain-maker presented to d'Arnaud in 1841. The object itself does not appear in the various installments of the catalogue of Nilotic objects which the author sent to Paris; perhaps the club too was lost on the long journey down the Nile. There is, however, a similar object housed in the National Archeological and Ethnological Museum "L. Pigorini" in Rome (cat. 48035). This object was transferred from the Royal Armory in Turin, where it had been deposited before 1891; with all probability it had been brought there around 1853 by Brun Rollet, who had donated it to the king of Sardinia (Castelli 1986, p. 19). The 90-cm-long object is tinted in a blackish color; the head is undoubtedly Bari, showing a hollowed-out face, well-defined by the superbly arched eyebrows and a mouth, partially filled with resin, in which the fragment of a tooth is embedded. Traces of a similar resinous substance mark the eye holes.

A second and similar object is mentioned by G. O. Whitehead in an article dedicated to the English traveler Mansfield Parkyns (1823–1894). The object (of which two photographs were published without any mention of its measurements) is the property of the Parkyns family (see Whitehead 1940). It would seem that Parkyns bought this club, together with two Bari statuettes, in Khartoum, at the house of the merchant trader Nicola Ulivi, around 1849 (cf. note 9). Yet a third club with carved human head and attributed to

12. Cf. Frobenius 1923 (table XLXXI); Sydow 1954; Holy 1967; Tcernova, G. A., and Old'erogge, D., 1967; Schweeger-Hefel 1969 et al.

the Dinka is housed in Leningrad (cat. 5225-19). The object is part of the Junker collection and is mentioned by Boccassino, also without indications as to the measurements (Boccassino 1966, p. 299). From the photograph, this last object appears to be of less certain origin; the attribution to Dinka, probably made by Junker himself, may be explained by the object having been bought outside its zone of production. One may also note that the acquisition date is thirty years later than that of the other two objects, which date from before 1850, the period of initial contact between a few European traders and the Bari.

These three clubs have enabled us to establish with some degree of probability that (a) human representation was not extraneous to Bari culture; (b) such objects were circumscribed to the family of the Bilian rain-maker, where they probably assumed the symbolic function of insignia of command; and (c) their extremely limited number and, above all, their total absence in other Bari sections or villages seem to indicate a circumscribed phenomenon (in terms of time and space) to be associated with the contribution of a single artist or group of carvers and/or a particular customer rather than with a cultural phenomenon on a tribal scale.

*   *   *

A comparative analysis comprising written testimonies concerning Bari sculpture, together with detailed study of the formal characteristics of all existing pieces, has enabled us to clarify certain facts regarding the nature of these objects and their function within Bari culture. It has been possible to distinguish a primary group of figured objects which, having been sculpted before the arrival of the white man, confirms the existence of an independent representation of the human figure based on precise aesthetic canons. The limited number of these sculptures has enabled us to connect their production with the figure of the Bilinian village rain-maker, a reference point of primary importance for the Bari in regard to the trading and production of iron manufactures. The objects, described in minute detail by d'Arnaud and Werne (who occasionally agreed in their evaluation of events they both witnessed), were the attributes of, or at least were associated with, the rain-maker himself; at the same time, the absence of any form of cult regarding them is also attested.

Thus two theories remain regarding the function of

these carvings: (1) that they were dolls or amusements, a thesis supported by similar human and animal representations found among other Nilotic populations (the Turkana, for example); (2) supported by the presence of carved clubs in the Nile area, that they would symbolize the chief himself and his special powers.

D'Arnaud's empirical description is of great value as it confirms the total absence among the Bari—as appears to be the case with all known African nomad and pastoral populations—of an ancestor cult allied to representations of the human figure. What Dupire, in fact, affirms regarding the Peul may be confirmed for the Nilotic populations.[13] The presence of both male and female figures in the first group of statues contrasts with the general characteristics of the second group of objects, which either show unmistakable signs of masculinity or lack any sexual definition at all. This restriction in the specifics of representation (about which there is insufficient ethnographic information to form any hypotheses) probably marks the transition from a privately oriented production to one destined exclusively for European markets. This second group of statuettes was produced in the port of Gondokoro, one of the major trading centers for river traffic and a bridgehead to Arab and Western European penetration, established close to the village of Bilinian.

The rather complex mixture of populations that was drawn to the area around 1850 should be emphasized: a never-very-peaceful coexistence between Arab agents and European traders and the presence of many leaderless tribes. Among them the mass of the Bari oscillated between its traditional reference point—that is, the Bilinian rain-maker—and the richest and most powerful exponents of a multiracial community of merchants and adventurers. A frontier town—never

13. "The Peul, even when sedentary, remain stateless, profoundly individualistic, ignoring the cult of the ancestors, fleeing from death, the very idea of which is odious to them, as in the face of epidemics and exactions" (M. Dupire, *Organisation sociale des Peul*, Paris 1970, p. 582). Among certain eastern Nilotic tribes (Turkana, Suk, Toposa), it was customary up to the last century to add the hair of one's direct ancestors to one's hairstyle, which the warriors mixed with earth and tinted. The enormous chignon that resulted, variegated and adorned with feathers, fell down the warrior's back. This practice is worthy of note as it consists in the incorporation of the dead warrior's attribute par excellence, that is, the hairstyle, into one's own —as a singular portable "memorial"—and it could almost be seen as analogous to a form of ritual cannibalism. A cult centered on wooden images, on the other hand, capable of containing or receiving as immaterial a presence as that of the spirits of the dead, corresponds to a different notion of ancestral worship.

governed by an authority strong enough to oppose the violence and robbery by which the old ivory trade would soon be replaced by the far more lucrative one of slavery—it became the haven for all those who survived the destruction of their traditional villages, their herds, and their cultures.

It was in this context that the second group of sculptures in question were most probably produced: first and foremost, they were objects destined for sale, manufactured to meet external demand. They would be shipped to Khartoum, then to Cairo, and finally to the museums of Europe. This connection—resulting from an original cultural adaptation to new locally created marketing possibilities—was limited to a select few. The result was the complete disappearance of the memory of the phenomenon, once trade relations were broken off with Khartoum. The development of an anthropological myth around this second group of objects—which would have them "fetishes" or "statues of the ancestors"—shows how Western imagination can, even though in direct contrast with known facts, change the data and bend reality to its ends.

The theory of cultural borrowing on the part of the Bongo tribe of Bahr-el-Ghazal, which accompanies the history of Bari sculptures, is also based on similar preconceptions. However, the Bongo objects, which are often of extraordinary dimensions (up to 4 m high), are in reality funeral poles, or totems, planted in the ground and therefore terminating in a solid foundation or base. This base may in certain cases begin at the bust itself, in which case one would define them as humanized poles; in others, it constitutes a skirting on which the feet of the figure rest. By contrast, all the Bari images—and this is one of their most salient characteristics—have widespread legs that laterally delimit an empty rectangular space that balances the volume of the trunk, almost replicating its proportions in inverted form (like an hourglass). It seems, then, that one must also exclude cultural borrowing in this instance, leading us to reiterate the theory of the existence of a single original "workshop" for Bari statuary, limited in all probability to a limited number of craftsmen having the rain-maker himself as "client."

It was the arrival of the white man that was to lead to the next phase: the establishment of a sort of subsidiary to the original "workshop" in Gondokoro. The production adapted to meet the demands of external markets; the number of objects increased; quality diminished with hasty workmanship, thus abandoning such fundamental aspects of traditional human representation as tattoos, bracelets, genitals, and so on, and resulting in a more and more abstract and vague vulgarization of these objects. In this way it reflected, on the formal level, the new encroachment of "money-making" over a tribal way of life.

BIBLIOGRAPHY

Bano, L.
1976 *Mezzo secolo di storia sudanese.* Bologna.

Bassani, E.
1977 "Gli oggetti figurati della collezione Gessi," *Africa* XXII, 1, pp. 29–46.

Beaton, A. C.
1934 "A Chapter in Bari History," *S.N.R., Sudan Notes and Records* XVII, pp. 169–200.

Boccassino, R.
1951 "Il contributo delle antiche fonti sulla religione dei Latuka, Obbo, Bari, Beri, Denka, Nuer e altre popolazioni," *Annali Lateranensi* XV, pp. 79–144.
1953 "Primo supplemento alla documentazione sulla religione e sulla magia delle popolazioni nilotiche fornita dai musei di etnografia," *Annali Lateranensi* XVII, pp. 9–54.
1960– "Contributo allo studio dell'ergologia della
1966 popolazioni nilotiche e nilo-camitiche," *Annali Lateranensi* XXIV-XXX.

Brun Rollet, A.
1855 *Le Nil Blanc et le Soudan.* Paris.

Cahier, A.
1869 *Essais sur les Musées de Douai.* Douai.

Castelli, E.
1981 "Early ethnographic collections from Sudan in the European Museums," *Atti del convegno L'Africa ai tempi di Daniele Comboni,* Roma, pp. 407–412.
1983 "Le spedizioni egiziane alle sorgenti del Nilo Bianco (1839–1842): i giornali di viaggio di D'Arnaud," *Africa* XXXVIII, pp. 264–276.
1984 "Origine des collections ethnographiques soudanaises dans les musées français (1800–1878)," *Journal des Africanistes* 54, I, pp. 97–114.
1986 "Antoine Brun Rollet in Africa: una collezione etnografica ritrovata," *Africa* XLI, 1 (in press).

D'Arnaud, J. P.
      In *Archives Nationales,* Paris Museum (A.N.P.M. AJ 45, Colis 20), unpublished.

Dupire, M.
1970 *Organisation sociale des Peul.* Paris, p. 582.

Emin Pasha
1888 *Emin Pasha in Central Africa* (G. Schweinfurth, F. Ratzell, ed.). London.

Evans-Pritchard, E.
1929 Review of "Seligman 1928," *S.N.R.* XII, pp. 268–271.

Frobenius, L.
1923 *Das Unbekannte Africa.* Munich.

Hodson, H. J.
1919 "Southern Abyssinia," *Geogr. Journal,* vol. 53, no. 2.

Holy, L.
1967 *The Art of Africa.* London.

Jensen, E.
1936 *Im Lande des Gada.* Stuttgart.

Junker, W. W.
1889 *Reisen in Afrika 1875–1886,* 3 vol. Vienna.

Leiris, M., et Delange, J.
1967 *Afrique Noire: la création plastique.* Paris.

Melly, G.
1851 *Khartoum and the Blue and White Niles.* London.

Miani, G.
1865 *Le spedizioni alle origini del Nilo.* Venezia.

Mounteney-Jephson, A. G.
1890 *Emin Pasha and the rebellion at the Equator.* London.

Old'erogge, D.
1947 "Bari wooden figures," *Collection of the Museum of Anthropology and Ethnology of Leningrad X,* pp. 207–212 (translation).
1953 "Ethnographic collection of W. W. Junker from the peoples of Africa," *Collection of the Museum of Anthropology and Ethnology of Leningrad XV,* pp. 416–446 (translation).

Paulme, D.
1953 "Carved figures from the White Nile in the Musée de l'Homme," *Man,* no. 172.

Schweeger-Hefel, A.
    1969   *Plastik aus Afrika.* Vienna.

Schweinfurth, G.
    1875   *Artes Africanae.* Leipzig and London.

Seligman, C. G.
    1917   "A Bongo funerary sculpture," *Man*, no. 67.

Seligman, C. G. and B. Z.
    1925   "Some little-known tribes of the Southern Sudan,"
          J.R.A.I. LV.
    1928   "The Bari," *J.R.A.I.* 58, pp. 409–479.
    1932   *Pagan tribes of the nilotic Sudan.* London.

Stigand, C. H.
    1923   *Equatoria, the Lado enclave.* London.

Sydow, E. (von)
    1954   *Afrikanische plastik.* Berlin.

Tcernova, G. A., et Old'erogge, D.
    1967   *L'art de l'Afrique tropicale dans les collections de
          l'URSS.* Moscow.

Werne, F.
    1848   *Expedition sur Entdeckung der Quellen des Weissen
          Nil.* Berlin.

Whitehead, G. O.
    1936   "A note on Bari history," *S.N.R.* XIX, pp. 152–157.
    1938   "André Melly's visit to Khartoum 1850," *S.N.R.* XXI,
          pp. 291–305.
    1940   "Mansfield Parkyns and his projected history of the
          Sudan," *S.N.R.* XXIII, pp. 130–138.

Whitehead, G. O. and Thomas T.
    1938   "Carved wooden figures from the White Nile,"
          *Compte-rendu du II Congrès Int. des Sci. Anthrop. et
          Ethno.* Copenhagen.

Wood, J. G.
    1870   *The Natural History of Man.* London.

3   4   5   6

7

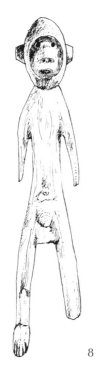

8

9

10

11

Figure 3. Musée de l'Homme, Paris, museum no. 30.54.344, coll: *Delaporte 1853*, ''red fetish as sign of mourning,'' h = 35.

Figure 4. Musée de la Chartreuse, Douai, museum no. 1382, h = ?.

Figure 5a, b. Merseyside County Museums, Liverpool, museum no. R.1.21, coll: *Melly 1854*, Bongo(?), h = 34.

Figure 6. Museum für Völkerkunde, Berlin, museum no. III A 785, coll: *Junker 1879*, ''Ahnenfigur,'' h = 34.

Figure 7. Staatliche Museum für Völkerkunde, München, museum no. 17.11.9, coll: *Schweinfurth*, h = 38.

Figure 8. Anthropologic and Ethnographic Museum, Leningrad, museum no. 5227-16, coll: *Junker 1888*, h = 31.

Figure 9. Musée de l'Homme, Paris, museum no. 30.54.335, coll: *Delaporte 1853*, ''fetish against the whites,'' h = 38.

Figure 10. Musée de l'Homme, Paris, museum no. 30.54.337, coll: *Delaporte 1853*, ''red fetish as sign of mourning,'' h = 32.

Figure 11. Musée de l'Homme, Paris, museum no. 30.54.340, coll: *Delaporte 1853*, ''large fetish for receiving strength,'' h = 47.

12

13

17

16

14

15

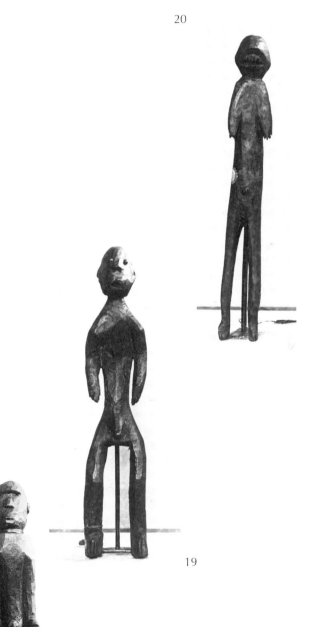

20

19

18

Figure 12. Musée de l'Homme, Paris, museum no. 30.54.342, coll: *Delaporte 1853*, "fetish to ward off eunuchs (to escape castration)," h = 34.

Figure 13. Musée de l'Homme, Paris, museum no. 30.54.343, coll: *Delaporte 1853*, "red fetish as sign of mourning. It goes from the 2nd to 6th degree." h = 39.

Figure 14. Musée de l'Homme, Paris, museum no. 30.54.1846, coll: *Delaporte 1853*, "fetish for a barren woman," h = 23.

Figure 15. Musée de l'Homme, Paris, museum no. 30.54.1847, coll: *Delaporte 1853*, "worn by children to help them grow," h = 47.

Figure 16. Merseyside County Museums, Liverpool, museum no. R.1.20, coll: *Melly 1854*, h = 43.

Figure 17. Merseyside County Museums, Liverpool, without museum no., h = 48.

Figure 18. Musée de la Chartreuse, Douai, museum no. 1378.

Figure 19. Musée de la Chartreuse, Douai, museum no. 1379.

Figure 20. Musée de la Chartreuse, Douai, museum no. 1380.

21

22

26

27

23

24

25

28

29a

29b

Figure 21. Musée de la Chartreuse, Douai, museum no. 1381.

Figure 22. Museum für Völkerkunde, Berlin, museum no. III A 784, coll: *Junker 1879*, "Ahnenfigur," h = 42.

Figure 23. Museum für Völkerkunde, Wien, museum no. 16923, coll: *Miramare 1883*, "Oberenweisse Nil," h = 45.

Figure 24. Museum für Völkerkunde, Wien, museum no. 16924, coll: *Miramare 1883*, "Oberenweisse Nil," h = 42.

Figure 25. Museum für Völkerkunde, Wien, museum no. 16922, coll: *Miramare 1883*, "Oberenweisse Nil," h = 36.

Figure 26. Museum für Völkerkunde, Wien, museum no. 10857, coll: *Buchta 1880*, h = 47.

Figure 27. Musée de l'Homme, Paris, museum no. 30.54.1848, coll: *Delaporte 1853*, "fetish worn by barren women. Worn between the breasts," h = 27.

Figure 28. Musée de l'Homme, Paris, museum no. 30.54.336, coll: *Delaporte 1853*, "fetish against the Whites," h = 31.

Figure 29. Museum für Völkerkunde, Berlin, museum no. III A 787, coll: *Junker 1879*, "Ahnenfigur," h = 26.5.

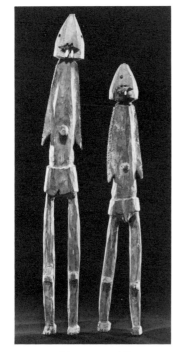

31a   31b

32

33a   33b

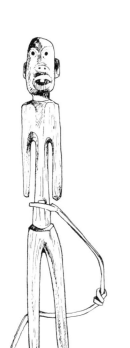

30

34   35

36   37

Figure 30. Anthropologic and Ethnographic Museum, Leningrad, museum no. 5227.13, coll: *Junker 1888*, h = 30.5.

Figure 31a. Museum für Völkerkunde, Wien, museum no. 14466, coll: *Hansal 1882*, h = 55.

Figure 31b. Museum für Völkerkunde, Wien, museum no. 14467, coll: *Hansal 1882*, h = 46.

Figure 32. Museum für Völkerkunde, Wien, museum no. 12847, coll: *Emin 1881*, "Male Figure," h = 50.

Figure 33a. Museum für Völkerkunde, Wien, museum no. 12848, coll: *Emin 1881*, "Male Figure," h = 46.

Figure 33b. Museum für Völkerkunde, Wien, museum no. 12849, coll: *Emin 1881*, "Female (?) Figure," h = 43.

Figure 34. Museum für Völkerkunde, Berlin, museum no. III A 4624, coll: *Speyer*, "Dinka (?)," h = 50.

Figure 35. Linden-Museum für Völkerkunde, Stuttgart, museum no. 118718, coll: *Ketterer*, "Dinka (?)," h = 43.

Figure 36. Museum für Völkerkunde, Berlin, museum no. III A 4624, h = 31.5.

Figure 37. Musée d'Ethnographie, Genève, museum no. 8912, coll: *Porte 1920*, h = 32.

38

39

40

41

42

43

44

46

47

48

45

Figure 38. Musée d'Ethnographie, Genève, museum no. 8913, coll: *Porte 1920*, h = 30.

Figure 39. Musée d'Ethnographie, Genève, museum no. 8914, coll: *Porte 1920*, h = 40.

Figure 40. Musée d'Ethnographie, Genève, museum no. 8915, coll: *Porte 1920*, h = 41.5.

Figure 41. Musée d'Ethnographie, Genève, museum no. 10768, coll: *1925*, h = 55.5.

Figure 42. Musée d'Ethnographie, Genève, museum no. 10769, coll: *1925*, h = 35.5.

Figure 43. Musée d'Ethnographie, Genève, museum no. 10770, coll: *1925*, h = 39.5.

Figure 44. Musée d'Ethnographie, Genève, museum no. 10771, coll: *1925*, h = 39.5.

Figure 45. Museum für Völkerkunde, Wien, museum no. 16925, coll: *Miramare 1883*, "Oberenweisse Nil," h = 34.

Figure 46. Anthropologic and Ethnographic Museum, Leningrad, museum no. 5227.14, coll: *Junker 1888*, h = 31.

Figure 47. Anthropologic and Ethnographic Museum, Leningrad, museum no. 5227.15, coll: *Junker 1888*, h = 29.

Figure 48. Anthropologic and Ethnographic Museum, Leningrad, museum no. 5227.18, coll: *Junker 1888*, h = 24.5.

51

50

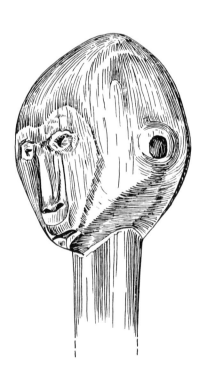

Figure 50. Museo Preistorico ed Etnografico "L. Pigorini," Roma, museum no. 48035, coll: *Brun Rollet 1853*, h = 90.

Figure 51. Private collection?, England?, coll: *Mansfield Parkyns 1849*, h = ?.

Figure 52. Anthropologic and Ethnographic Museum, Leningrad, museum no. 5225.19, coll: *Junker 1880*, h = ?.

52

The image and its setting

A study of the Sacro Monte at Varallo

DAVID LEATHERBARROW

Sacred places are always both remembered and invented. Bernardino Caimi's discovery of the site for the Sacro Monte at Varallo is a case in point. Samuel Butler described Caimi's find as follows:

> For a long while he sought in vain, and could find no place that was really like Jerusalem, but at last, towards the end of 1491, he came to Varallo alone, and hardly got there before he felt himself rapt into an ecstasy, in which he was drawn towards the Sacro Monte: when he got up to the plain on top of the mountain . . . perceiving at once its resemblance to Jerusalem, even to the existence of another mountain hard by which was like Calvary, he threw himself on the ground and thanked God in a transport of delight.[1]

The purpose of Caimi's search and final building of the pilgrimage route was devotional. The design, however, was mimetic. "The object [was] to bring the scene as vividly as possible before people who [had] not had the opportunity of being able to realise it to themselves through travel or general cultivation of the imaginative faculty."[2] The project was immediately successful; moreover, the route continues to be used and is beautifully mimetic. In what follows I would like to focus on the correspondence between a mimetic site and devotional pilgrimage. Imitation and pilgrimage are subjects that can be clarified when considered complementary, particularly when ideas of image and setting are joined in consideration of bodily movement through exemplary places. I propose that the Sacro Monte can be seen as a key to understanding the mutual dependency that exists between image and location in any meaningful architecture.

The pilgrimage route at Varallo not only was discovered by Fra Bernardino, a Franciscan friar, but was also planned and laid out by him.[3] Fra

Bernardino's idea for the Sacro Monte seems to have come to him as a result of his stay in Jerusalem, where he acted as one of the guardians of the Holy Sepulchre in 1477. At this time, and in the decades that followed, fewer pilgrims traveled to the Holy Land than previously. With the shifting of trade routes, passage from Venice to Jerusalem was becoming more difficult, and the military pressure from the Turks on the frontier discouraged many would-be penitents.

Saint Ignatius Loyola has left us a revealing account of the difficulties that faced him on his voyages to the Holy Land in the 1520's.[4] Loyola found that ships were infrequent, tickets were costly, and the hospitality of the sailors was discouragingly disagreeable. In Jerusalem, however, he was well cared for by the Franciscans, and he enjoyed staying in their monastery. The monks provided his lodging and daily food and gave him tours of the holy places. Even earlier, in the time of Fra Bernardino, the monks had set up "stopping places" at the most important and frequently visited sites. The stopping places, or "stations" along Christ's road to Calvary, inspired the "stations of the Cross," which were built into every Roman Catholic church after the seventeenth century. These stations became a standard form of Catholic devotion, whereby the faithful passed from station to station saying certain prayers at each and meditating on the various incidents in turn. The sites along the original way of the Cross also inspired the design of the little chapels that were built on the hillside at Varallo.

When Fra Bernardino returned to Italy in 1478, he conceived a plan to build an imitation of the original *sacra via* in the foothills of the Alps. His aim was to provide a setting for retreat and pilgrimage for those

1. S. Butler, *Ex Voto: An Account of the Sacro Monte or New Jerusalem at Varallo-Sesia*, London, 1888, p. 41. The *Dizionario Biografico degli Italiani*, Roma, 1973, v. 16, p. 348, uses the term *vagheggiore* to describe this initially unsuccessful searching for the best site. We should think of Caimi wandering and longing as if in a dream.

2. S. Butler, *Alps and Sanctuaries*, London, 1920, p. 250.

3. See R. Wittkower, " 'Sacri Monti' in the Italian Alps," in *Idea*

and Image (London, 1978), pp. 175–184, for a recent and helpful introductory account. The most thorough collection of documents on Varallo remains P. Galloni, *Sacro Monte di Varallo*, Atti di fondazione, Origine e svolgimento della opere d'arte, 2 vols., reprinted 1973. Also see William Hood, "The Sacro Monte of Varallo: Renaissance Art and Popular Religion," in T. G. Verdon, *Monasticism and the Arts* (Syracuse, 1983), pp. 291–313.

4. Loyola's autobiographical account is summarized in P. Van Dyke, *Ignatius Loyola: the Founder of the Jesuits*, 1968, pp. 46–62.

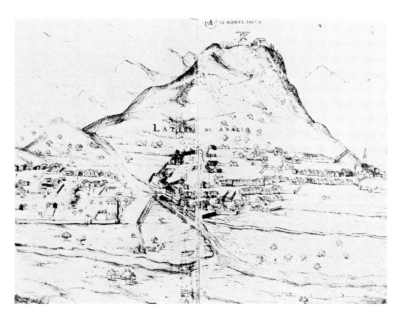

Sacro Monte, Varallo, from Galeazzo Alessi, *Libro dei Misteri*, 1569.

who were unable or unwilling to make the difficult and dangerous voyage to Jerusalem. Popular religious fervor was increasing at this time, and many Catholics were seeking a more direct and personal contact with the Saviour than existing liturgical forms could provide. Pilgrimage routes had been set up in Cordova (ca. 1420), Messina (ca. 1420), Gorlitz (1465), and Nuremberg (1468). Much earlier, in the fifth century, St. Petronius had constructed a group of connected chapels at the monastery of San Stefano in Bologna, which was supposed to represent the most important shrines of Jerusalem. In the late fifteenth century, Fra Bernardino's idea for a pilgrimage route in the foothills of the Alps found immediate and welcome response. His "new Jerusalem" was to be a place where the faithful could go on "holy pilgrimage" without leaving their own countryside.

At this time the practice of making a pilgrimage to the Holy Land, or any other sacred shrine in Europe, had a long history. The pilgrimage at Varallo can be understood as part of this long history when certain qualifications are acknowledged. In earlier pilgrimages the sanctity of the site was primary; the actual presence of the place and the events that had occurred there attracted the faithful. When the pious set off on their journeys, they expected to stand before the tomb of a saint, enter into the cave of a hermit, or kneel before the birthplace of the Redeemer. The holy spot was individual and geographically fixed; it had a spatial identity and was nontransferable (although relics were commonly transferred from one site to another). Varallo, however, was neither unique nor sanctified; before Fra Bernardino laid out his pilgrimage route, nothing sacred had occurred there. There was, thus, a degree of abstraction in Fra Bernardino's siting of the "new Jerusalem"; sanctity was abstracted from place. This is significant. The route was built upon uninhabited and otherwise unimportant hillside, the topography of which, the friar maintained, resembled the Holy Land; the distances between the stopping places were supposed to equal those between the Jerusalem stations. The pilgrims who visited Varallo, however, had no illusions about the prior sanctity of the place. It was visited because pilgrimage was important.

This too was neither unusual nor novel. Pilgrimage had always been important to Christians, and this is why the Sacro Monte is part of the tradition of Christian retreat. Pilgrimage is the way of life of the wayfarer, the *homo viator*, or the wanderer, and has countless precedents in pre-Renaissance thought and life. The Crusades are only the most famous pilgrimages; the monastic rule, for example, also encouraged voluntary retreat and self-imposed exile, which was believed to be salutary. The idea that man is never more than a traveler in this life, that the world around him is really an unknown and unknowable place, and that his true home is elsewhere is an essential ingredient in Christian doctrine. Of the many documents that testify to the importance of this complex of ideas, perhaps the following passage is most explanatory. The terrestrial lot of Christians is eminently that of strangers:

> They reside in their own fatherlands, but as if they were noncitizens; they take part in all things as if they were citizens and suffer all things as if they were strangers; every country is a fatherland to them and every fatherland is to them a foreign country. . . . They dwell on earth but they are citizens of Heaven.[5]

Gerhart Ladner has written that "the *topoi* of *xeniteia* and *peregrinatio*, or pilgrimage, of homelessness, of strangeness in this world, are among the most widespread in early Christian ascetic literature, and not a few ascetics, monastic or otherwise, practiced it by voluntary and migratory exile from their fatherland" (ibid.). Pope Gregory the Great wrote that "temporal comfort on this earth is to the just man what the bed in an inn is to the viator . . . he will rest in it bodily, but mentally he is already somewhere else" (ibid., p. 235). This observation helps explain why pilgrims would actively seek out solitary, unfrequented, and even the most difficult places: the fear of worldly delights, the desire to escape temporal comforts, and the longing for extramundane orientation estranged the pilgrim. Thus the piety of the pilgrim's journey was important, as well as the attractiveness of his destination. Since the hill at Varallo had no special historical meaning, the themes of voluntary exile, self-imposed difficulty and wandering must serve as the starting point for an interpretation of the Sacro Monte.

What sort of place would be well suited for experiences of this kind? Where would a pious believer best come to realize or remember his essential solitude, homelessness, and alienation? What sort of place would naturally act as a spatial framework for pilgrimage? Certainly mountains and steep slopes possess the spatial characteristics that form settings for voluntary exile. There is no more difficult road than that up the side of a mountain. Mountain routes are solitary and can be strange enough to be disorienting. But there are other considerations that recommend the mountain as a place for spiritual retreat: the rich and elaborately developed symbolism of the mountain in Christian and pre-Christian mythology.

The mountain has been an important symbolic form since remote antiquity. In pre-Christian belief the mountain symbolized not only ascent, separation from mundane things, and striving for the transcendent and absolute, but also that which is permanent, solid, and everlasting, the marker of the center of the world. Biblical writers accepted and elaborated this symbolism. Mount Tabor was the site of the Transfiguration, and Mount Sinai was the site of Moses' ascent into the presence of the Law-giving God. Old Testament epiphanies were generally sited on mountaintops. In the life of Christ there exist numerous important mountaintop scenes: a mountain was the site of the announcement of his birth to the shepherds, the miraculous feeding of the five thousand, His death, and, as already noted, His ascension. In each case, we are presented with a place that joins the Heavens to the earth. The mountain is the site of an interruption in the spiritually bankrupt expanse of profane space;[6] it can act as a center or point of reference that gives orientation and stability to the world. The soul of the saint or holy man is the exact spiritual center of this joining and stabilizing. Mircea Eliade and other historians of religion have documented copiously the mythical meaning of the cosmic mountain as the center of the world. It remains to be seen how much of this ancient tradition was preserved and rearticulated in the Sacro Monte at Varallo.

When, in my discussion of Varallo as a "new Jerusalem," I concluded that the hill possessed no special historical meaning, I said nothing about the way in which it — as opposed to a valley or a piece of flat terrain — was meaningful. Sanctification is not the only grounds for spatial meaning. The pilgrims who spent days climbing the slopes and walking from chapel to chapel were reenacting an ancient form of ritual with very specific spatial and topographical meanings. Independent of the representational content of the images in the chapels, the very act of making an ascent, separating oneself from one's normal surroundings, searching for an other-worldly orientation, wandering, becoming lofty, and reaching the summit and center of the world was the way in which these pilgrims, like countless others before them, realized for themselves what they believed to be their true nature.

---

5. G. Ladner, "Homo Viator," in *Speculum*, vol. xlii, April 1967, p. 236.

6. Luigi Zanzi in " 'Cosa Miraculosa,' Per la storia di una 'Fabrica del Rosario' in una terra Lombarda all'epocha della Controriforma: il Sacro Monte sopra Varese," *Il Sacro Monte sopra Varese*, Milano, 1985, p. 159, has cited M. Eliade and referred to this alteration of the expanse of profane space as "una esperienza di consacrazione dello spazio" and the "creazione del mondo."

Carlo Borromeo, by Daniele Crespi, ca. 1626.

This attitude toward the mountain must be distinguished from more recent attitudes toward alpine scenery. We tend to see mountains as beautiful and magnificent natural wonders. This is, however, a very recent sentiment. Before the seventeenth century, mountains were seen as evidence of man's fall from grace, ugly obstacles to free passage.[7] In Caimi's time the terms used to describe the Alps included *horrido*, *selvatico*, *disastroso*, and *terribilissimo*. The mountains were notable for their unmatched topographical difficulties. This, of course, is also what made them suitable for pilgrimage.

The significance of the mountain can be understood more fully when the pilgrimage route is examined in more detail. This can be accomplished most easily by reviewing the use to which the route was put by a particular individual. Perhaps the most illustrative case will be that of St. Carlo Borromeo. St. Carlo was the Archbishop of Milan, the author of the *Noctes Vaticanae* and a number of sermons and discourses (including one on church building), and an immensely popular figure among the pious populace. He was an influential figure in the final proceedings of the Council of Trent, and a financial supporter of building works at

the Sacro Monte at Varallo—for the construction of the Palazzo di Pilato, which contained nine chapels, he spent the considerable sum of 80,000 lire. Other sacred sites, such as Varese and Orta, received his support too (Zanzi, p. 152). St. Carlo had a passion for making pilgrimages to Italy's sacred shrines. One of his biographers has written that "he considered pilgrimage a valuable element in that grand design of counterreform which was the real programme of all his pastoral activity."[8] This understates St. Carlo's fiery zeal. St. Carlo wrote: "Even though in our unhappy times, when the religious exercise of making pilgrimages has diminished to so great an extent, you must not become tepid, my dearest brethren, but you must become more enkindled because this is precisely the time when real Catholics and obedient sons of the Church show the zeal of their faith and piety." (ibid.). And they did show the zeal of their faith. Pilgrimage to such sites as Varallo, Orta, Oropa, and Varese increased greatly in Borromeo's time. This was especially true in areas north and west of Milan— throughout Lombardy and Piedmont. While each site differed in layout, dimension, and subject, all shared the purpose of facilitating Borromeo's idea of Catholic faith and piety. But St. Carlo's actions were far more influential than his writings; his pilgrimages to Varallo are the best case in point.

St. Carlo visited the site on many occasions. During each visit he spent entire days and nights climbing the mountainside. At each chapel he would meditate under the direction of the resident Jesuit, Father Adorno. His memoirs contain numerous references to visits to Varallo, but his last visit, days before his death, is perhaps most illustrative. When he arrived at the site of his retreat, the pilgrim restricted his nourishment to bread and water, and for a bed he used a plank of wood, although he slept only a few hours each night. Throughout the day he would visit those chapels which contained representations of the passion and death of Christ (for guidance on the Christian way through these experiences, in anticipation of having to face death himself). At each chapel he kneeled before the scene to be contemplated, and meditated on the points of Loyola's *Spiritual Exercises*, which were suggested by Father Adorno. Also, there were guides to Varallo in Borromeo's time; the first was published in 1514. In

7. On this older view of the mountains, especially in English literature, see M. H. Nicolson, *Mountain Gloom and Mountain Glory: The Development of the Aesthetics of the Infinite*, Ithaca, 1959.

8. C. Orsenigo, *Life of Charles Borromeo*, 1945, pp. 302–330. See also William Hood, op. cit. Both authors are citing *Della Vita di San Carlo Borromeo*, Bologna, 1614.

particular he may have used one by Sesalli called *Breve descrittione del Sacro Monte di Varallo di Valsesia*.[9]

Sequence was important. From chapel to chapel Borromeo ascended the hillside, meditating, examining his conscience and following the holy path. At night, when the others had gone to bed, St. Carlo would journey from chapel to chapel by candlelight. On the fifth day of his retreat he made a confession of the whole of his life, which he had prepared for in an entire night of kneeling prayer. But his further spiritual progress was interrupted by repeated and increasingly more intense attacks of fever. He was compelled by his friends to come down from the mountain and return to his home in Milan. He did, but did not recover from the fever and died shortly thereafter.

I shall summarize St. Carlo's use of the mountain and route. His retreat involved self-imposed solitude, climbing the mountain, the limitation of bodily comforts such as eating and sleeping, meditation according to Loyola's instructions, contemplation of the scenes depicting the life of Christ, and confession. It should be apparent how this set of activities conforms to and amplifies my outline of mountainside pilgrimage. We have the abstraction from customary surroundings, the denial of temporal comforts—that is, the acceptance of all difficulties—the difficult upward movement and striving to approach the transcendent through contemplation. Here these activities have been made into a specific program for spiritual exercise. And it was a program for everyone, for all classes together. It combined simple piety with the cultivated discipline of the Jesuit method; it joined the habits of the populace to the regulations of the counter-reformation church. The unifying and mediating power of mountainside pilgrimage contributed to its great popularity.

The importance of Loyola's text for understanding the use of the route of Varallo should not be underestimated. It is unlikely, although not impossible, that Loyola visited Varallo and had in mind images of the kind represented there when he worked on his program for retreat. It is known that he visited other monastic retreats, the most famous being Montserrat, where he met Garcia de Cisneros and was instructed in his form of spiritual exercises. After Montserrat and Manresa, Loyola traveled north to Paris, where he made his famous journey up Montmartre; then he traveled back through France and northern Italy on his way toward Venice and ultimately Jerusalem. In later years he passed by Milan and the neighborhood of Varallo a number of times, but the name of the already famous pilgrimage site is not mentioned in his autobiography.

Loyola's *Exercises* were in the tradition of *devotio moderna*, which is very different from older forms of mystical contemplation and quietism. He encouraged the creation of vivid and concrete imagery; special places, both found and invented, suited the practice of his *Exercises*. Loyola instructed his students accordingly:

> The first prelude is a composition, seeing the place. Here it is to be observed that in contemplation or visible meditation (that is, meditation on a visible thing) as contemplating Christ our Lord, who is visible, the

9. W. Hood, op. cit., has explained that these guides outlined not only spatial sequence and procession, but also appropriate thought and feeling, p. 299.

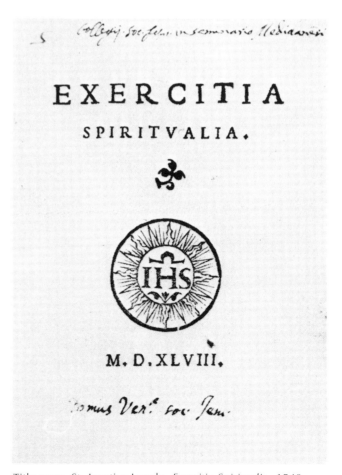

Title page, St. Ignatius Loyola, *Exercitia Spiritualia*, 1548.

Sacro Monte, Varallo, on route between chapels.

Sacro Monte, Varallo, entry to the Basilica Square.

composition will be to see with the eye of the imagination the corporeal place. I mean, for instance, a temple or a mountain where Jesus Christ is found, or our Lady, according as I wish to contemplate.[10]

Loyola repeatedly stressed the importance of "seeing the place." This "seeing" amounted to a sort of mental exercise whereby the imagination struggled to clothe an idea with visible form. The success of the meditation depended upon the penitent's ability to produce a clear and distinct image of his subject so that it could be studied, retained, and used in the future as a guide to conduct. Every "composition" had two parts: the image and its place. If the subject was to be the crucifixion of Christ, then the image would be the suffering body on the cross and the place would be the hill outside Jerusalem. Meditation on the wickedness of the fallen angel would involve the production of an image of the devil standing in the fires of the underworld. Images in their places were the means by which the penitent could know, remember, and anticipate what is good and bad.

One writer on Loyola's method has described the *Spiritual Exercises* as "a manual, and the best ever written, of Christian prudence" (Van Dyke, op. cit.). When we remember that prudence was understood at this time as a compound of memory, intelligence, and foresight, we realize that prudence was indeed the main object of the *Spiritual Exercises*. St. Thomas Aquinas, in his commentary on Aristotle's *De Memoria et Reminiscentia*, said that the parts of prudence are *memoria*, *intelligentia*, and *providentia*.[11] He also wrote about the composition of the image and the place. In

10. St. Ignatius Loyola, *The Spiritual Exercises*, the first week, first exercise.

11. St. Thomas Aquinas, *Opera Omnia*, Parma, 1866, vol. 20, p. 198ff.

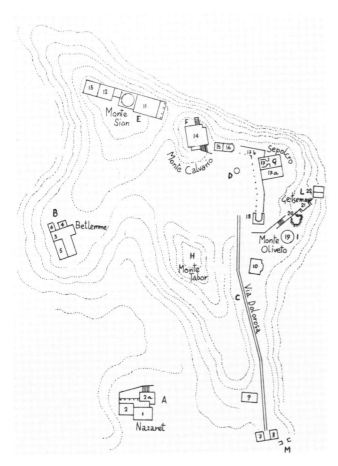

Reconstruction of Bernardino Caimi's plan for the "Nuova Gerusalemme" Sacro Monte at Varallo, ca. 1486–1530.

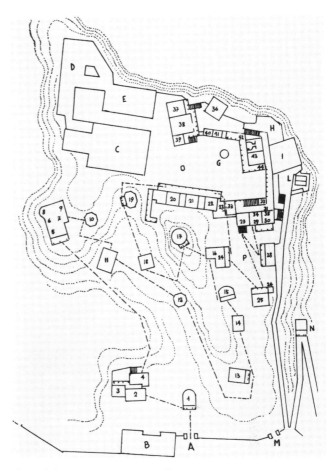

Plan of the Sacro Monte, Varallo.

his commentary on Aristotle's treatise *de Anima*, we read that "man cannot understand without images (phantasmata), the image is a similitude of a corporeal thing, but the understanding is of universals which are to be abstracted from particulars" (ibid., p. 200). In anticipation of Loyola, Aquinas stressed the necessity of images for the acquisition and preservation of knowledge. Similarly, he stressed the importance of place:

> It is necessary for reminiscence to take some starting point, whence one begins to proceed to reminisce. For this reason, some men may be seen to reminisce from the places in which something was said or done, or thought, using the place as it were as the starting-point for reminiscence; because the access to the place is like a starting-point for all those things which were raised in it. Whence Tullis (Cicero) teaches in his Rhetoric that for easy remembering one should imagine a certain order of places upon which images (phantasmata) of all those things which we wish to remember are distributed in a certain order.[12]

Thus we see that Loyola's method of forming vivid and concrete images in specific places was based upon an ancient tradition of Christian and pre-Christian epistemology. Loyola may have been only vaguely familiar with this tradition, but doubtless his teachers, such as Garcia de Cisneros—the author of the book on spiritual exercise which probably formed the basis of Loyola's text—were familiar with this tradition and well versed in the writings of Aquinas and Cicero. It is possible, therefore, to establish a close connection between Loyola's method and one of the strongest currents of medieval and ancient philosophy: spiritual exercise was a form of Christian prudence, prudence

12. English translation cited in F. Yates, *The Art of Memory*, 1966, p. 72. For Aquinas's original, see *Opera Omnia*, p. 199.

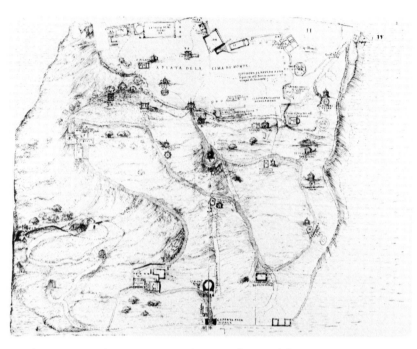

G. Alessi's project for reorganizing the central area of the Sacro Monte, 1576–1580, from his *Libro dei Misteri.*

was composed of memory, intelligence, and foresight; and memory, according to such writers as Aquinas and Cicero, involved the formation of mental images and places. Now, to the degree that Loyola's program for spiritual exercise was motivated by the same sentiments that inspired Fra Bernardino's design for Varallo, we have another way of making our description of the pilgrimage route more specific: namely, the rules for the formation of the kind of images and places that could be stored best in the prudent memory.

Dame Frances Yates has, in her classic study of the art of memory, clearly set out the rules for making mental images which would lodge in the memory (Yates, pp. 6–7). The rules for forming places that could act as settings for mental images are as follows: places should be deserted and solitary, individual and distinct, neither too bright nor too dark, and placed apart from one another with moderate intervals between each. It is surprising how easily these rules can be used to describe the layout of the chapels or stopping places at Varallo. As has been said already, the hillside was a place of self-imposed solitude. This quality fulfills the first rule for the formation of memory places.

Secondly, each chapel, as well as the landscape setting for each chapel, was unique. This is a

consequence of the site being a hillside. Up steep slopes and across the terraces the pilgrim was directed through dense woods, openings in tree screens and architecturally built-up areas. From a temple with a colonnaded porch, toward and beyond an arcaded rotunda, the pilgrim entered, contemplated, and passed through a sequence of clearly distinct spaces. The rule of uniqueness of place is beautifully celebrated at Varallo. The lighting of the places varies with the characteristics of the landscape setting and the architecture; but there is no place that could be judged to be "too bright" or "too dark." So much for the third rule for the formation of memory places.

Finally, the spacing and the sequence of the spaces must be considered. At Varallo the pilgrim started the route on the lower side of the hill just outside the limits of the village farm buildings and advanced along the route of the chapels toward the Basilica at the top.[13] Far from being crowded in upon one another, the chapels and places are situated so that the visitor is always apart from, but in sight of, neighboring chapels when stopping at any particular spot. Thus the stopping

13. This was the case at all of the important Sacri Monti. See, for example, Zanzi's description of S. Maria del Monte e "sopra" Varese, in Zanzi, op cit., p. 156.

places were interconnected visually, but independent spatially.

In its present form the landscape and its material configuration set up a number of views that, seen in sequence, establish the continuity of the route. Leaving one temple the visitor is presented with a row of trees that lead him to the next. In such a situation tree screens block off views to neighboring chapels that are out of sequence, and the topography prohibits movements that would take the pilgrim off course. From the exit of another chapel the visitor can see through an archway in a wall with illusionistic frescoes to the entrance of another stopping place. Framed openings, vistas, changes in surface, lighting, and degrees of enclosure structure views that lead the pilgrim from place to place. The layout and spatiality of the whole route is a perfect example of the way memory places should be "placed apart from one another with moderate intervals between each."

This arrangement is neither haphazard nor accidental. According to the documents that survive from the period of the early history of the Sacro Monte, especially Galeazzo Alessi's *Libro dei Misteri*, it is clear that the route up the hillside was designed very carefully to structure the sequence of spaces that would aid the memory of the pilgrim. After the death of Fra Bernardino, building work at Varallo continued under the direction of the *fabbriciere* and Giacomo d'Adda. The history of this period of building is documented poorly, but it is clear that by the middle of the sixteenth century Fra Bernardino's *schemi topomimetici* had been disrupted entirely. In reaction, then, Alessi proposed "*il totale riordino del Sacro Monte*," which involved both the articulation of "*un organico piano*" and the reconsideration of the site "*ex novo*."[14] In the reorganization of the route some of the temples were demolished, others were altered, new temples were built, and the paths that joined the temples together were redirected. All of this work was undertaken in order to clarify the representation of the chronological sequences of the sacred drama. Alessi's work can be seen thus as a reordering of the memory places.

Alessi proposed to divide the hill into three areas. His proposal acknowledged the differing ambient circumstances, the separate parts of the narrative, and the various types of spatial enclosure that were needed for the memory places. In the first area, a densely planted, uneven terrain, Alessi suggested grouping representations of events such as the annunciation, Christ in the garden, and the entry into Jerusalem. In the second area he proposed to build the monumental and more strictly geometric buildings of the city of Jerusalem. The third area was to include images of purgatory, limbo, and the inferno. While Alessi's scheme was realized only partly and many buildings not included in his design were added after his "*riordino*," the narrative sequence of the spaces up the hillside has been preserved.

Now we must consider the images to be stored in the memory places. Concerning the formation of memory images, Dame Frances Yates has cited the oldest surviving treatise on the art of memory:

Memory image of the "Devil and His Friars," from the *Swiss Chronicle*, 1548.

14. See G. Alessi, *Libro des Misteri*, Bologna, 1974, the Proemio especially; also S. S. Perrone, "l 'Urbanistico del Sacro Monte e l'Alessi," in *Galeazzo Alessi e l'architettura del cinquecento*, Genoa, 1975. In the same publication see also A. Cavallari Murat, "Scelte formali di G. Alessi per una moderna aggregazione edilizia," especially pp. 64–65. Also see Cavallari Murat's discussion of Varallo in his *Forma Urbana ed Architettura nello Torino Barocca*, vol. 1, pp. 38–42. And finally, the catalogue that resulted from the International Conference of 1980 at Varallo, entitled *Sacri Monti, itinerari di devozione fra architettura, figurativa e paesaggio*, by F. Fontana and P. Sorrenti, has a helpful section on Alessi's projects, as well as a good bibliography. In addition to these texts, the author has benefited from discussions with a number of his colleagues: Joseph Rykwert, Dalibor Vesely, Peter Carl, and Marco Frascari.

We ought, then, to set up images of a kind that can adhere longest in memory. And we shall do so if we establish similitudes as striking as possible; if we set up images that are not many or vague but active (*imagines agentes*); if we assign to them exceptional beauty or singular ugliness; if we ornament some of them, as with crowns or purple cloaks so that the similitude may be more distinct to us; or if we somehow disfigure them, as by introducing one stained with blood or smeared with red paint, so that its form is more striking, or by assigning certain comic effects to our images, for that, too, will ensure our remembering them more readily.

Yates, op cit., p. 10

The principal characteristic of the memory image so defined is its strikingness. Reminding us of Loyola's insistence on the formation of vivid and concrete imagery, the author of this treatise on memory claims that a distinct image is a memorable one. The meaning of this strikingness is complicated, involving us in the touchy issue of the realism and illusionism of the

Varallo images. These images can be distinguished from earlier memory images in that the latter were "disfigured" to the point of becoming "abnormal." The Varallo images were instead "extraordinary" in the sense of being combinations of the parts of beautiful women to make an image of Venus or the Madonna. They were striking, and strikingly beautiful. For present purposes it will be sufficient to state that the images depicted in the chapels at Varallo were certainly striking and (in theory they were therefore) memorable. This being so, it is now possible to summarize the interrelations between the architecture of the Sacro Monte, spiritual exercise, and the art of memory. After this summary I shall return to the problem of the strikingness of the image.

Considering the geography of the Sacro Monte, we are not surprised to discover that the place was meant to act as a setting for retreat and spiritual exercise. Being situated at the edge of the village, on a mountain

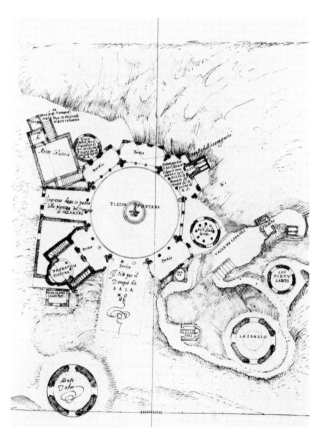

G. Alessi's preliminary project for the reorganization of the piazza in front of the Temple of Solomon, 1565–1569, from his *Libro dei Misteri*.

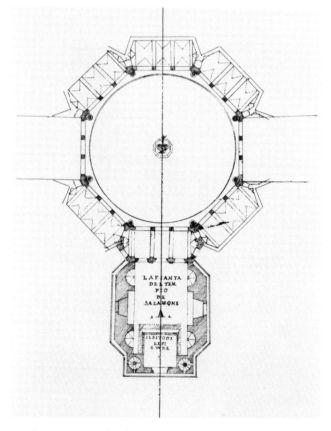

G. Alessi's project for the organization of the piazza in front of the Temple of Solomon, 1565–1569, from his *Libro dei Misteri*.

The Road to Calvary, chapel 35, ca. 1599.

slope, it was well suited, both physically and symbolically, to the solitude that is required for spiritual exercise. Loyola's method required separation from friends and customary surroundings, as we have seen; Varallo was a place where pilgrims such as St. Carlo Borromeo could go to escape the distracting influence of daily concerns and friends. The purpose of this self-imposed solitude was to fortify the soul. Part of the Christian's duty, it was one of the four cardinal virtues: prudence, which consists of knowing, remembering, and intending what is good and right. Loyola's text, as we have seen, was a program for specific meditation on the life of Christ, which formed the substance of the Christian idea of the good and right. The means by which these ideas were meditated upon brings us back to the architecture of Varallo; they include the use of concrete images and places. While Loyola's images were never more than the products of the imagination, those at Varallo were built, carved, and painted. Varallo was designed so that distinct images of the exemplary life of Christ could be *placed* in unique and well-lighted buildings and visited along a route up a mountain. As such, I think it is described best as a large scale "theater of memory" for "spiritual exercise."

The drawings and explanatory passages in Alessi's *Libro dei Misteri* confirm this. He devoted his attention most often to the complex of buildings organized around the Temple of Solomon, contrary to the relatively minor importance of the clearing of the Temple episode in the life of Christ. The importance of remembrance and the idea of the theater of memory clarifies Alessi's interest. In the late Middle Ages and the early Renaissance, Solomon's Temple was referred to often as the Temple of Wisdom; Giulio Camillo, for example, called it a House of Wisdom that was founded on seven pillars. Seven pillars plus an entrance come together naturally into the form of an octagon, which was the shape of the central space of Alessi's designs for the Temple of Solomon, as well as other well-known early Renaissance designs (such a circular temple was illustrated in the *Hypnerotomachia Polyphili*). Many historians have described the symmetry, centrality, and uniformity of Alessi's designs for the Solomonic piazza. It has been discussed as a typical early Renaissance space embodying familiar design techniques and expected architectural symbolism. On entry into this space, however, the spectator was to be confronted with images of the important events in Christ's life. It seems that what might be called the geometry of memory is also important here. Solomon was thought of by many of this time to be the originator of a memory system, called the *Ars Notoria*. It is the representational economy of the memory theater that accounts for

Pilate Washing His Hands, chapel 34, 1600, frescoes by Tanzio da Varallo.

Christ before Pilate, chapel 29, ca. 1610, frescoes by P. F. Granoli and G. Grandi.

Christ Healing the Cripple, chapel 15, 1583, frescoes by Cristoforo Martinolio.

The Canonization of St. Francis, chapel 20, Sacro Monte at Orta, 1607, sculpture by D. Bussola, frescoes by Busca.

G. Alessi, design for the Temple of the Pentecost, 1565–1569, from his *Libro dei Misteri*.

Alessi's strong interest in the Temple of Solomon, and for its central position in the Sacro Monte at Varallo, too.

The images in these buildings have fascinated many writers. Samuel Butler was one of the first English writers to comment on the realism of the Sacri Monti representations. Concerning the Sacro Monte at Oropa, Butler wrote that "the founders of these chapels aimed at realism. Each chapel was intended as an illustration and the desire was to bring the whole scene more vividly before the faithful by combining the picture, the statue, and the effect of a scene upon the stage in a single work of art" (Butler, op cit., p. 176). Rudolph Wittkower elaborated on this observation, writing that the aim of this art form was to "reproduce visually and exactly the events believed to have taken place along the via dolorosa. Each chapel may be likened to a scene from the *sacra representazione* frozen into

permanence" (Wittkower, op cit., p. 178). Yet despite the apparent desire for accuracy and historical realism, many figures are clothed in the regional dress of the time and others—a surprising number, in fact—exhibit a then typical (and characteristic) physical malady, the goitre. Many of the background figures in the paintings of Tanzio and Morazzone are dressed similarly. This eases the spectator's participation. The figures are both foreign and local, historical and contemporary; their makers were striving for more than a depiction of historical events. Moreover, all of the representations make use of the techniques of pictorial illusionism: foreshortenings, distortions, and so on. While some of the life-size clay figures are wearing real shoes and clothes made out of real cloth, others, painted on vaults, emerge from the artificial depth of two-dimensional space and become, in part—as they pass through the picture plane—three dimensional and solid. This is not an objective or even historical realism, but a realism of meaning or content in response to interests and expectations current at the time. Versimilitude was important because the use of these spaces, spiritual exercise, required it. And here we return to the issue of vivid and concrete images of the exemplary life of Christ.

What is it about spiritual exercise that required this blending of realism and illusionism? What are the visual requirements of counter-reformation contemplation? What must be revealed in the image? Wittkower has described each image as a scene from the "*sacra representazioni* frozen into permanence." We know that each image embodies a moment in the life of Christ. But what is the spiritual meaning of this moment and how was it made concrete? Here my earlier use of the term "exemplary" is helpful. The life of Christ was the subject of meditation because it was a model for Christian behavior; a prudent life was one lived in imitation of the conduct of Christ. But this is not allegorical, nor does it refer to "other" events and individuals: the settings facilitated more direct experience. Therefore, the value of the image was its ability to make the pilgrim feel as though he were actually witnessing or virtually participating in the event. As we have seen, a distinct and striking image is a memorable one.

The techniques by which the spectator was brought into the scene were those of perspective and stage set design. At Varallo the contemplative pilgrim is expected to take up the posture of a spectator placed in front of the theatrical illusion of a moment in the life of Christ.

This is where the false perspectives, hidden and indirect lights, and illusionistic paintings amplify the realism of the carved figures. The effect of this illusionism is to bring the spectator into the scene, or as far into the scene as the representational possibilities of perspective art would allow.

The peripheral field of the three-dimensional representations — that is, the surface of the surrounding walls, ceiling, and subordinate spaces that form the limits of the interior — is the place where the techniques of illusionism were put into practice. In some cases the architectural forms of the exterior of the chapel were painted onto the unbroken surfaces of the inner walls of the space. In the chapels built later, the techniques of illusionism are more sophisticated. Between the painted pilasters the scene is allowed to extend beyond the surface of the room by use of painted perspective depth, as appears in Alessi's drawings. Walls are covered with street perspectives; ceilings become either galleries, rooftops, or the heavens; and in some chapels the rear wall is broken down into a series of planes, like flats in a theater, which act as superimposed perspective frames. All of this presupposes a localized spectator and reminds us of Renaissance and early Baroque theatrical spaces, such as those in Peruzzi's and Serlio's drawings, Palladio's and Scamozzi's set designs, and Bernini's church interiors, the Cornaro Chapel in particular. Perhaps even more relevant is Bramante's choir in S. Maria presso San Satiro, which was built not far from Varallo in Milan.

In fact, it is at the limits of the interior space that all the representational difficulties of the scene arise. The techniques mentioned so far overcame most of these difficulties. Thus the technique of the figure emerging through the picture plane into the space of the room (best executed at Orta rather than at Varallo) is an attempt at removing the division between the space of the scene and that of the image. It is, perhaps, the best indication of the limits of perspective or theatrical representational techniques. This figure, ambitious and finally unsuccessful as it is, indicates the desire to bring the illusory space of perspective depth (and narrative time) into the space of the clay figures, and by virtue of the "point of origin" of the perspective construction, into the space of the penitent/spectator as well. The figure works when seen frontally by joining the two-dimensional representation of depth to the three-dimensional space of the sculptural figures. But being part of the peripheral field, as are all of the fresco

Mount Tabor, chapel 17, G. Alessi, ca. 1569.

figures on the perimeter walls, it is not seen this way normally; when looking straight ahead through the viewing screen into the center of the room where the principal figures are standing, this figure is marginal — oblique — certainly not frontal. Thus, although composed frontally, it is experienced peripherally, by virtue of the spatiality of the setting. The difficulties of this figure point to a tension between different types of representation and forms of participation; that is, visual and stationary participation in pictorial surface representations in the chapel interiors, and bodily and active participation in the spatial and topographical representations up the mountainside.

The subject of the image and its representational power brings me to the end of this study. My purpose has been to demonstrate the way in which Renaissance accomplishments in representation and perspective design were interrelated with "pre-Renaissance" and "pre-perspective" spaces and settings. In my study of

Varallo I have discussed the way in which perspective interiors were set within the spatial order of the pilgrimage route and the landscape of the mountain side. The interiors were made for the eye trained in perspective, the pilgrim who participated in the event as a spectator. Yet, despite the power of the image and the sophistication of the representation, the spectator/ pilgrim was still an outsider, still somewhat out of touch with the exemplary life of the Saviour. The full-size figures and illusionistic frescoes are palpable but stiff—they are "frozen into permanence." However, when the pilgrim withdrew from the perspective construction and went back to the mountainside, along the route, the situation and the means of participation in the representation were very different. Here the techniques of perspective art had less of a part to play; here the pilgrim participated in the setting in a more direct and more immediate way—bodily participation. Solitary ascent and the search for a world-transcending orientation was the way the pilgrim reenacted the Christian way of life: the mountain is hard work. The more direct spatial and bodily meaning of the route and setting acted as a complement to, perhaps a foundation for, the more indirect representational significance of the images. Both are symbolic forms, the first perhaps being less articulate but more powerful. If we abstract these beautiful perspective interiors from their field of spatial meanings we deprive them of what, in great part, made them and continues to make them memorable.

And this observation can be generalized. If the recollection of a visual figure is improved when the figure has been located as part of an integrated topography, the power of pictorial and plastic figures generally can be improved in consideration of spatial and topographical conditions: images make more sense in specific and suitable settings. For example, the removal of a painting of a madonna from an altar changes the sense of the painting. In a museum many madonnas are both secularized and difficult to remember; no museum can compete with a differentiated spatial setting such as the route at Varallo. Nor can architectural figures. When architectural settings are considered abstractly as two-dimensional frontal surfaces, when designers compose internal and external façades pictorially for presentation as part of a sequence of views (marche) through a building, architectural figures become less memorable and spatial experience loses its force and integrity. Façades, like paintings, are memorable when situated; unlocated figures are unmemorable. The site at Varallo demonstrates that considerations of the presentation of architectural meaning in visual figures must be seen as part of more comprehensive and radical considerations of bodily meaning in spatial settings. Every image must have its place.

The body and architecture in the drawings of Carlo Scarpa

MARCO FRASCARI

In contemporary architectural drawing, the presence of the human figure, to give scale, is absolutely indispensable. This has not always been the case. In older representations, the scale relation between drawing and building itself was mediated by a design method in which the human figure was incorporated into the elements of architecture by simile and metaphor, by an organic use of stone and rendering. The goal was the transubstantiation of architectural artifact into human presence, and vice versa; it was possible because technology was understood as a productive system that operated simultaneously on two levels, the rhetorical and the physical one (Frascari 1985: 4). The world constructed by this twofold process of view thus became experience translated into a visual and tactile manifestation of thinking.

The theoretical drawings developed by the Tuscan Renaissance architect Francesco di Giorgio Martini (1961) to illustrate his architectural treatises are ideal examples of such an interpretation of the world as a product of the twofold technology resulting from the projection of the human body. A building is as it is because it is both constructed by man and interpreted through the human form (fig. 1). The logic of the constructive technique is part of the technique of verbal logic, and vice versa. In this procedure the body is the most general and perfect means for arriving at a sizing of the reality of the architectural world. The body as reality becomes the unit of architectural production since it sets brick upon brick. It is also the formal basis for the configuration from the elements of construction to whole cities (figs. 2, 3).

Architectural anthropomorphism—the ascription of human characters and attributes to buildings and edifices—has a long tradition in architectural theory. Vitruvius, a rhapsodic architect from the first century B.C., describes the diverse forms it took in the Hellenistic-Roman tradition of his day. It was a practice suggested for the determination of both measure and proportion to stimulate the imagination of the designer and the builder. In our own time Leon Krier (1984), an aggressive postmodern architect from Luxemburg, returns to the metaphor and the anthropomorphic conception in his battle against the deleterious modernist city (fig. 4) and its poorly organized body,

patched up as it is by mechanistic and functionalistic protheses and the transplant of organs to improper sites (fig. 5).

The abstracting of architectural representation in the modern movement is required by the alienation of human corporality from the business of building. Thus the elaborations of modern projects favor a Cartesian rationality; they produce mathematical constructions but lack human reality. If one compares drawings by Krier with those by Francesco di Giorgio, one can see how the decline in the anthropomorphic construct both has produced, and is produced by, a corresponding

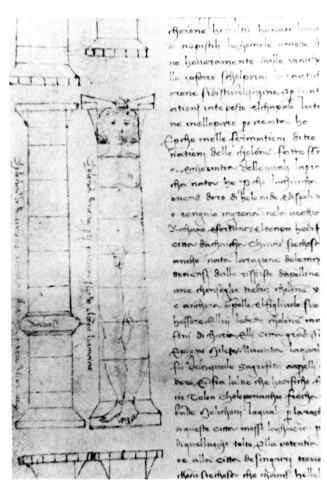

Figure 1. Francesco di Giorgio Martini. Proportion of columns, *Trattati*.

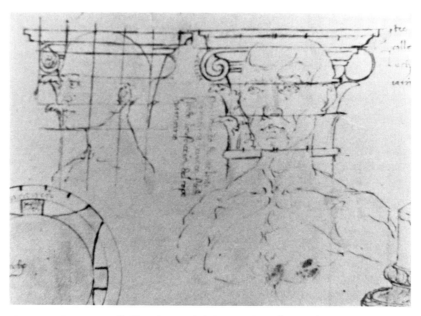

Figure 2. Francesco di Giorgio Martini. Proportion of capitals, *Trattati.*

change in human self-identification. In antiquity, man could represent his universe through topological projection of his own body, and understand his body in this projection. Contemporary architecture, however, is constructed according to the dictates of modern rationalism, and therefore no longer adheres to this topology. Figures and anthropometric sections used by architects in their drawings are the last—and least—of the approaches to the reintegration of human presence into the architectonic artifact.

The figures in the drawings of the modern architects can be grouped into three categories. The first includes all the possible naturalistic representations of the human figure and all artifacts that can help the nonarchitect imagine a three-dimensional future reality in a two-dimensional rendering—that is, to understand the project on paper, within the context of presentation drawings for clients. The second category includes all the abstract representations used to verify the anthropometry, a graphic process that eliminates errors of dimension during the project's formulation. The third category is a result of the interaction of the first two, with representations of the human figure based on pseudoformal abstractions generally favored by architecture students. Men, women, and children become biped balloons with pointed feet and floating heads, sometimes with a bow tie below the head of the largest figure to distinguish it as male (fig. 6). In any case, these three categories present only stereotypes

that have lost any ontological dimension; they are simply a form of communication oriented to the common man and to the technician, or a formal representation to other architects of the possible problems of scale and dimension.

Despite the present limitations of the role of the body in architectural drawing, I would like to suggest that architects cannot do without the anthropomorphic practice of identification of the human body and its elements in the architectural body. A new practice of body/building topology is now required—one that avoids the all too simple road of isomorphism, isotopy, and the metaphoric analogies of the architecture of the past, but will, instead, use the body as the element of reference for architectural metonymy.

In rhetorical usage, metonymy is a semantic shift based on a relationship of logical and material contiguity between literal and figurative terms. While in metaphor the relationship established is pragmatic and extrinsic (city = body, head = seat of government, stomach = market, church = heart, and so on), in the metonymy the relationship is syntagmatic and intrinsic: effects substitute for causes, materials for objects, the contained for the container, the abstract for the concrete, or vice versa. In architecture, vision is dominant; its morphological characteristics are perceived as nonvisual qualities that give privileged status to various forms of perception. A sound is grave or acute; a tactile sensation is soft or cold. The metonymy works through the privileged status of perception, while the metaphor is based primarily on judgment, which depends on other forms of knowledge. In a metonymic procedure, the drawing of a handle results from a mold in the form of a hand that grasps, rather than from a formal representation of the hand itself. Another metonymy, primarily synecdoche, is exemplified by an illustration by Teofilo Gallacini for his treatise on fortifications. In his drawing of a rampart, the architectural form is anthropomorphized into a head, based on the metonymy for look-out, rather than on the metaphoric isotopy of "headship" in a bastion (fig. 7).

The drawings and architectural production of Carlo Scarpa (1906–1978) are an ideal source for characterizing the method, processes, and elements of this practice of architectural metonymy. Scarpa, a great *Dilettante Veneto*, was one of the few original masters of Italian contemporary architecture, cultivating in almost complete isolation, in the calm and potent Venetian mixture of *otium* and *negotium*, his extraordinary vocation. The anthropomorphism in Scarpa's architectural procedures is neither the cosmological isomorphism of Francesco di Giorgio nor the metaphoric imagery of Krier, but is based on an understanding of the human being as *homo viator*. In Scarpa's architecture, the human figure is both the subject that produces the buildings *sub specie corporis*, and the object starting from which the building is made. As Hubert Damish has pointed out (Dal Co 1984: 210), Scarpa's drawings are not static images; they are dynamic demonstrations of an act of projection that has the world-construct for its final goal. In his design development drawings, Scarpa uses representations of human figures and their parts to recount the story of the vicissitudes and accidents of the project. The images of human bodies in these drawings are at once abstract and concrete, generalized and specific. They act within the representation, mediating the semantic transfer through a logical and material connection between human behavior and the specifications required by the work, the terms of the work as transferred in the architectural workings.

One of Scarpa's favorite sayings was a Latin tag: *nullo dies sine linea*. Originally, this motto of Plautus's was an invitation to the everyday literary practice. In his appropriation of the phrase, Scarpa, like others before him (e.g., Viollet-le-Duc in *Histoire d'un Dessinateur*, Paris, 1879), modified the meaning of "line," extending the sense of the motto to the everyday practice of drawing, which he saw as the basic instrument of theoretical and practical architectural activity.

Among the various ways of analyzing an architect's work, the study of drawings, by itself, usually results in an incomplete assessment—the final construct, as an artifact, must always be implicit. Real architectural drawings are not limited to simple presentations of a future construction, but are privileged representations of a conceptual elaboration of architecture. Even so, since the final aim is the construction of the building, these representations are limited. Consequently, while analysis of the traditional detailed project drawings can permit the characterization of a theory, they do not ordinarily permit its verification *in corpore vili*, that is, in the construction. Scarpa's drawings, however, do not generate such ambiguity. The heavy wing card, light

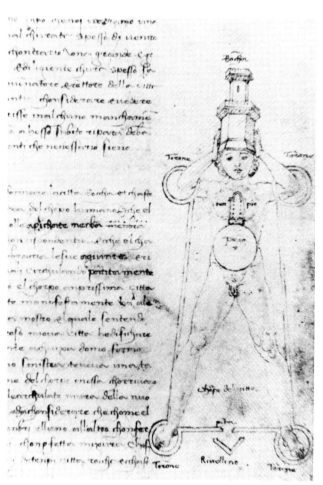

Figure 3. Francesco di Giorgio Martini. Design of a city, *Trattati*.

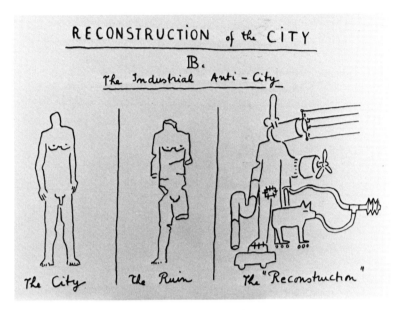

Figure 4. Leon Krier. The Reconstruction of the City.

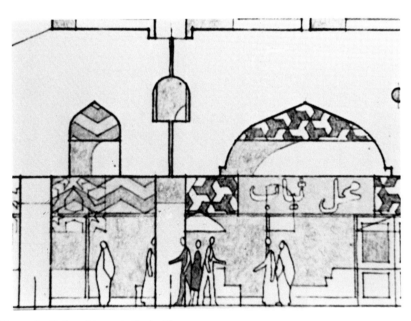

Figure 5. Robert Venturi. Scale Figures.

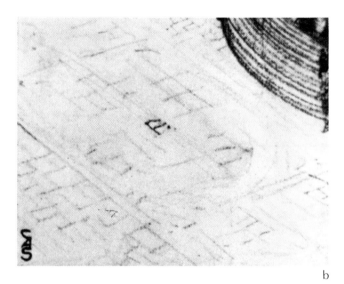

Figure 6. a. Carlo Scarpa, perspective drawn for a school exercise. b. Detail.

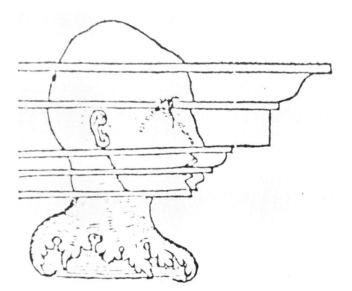

Figure 7. Diedo da Sagredo. Anthropometric proportion of a cornice, *Epitome*.

tracing paper, backs of cigarette boxes used as support and vehicle for his architectural ideas, are transformed into representations of a continuous meditation on the union of a theory with a practice. It is a theory that cannot be verbalized, but that communicates by means of the dialogue between the drawn line and the surface that is its vehicle, an entire process of construction. Each of Scarpa's drawings is proof of the Vitruvian motto ex *fabrica ratiocinatione*. The signs traced on the paper coalesce and crystallize in continuous theoretical explorations of architecture, in representations that are proposed as possible architectural realities. The drawings are themselves an architecture. These sketches omit tones and conventional efforts to communicate, assuming the significance of an iconic message reserved for the construct. We might say, figuratively, that these sketches are the result of eliminating the gulf between the "saying" of theory and the "doing" of construction. They are instruments whose function resembles that of the supervisors, craftsmen, bricklayers, carpenters, and stonecutters who transform the construction drawings into physical objects. In Scarpa's particular case, the lines (like words) turn to stones, or better still, become the account of the process of putting the stones on each other. This kind of writing weaves a multitude of more or less subtle relationships between architectural details, bringing the mind to see and feel the links that unite ways of being with ways of building. In these drawings marks and lines stand for the pegs and lines of a site layout; on them walls are built, demolished, and restored. Destruction is accomplished by rapid erasures, and the reconstruction sometimes follows the incised marks left by lines drawn in hard pencil and then erased. On these wonderful surfaces, the process by which the Basilica of Vicenza or the Ducal Palace in Venice were created, is condensed into a few brief movements. The making and unmaking of history is re-created with pencils, colors, and erasers.

Scarpa's designs are drawn on heavy drawing card stretched on a board—his favorite support for the formulation of his architectural thought, where architecture is the result of successive "strata" of meditation. On the precious surface of a heavy card are set and superimposed the nervous marks of charcoal and pastel, the deeply incised marks of the hard pencil—memories that remain, despite erasures. Finally, there are the definitive signs of the India ink, diluted so as not to be antagonistic to the pencil. Next to heavy paper is white or yellow tracing paper, the translucent support of a quick dialogue, for superimposing onto ideas already recorded on the opaque card. Beyond these desk drawings are pen sketches traced with the quick, masterly gesture on the backs of boxes of cigarette boxes of his favorite Oriental tobacco. These drawings record a constant architectural thought, and became his lifeline. Scarpa produced thousands of drawings for each of his projects; in them, human figures emerge as a continuous presence and as favorite images. An analysis of these figures in their various roles can demonstrate what might be a valuable modern usage of anthropomorphic practice. As Scarpa stated in the course of a lecture in Madrid:

> I want to make a confession: I would very much like some critic to discover certain intentions in my work that I have always had. That is to say, a powerful desire to work within tradition, but without making capitals and columns, because these can no longer be made.
>
> Dal Co 1984: 287

The first indication of Scarpa's use of the human body as fundamental for his understanding of architectural creation was a scholastic exercise at the Accademia in Venice—a detailed view drawn for a course taught by Professor Guido Cirilli (fig. 7). The drawing presents a pen drawing of a central-plan building of Late Venetian Renaissance flavor with geometric nuances that recall Longhen. The view is framed by a line marked in pencil. Scarpa uses the space outside of the frame for notes on ideas, checks, and analytical studies of details of the building presented in the view. Near the lower left corner of the

frame, embedded in the sketches, is the clue we seek: a human profile opposite that of a molding. The inane face of this architectural personage recalls, in its expression, the astonished face superimposed on a composite molding designed by Diego de Sagredo (1564: 14) to indicate anthropomorphic proportions (fig. 8). This superimposing of a human profile over a composite molding profile as a constant in judging the value and character of architectural elements from a physiognomic point of view was again used, toward the end of the eighteenth century, by Jacques-François Blondel. In his treatise, Blondel criticizes a Tuscan cornice by Palladio, demonstrating that the combination of molding profiles produced by the great Vicentine architect displays a discordant physiognomy: "the nose of an infant of twelve years sustained by the chin of a venerable gentleman of twenty-four years and crowned by the forehead of a man of fifty years" (Blondel 1771: I, 261) (fig. 9). The inane face drawn by Scarpa shows how the role of the human body in relation to the construct developed in his drawings. It is not only isomorphic and metaphoric; in the undoubtedly intentional irony of the expression selected—the dull face for a dull scholastic architecture—there is the seed of the metonymic system of the use of bodies in his more mature works.

The transition in Scarpa's work from a classic anthropomorphism to a modern one undoubtedly

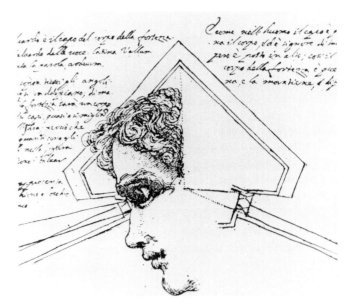

Figure 8. Teofilo Gallacini. Plan of a bastion, *L'Idea della Fortificazione.*

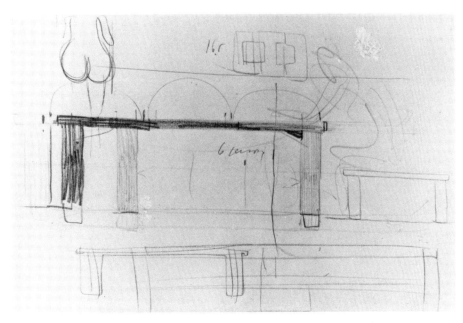

Figure 9. Carlo Scarpa. Table "millenovecentotrentaquattro" (1934), for six persons.

occurred during his preparatory retreat to the world of Venetian glass. Almost all of the critics of Scarpa's architecture agree that between the period 1926 and the early 1940s was a time of meditation and productive silence: a pause in architectural production during which Scarpa

> patiently contemplates human labour in the furnaces of the glazier: his silence that is understood and appreciated all the more as you consider the early works of some of our best-known architects in the official journals of the 'Thirties.
>
> *Brusatin 1972: 5*

In these drawings Scarpa transformed his approach to the role of the human body through a different material. In drawing figures prepared for incising on the glass wheel, Scarpa used both the dynamic dimensions of construction and a vision of the outlines of the glass to present the bodies and their members in a constant play with the materiality and reflections of the incised glass body. In a preparatory sketch for a series of vases dedicated to the four seasons, summer is represented by a woman seen from the back, who is undressing—a curly, callipygean motif reflecting the dominant form, which in turn determines the background beyond the figure. The drawing is for a double-jacketed vase of glass, curled and then unfolded. Beside the drawing there is a quick note: "You remember that verse by Valery, *'un frisson entre deux chemises'* " (fig. 10).

Scarpa used the same callipygean motif in the drawing for a table designed in 1934 and produced by Cassina in 1976. The motif is rapidly sketched in the upper left of the drawing and floats freely over the table. The notation is not casual, but emphasizes being seated as the dominant theme of the order of the table—a theme repeated in the figure at the head of the table in the same drawing, a study of the dimensions of a table for six (fig. 11). In the study sketch of the same table for eight, the callipygean motif appears again, here assuming a dynamic presence rocking on the seat of an invisible chair (fig. 12).

Figures of women predominate in Scarpa's drawings: stupendous nudes of contours and lines in constant dialogue with the architectural artifacts proposed in the drawings. For Scarpa, architecture is undoubtedly woman, but not prosaic and middle-aged with nude arms and iridescent dress, as in the Baroque iconological representation developed by Carlo Ripa (1675: 115). For Scarpa the image is poetic; his architecture, like his figures of women, is a continuous research into a tangible beauty, not a canonical and abstract one. This poetic relationship between the body of woman and architecture was expressed by Scarpa in a lecture at the Academy of Fine Arts in Vienna: "We can say that the architecture that we would like to be poetry should be called harmonious, like the beautiful face of a woman" (quoted in Dal Co 1985: 283).

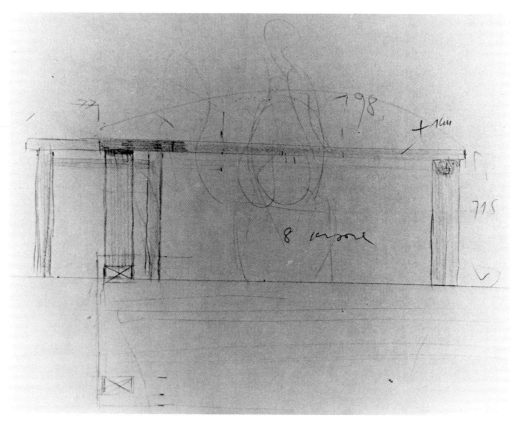

Figure 10. Carlo Scarpa. Table "millenovecentotrentaquattro" (1934), for eight persons.

In many of Scarpa's drawings, the figures of women are in groups of three, like the Graces or the Parcae. In a design Scarpa devised for an opening outlined by crossed circles in the wall facing the entrance to the Brion Tomb in the Cemetery of Altivole, three female figures, with the lineaments of thirties-style figurines, give a rhythm to the tripartite construction of this "impassable" window (fig. 13). The opening is generated by two intersecting metal-edged rings decorated with rose and blue mosaic mounted on either side of the window, within the channel of the metal profile. The geometry of the face of the central figure regulates the intersection of the circles. The geometry of this wonderful female face is the origin of the minimal system of the relationship between the two circles. The face, with its forehead set at the intersection of the two circles, determines the rule for the intersection by means of the position of the eyes, nose, and mouth. In these circles, the canonical relation of the diagonal of the square and the golden mean are disregarded. Instead, a two-faceted relationship is approached but not attained, just as a perfect symmetry in the human face is never achieved. This drawing indicates, furthermore, Scarpa's great attention to microarchitectural conditions; a forehead set against the cool metal of the window frame is most probably at the beginning of the architectural reflection that produced the geometric thought of the intersection of the circles. This attention that avoids the macro in favor of the micro is at the base of this new embodiment of architecture. A "being" and a "making" that focuses, as Manlio Brusatin has indicated,

> the minimal mechanisms of small systems that subtend— as in biological life—to the production of larger systems of artificial and artistic forms. A sensibility in designing that takes note of the union of all the small things which have great effects and the discontinuity of the great that finish in miniature (minima crescunt maxime maxima descrescunt).
> Brusatin 1984: 24

The small things of the body and its habits constantly regulate Scarpa's planning.

In another drawing for the Brion Tomb entrance, a rapid note at the foot of the three entrance steps—"if moved to the right everyone will go to the right'' — again indicates the remarkable attention Scarpa pays to minimal but fundamental facts of humanity in the use of the constructed space (fig. 14a). Guido Pietropoli has analyzed the idea that generated the decision for this detail masterfully: The building at the entrance to the tomb is based on an axial directrix grafted orthogonally on a narrow passage that leads to the left, to a site of reverence, to the arch-volt which protects the sarcophagus of the Brion; and to the right, a site of meditation: a platform with a canopy placed in the center of a large water basin. The walls of the entrance

are of concrete, decorated with squares of plaster whitewashed with clear stucco. The base of the two crossed rings is on the axis. The note mentioned above refers to three small steps interposed in the larger steps that break up the entrance space. In the drawing of the long section, the three small steps are moved considerably to the left. The note is undoubtedly correct from the formal point of view of axial composition; the displacement to the left is inexplicable unless one reconsiders the body and its manner of communication, using its own nature as a matrix for all information. Scarpa's note indicates his reflection, but in the end he retains his first intuitive choice. The body,

> without the schemes of the mind, knows how to see what it looks at and will understand that this stairway moved from the side of the heart suggests the imitation of a sorrowful ascent/descent to the city of the dead, turning to the left to encounter the affections most dear: father and mother.
>
> *Pietropoli 1983: 5*

Many heads crowd Scarpa's drawings: heads of beautiful women, indeterminate adolescent faces, classic profiles, and sometimes caricatures, most often self-caricatures that are always (extremely) significant. The presence of Scarpa himself in a drawing is a sign that something special is reserved for that particular space. In the same drawing of the entrance to the Brion Tomb where he notes the movement of the steps, a head looking up floats bodiless in the air of the transverse section of the building. A visible line is drawn from the eye of this figure fragment (fig. 14b). This line delimits the outline of the internal part of the flower stand that spans the entrance threshold. The eye is indicated in the sketch of the head by a point in a small circle. The same notation, the small circle and the point, is repeated through all of the section, many times with quick diagonal lines radiating from them, determining the opening and outline of various moldings and steps that give rhythm to the space. The path that the visitor takes through this monument has been attentively studied by Scarpa; the way in which the architecturally inattentive visitor perceives them becomes the pretext for the relationship between space, light, and shadow that he generates. The small head, which he creates with a few quick strokes, is a self-caricature. The expression is cunning, as if to say, ''I know something that you do not, but which in any case will captivate your eye through a reflection of shining brass or a shadow darker than the others, which I—

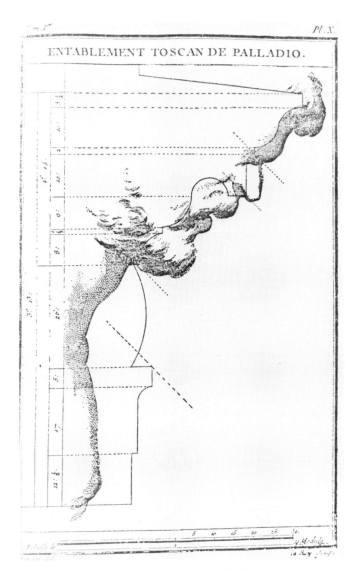

ENTABLEMENT TOSCAN DE PALLADIO.

Figure 11. Jacques-François Blondel. Palladio's Tuscan Entablature, *Cours d'Architecture.*

Figure 12. Carlo Scarpa. Sketch for a glass vase.

who have put myself into this drawing—have devised.''

In a sketch project for the large door inside the chapel in the garden of the Brion Tomb, two heads inserted into the composition demonstrate the internal rule of the artifact (fig. 15). The door is made up of a metal section over a square grid, asymmetrically pivoted. Each square is filled with white cement cast in glass shuttering (a technique that produces extremely smooth surfaces), then decorated with small Greek crosses in brass, produced by shuttering spacers cast into the panels. In the center of gravity of the door a smaller one of veneered wood opens and has a central vertical aperture of transparent glass. In the drawing, two heads are inserted in this small door. One face emerges, as though from behind misted glass, looking through the glazed aperture. This physiognomy is very

unlike the evanescent one behind the opaline glass. Instead, it has the slightly mocking expression of a youth who has gotten away with a playful prank. The other figure is a profile caricature of Scarpa himself, observing from above, not in the background where one might expect him to be. (This profile is not sketched in the background where one would expect it, considering the vision of the object and the space that encompasses it.) Scarpa's head is a part of the material of the object itself, the door and Scarpa unified in an ambiguous representation of architectural reality, an affirmation of the being in the reality that is architecture. The frustration of scenographic presentation, easing the fusion of reality with what is done on a perceptual act which is *donné*, is given as a first form of knowledge, a manifestation of being in building. The door in question is an *ianua*; the two heads represent the two-sided nature of Janus-Scarpa, the master and the playful pupil. In fact, the small door itself presents this two-sided nature of the building: on one side the veneered panel is placed on the bottom while on the other side it is placed in the upper part of the door. The presence of the smaller door in the larger one, furthermore, indicates the role played by the threshold of this opening to the chapel—the last stop on our earthly voyage—and our continuous need to remember this rite of passage.

Another example of Scarpa's use of the human figure in the traditional identification with interior furnishings is in his drawing of the fireplace projected for the Balboni House (fig. 16). In his detail drawing for the fireplace, Scarpa and the patroness are present next to the object. The best-defined parts of the two figures are the heads that, drawn with nervous sinuous lines, are sustained by giant wings. Traces of the real bodies are indicated by fine, vague lines. The two bodies as projections of giant wings are a part of the fireplace. A similar, perhaps more persuasive image of the process of identification of the body as norm and as indirect element of every space and object constructed is in the preparatory drawing for the arrangement of a wall in the gallery in the Accademia in Venice (fig. 17). In the elaboration of this project, two paintings—attentively delineated by Scarpa—have been mounted on fabric-covered panels. He uses the pyramidal composition of these pictorial images to generate the geometric construction of the panels. A series of intersecting squares is rotated forty-five degrees in respect of the perpendicular determining the dimensions, proportions, and the salient points of the project. While the use of rotation of the diagonals can be seen clearly in the construction of the drawing, the geometric concept is indicated by the triangular joint, a square cut on the diagonal and rotated, which brackets the horizontal beam supporting the panels to the bearing wall. At the extreme right of the drawing a female figure seen from the back and characterized by the light pose of a classical dancer determines the hanging line of the paintings by the upper line of her coiffure. To the right of the drawing, beyond the representation of the vertical section of the panels, there is a pole that supports a mask of powerful outline with a shadow that suggests almost metallic reflections. The eye of this mask is in front of the dotted lines that indicate the niche where the paintings will be placed; the eye organizes the form of this mask/helmet in balance on a vertical support. The abstraction of this static personage, in contrast to the dancing figure's celebration of movement, both points to and guides the process of rarification of the space — from the two-

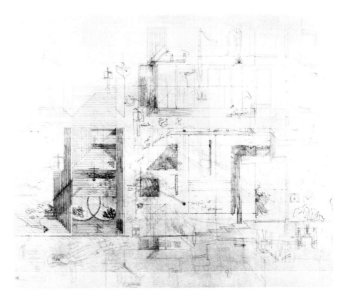

Figure 13. Carlo Scarpa. Entry, Brion Cemetery, Elevation and Section.

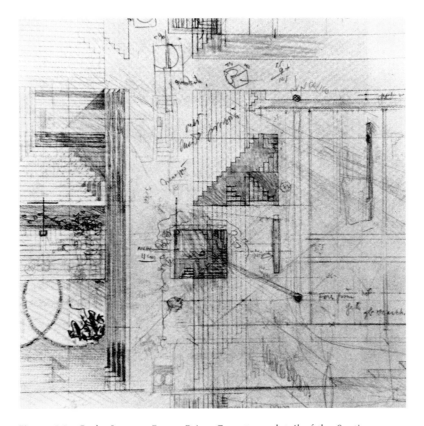

Figure 14. Carlo Scarpa. Entry, Brion Cemetery, detail of the Section.

Figure 15. Carlo Scarpa. Sketch for the crossed ring window. Entry, Brion Cemetery, Elevation.

dimensional representation into panels to three-dimensional movement—for seeing the works of art. Here there is a play to discern the predominant form of architectural disposition between the real and virtual (conceptualized?) figures of a constructed environment. The geometric characteristics of the figures' composition delineated in the paintings become the *forma eximia*; the other figures are momentary appearances. The dancer and the mask are elements borrowed from the theater—the supreme form of human representation. They are the *corpi incerti* and dynamic of the space of an exhibition, a representation of a representation.

Scarpa celebrates the dynamic condition of the human presence in a sequence of study drawings for the covered footbridge that links the *Mastio* to the *Reggia* in the Museum of Castelvecchio in Verona. In a drawing showing one of the first solutions for the suspended passage, two female figures are represented on the inside of the transverse section (fig. 18). One is a female nude shown from the back and walking with a certain majesty. The other is a feminine bust with sketchy bosom, looking out of the continuous window

that delimits the passage toward the courtyard. These two figures indicate the two major architectural problems Scarpa faced in his search for the solution to the brief suspended passage, a dynamic joint between the two parts that compose the Castelvecchio Museum. The nude seen from the back indicates the dynamic kinaesthetic of the passage: the majestic stride is manifestation of the resonant step on a sound box created in the space between the pavement and the external covering that accommodates the carrying structure, which is made with stone slabs suspended on a third level. The frontal head demonstrates the problem of looking out, an act of reorientation necessary at that point in the museological path. To capture the eye of the passing visitor, an anomaly is inserted into the composition: the upper edge of the internal windowsill covers the view of the lower frame of the fixture. In the drawing of the transverse section of this passage, the resonant slabs of the pavement are no longer a problem; they are set up over the mitered edges of the cement slab of the parapet and of an intermediate beam. The problem of looking out, however, required further thought (fig. 19). The visual

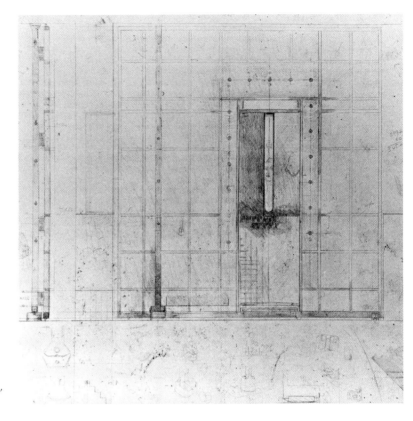

Figure 16. Carlo Scarpa. Interior Door of the Chapel, Brion Cemetery.

Figure 17. Carlo Scarpa. Fireplace, Casa Balboni, Elevation and Section.

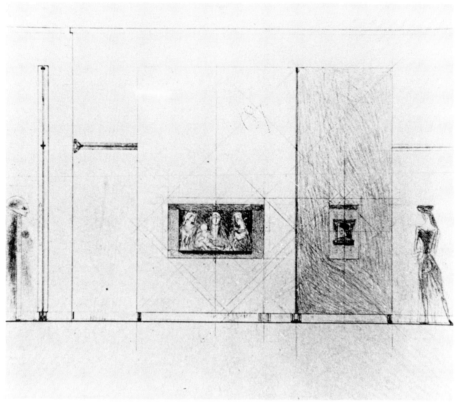

Figure 18. Carlo Scarpa. Study drawing for exhibition panels, Gallerie dell'Accademia, Elevation and Section.

line generated by the upper edge of the internal windowsill is linked to the eye of the head with its Renaissance profile. The head is positioned in counterpoint to the circle created by the rotation of the internal fixture. Simple human attention is at the base of this ultimate architectural meditation; the concern that, in the act of opening the window for ventilation or cleaning, there is the danger of banging one's head during the rotation of the glass panels of the fixture. This consideration leads to the creation of a panel with an inclined edge that gently averts the risky circle of rotation. The small head is the expression of this final reflection, in which the windowsill edge results as much from the reality of the idea as from the mechanics of construction.

This interaction between fact and reality as an excuse for the ingenuities of an architectural machine is celebrated by Scarpa in a studio drawing prepared for

his own *Personale* in the *Mostra Ambiente* at the Thirty-fourth Venice Biennale (fig. 20). Scarpa's idea of the architectural machine does not arise from a Corbusian *esprit*, but relies on an inventiveness, as of the *Proti* of the Venice Arsenal. The drawing of the Scarpian machine is a section and represents the part of the show dedicated to the exhibition of his own architectural *oeuvre*. The dominant motif is a movable beam, a mechanism that localizes objects in space by its rotation. The line of rotation created by the ends of the beam and by the counterweight located at three-quarters of its total length is the recognized matrix of the dimensional and spatial order of the room of the exhibition. In the drawing of the longitudinal section a figure of a young girl evidences the importance of this geometry, not solidified, but present in the construction; it is the face with its receding outline set against the circle generated by the trajectory of the

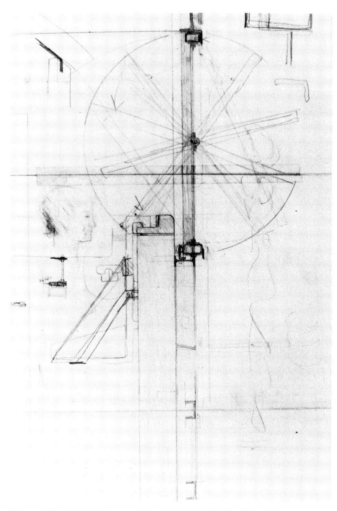

Figure 20. Carlo Scarpa. Detail of the Wall of the Passage between the Reggio and the Mastio, Castelvecchio di Verona. Section.

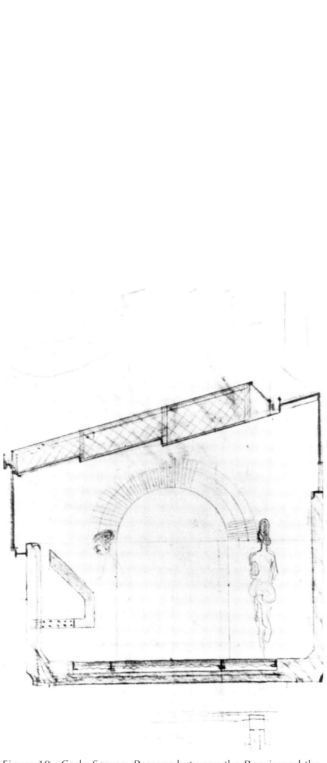

Figure 19. Carlo Scarpa. Passage between the Reggia and the Mastio, Castelvecchio di Verona.

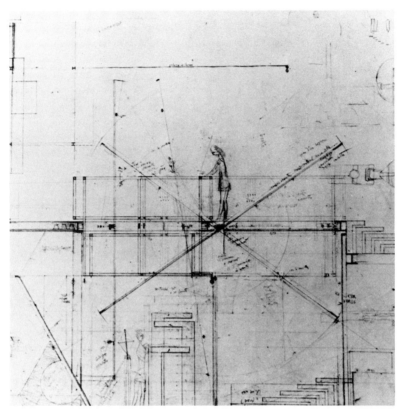

Figure 21. Carlo Scarpa. Study drawing for the design of his personal exhibition, Biennale 1968, Longitudinal Section.

intermediate counterweight. The beam is mounted on a platform-scale joint so that it has an oscillating movement from the plane of rotation. In the transverse section a figure of partially indeterminate outline reacts to the final possibility of movement by withdrawing brusquely, but at the same time grasping the railing and assuming a dynamic position. Just as this beam is dynamic, the lower counterweight is the *oiseau bleu qui dorme* (fig. 21).

Scarpa makes similar use of the figure of the circle — related to the movements of the architectural machine — in his plan for the tomb-chapel of the Galli family in the Monumental cemetery in Genoa. The generating figures of the plan are the stretched-out bodies of the parents and the dead son. The commission touched Scarpa particularly, especially the fact that the young Galli was the first Italian child kept alive by a pacemaker. The circle and the square of the composition of the plan became the absolute motif of

the reality of death expressed in an architectural artifact (figs. 22, 23).Scarpa in fact defines the fundamental terms of the architectural machine, affirming that "the funerary tabernacle for the Galli family represents the extremely essential structure that agrees with the idea of the absolute that comes with death." In the elaborate images drawn by Scarpa for this plan, the architectural absolute is restored to its original dimensions. In the studio drawing of the tabernacle, the analogical thought in plan uses the human body as the "symmetrical" base from which the "proportions" are born. In these drawings — the only ones where he represents human figures in plan — Scarpa has regenerated and reinterpreted the proportional process of the so-called Vitruvian man. The outstretched body of the youth becomes the origin of the geometry of the square and the circle, and the localization of the center is extremely significant. What is only a tension in the representation of the Vitruvian Man by Cesare

Cesariano (1521: 45) is, in Scarpa's drawings, realized (fig. 24). In a summation of iconological references recalling to mind (physiognomies of) Medieval and Renaissance saints or modern notations of the Neo-Primitives, the figure of the young Galli interacts with the figures of the mother and the father to determine the transformation of the plan to the elevation of this architectural machine. The bodies of the parents superimposed orthogonally over the body of their son are parallel to one another and to the façade of the tabernacle. This disposition of bodies establishes in this simple but powerful block of stone an ancient symbol of salvation—the opening of the TAU (figs. 25, 26). This opening in the form of TAU is the result of the proportional openings that introduce the bodies into the block of stone. Its operation is guillotinelike; it will be opened and closed three times, then the cables of the counterweights will be cut, so that the family that death has prematurely separated will be definitively reunited. In these project drawings the idea of proportion goes beyond "*ratio pro parte*"—Cicero's reductive translation of a Greek term without direct Latin equivalent—to the complete extension of the Greek concept of analogy that includes within itself a relationship of formal contiguity (Vitruvius 1960: 94 n.a.).

*   *   *

Thus the presence of the human figure is an indispensable requisite in contemporary architectural drawing. It not only helps us to understand the dimensions and scale of the proposed project; it is also essential for introducing into the construction a dimension in which human fact and architecture are integrated, in a poetic reality made possible by our twofold comprehension of architectural technology. From this point of view, a building is such because it is constructed by man and interpreted by means of human form. The logic of constructive technique is encompassed by the techniques of verbal logic, and the techniques of verbal logic are encompassed by the logic of constructive technique. It is a procedure that accepts the body as the most perfect and general means for attaining the architectural world. The body as reality thus becomes the basis of architectural facticity, its action/thoughts determining—through material and logical contiguity—the configuration of the constructive elements.

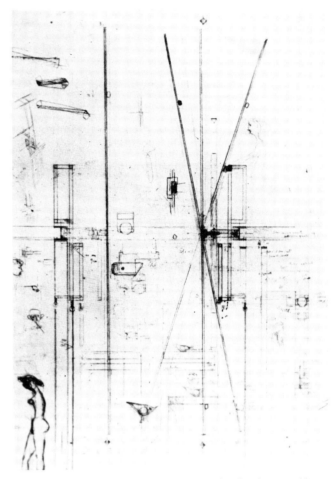

Figure 22. Carlo Scarpa. Study drawing for the design of his personal exhibition, Biennale 1968, Transverse Section.

BIBLIOGRAPHY

Blondel, Jacques-François
   1771   *Cours d'Architecture*. Paris.

Brusatin, Manlio
   1972   "Carlo Scarpa Architetto Veneziano." *Controspazio*, 3–4, pp. 2–85.
   1984   "I minimi sistemi dell'architetto Carlo Scarpa." *Carlo Scarpa: Il Progetto di Santa Caterina a Treviso*. Vianello, Treviso.

Cesariano, Cesare
   1521   *Di Lucio Vitruvio Pollione De Architectura*. Milano.

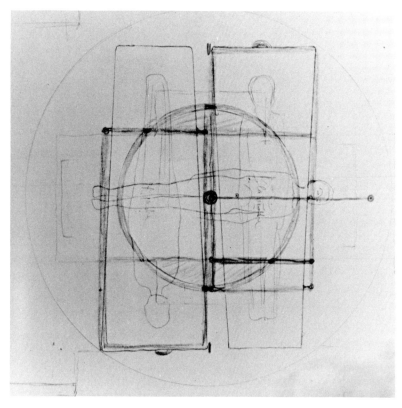

Figure 23. Carlo Scarpa. Study drawing,
Tomba Galli, Genoa. Plan.

Figure 24. Cesariano Cesare.
Vitruvian Man, *De Architectura*.

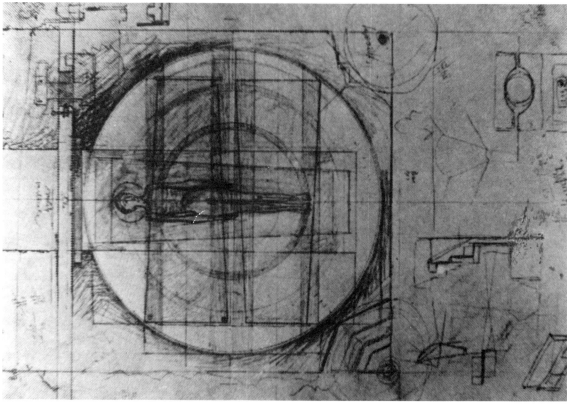

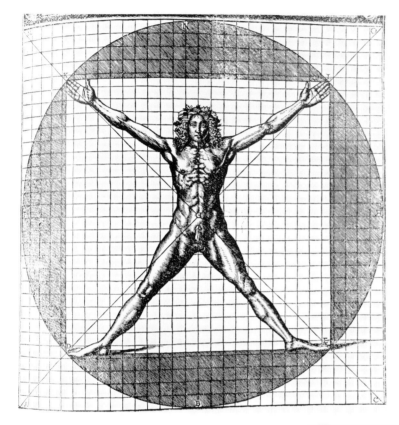

Figure 25. Carlo Scarpa. Study drawing, Tomba Galli, Genoa. Plan.

Figure 26. Carlo Scarpa. Study drawing, Tomba Galli, Genoa. Elevation.

Crippa, Maria Antonietta
  1984 *Carlo Scarpa*, Jaca Book. Milano.

Dal Co, Francesco, and Giuseppe Mazzariol
  1984 *Carlo Scarpa Opera Completa*, Electa. Milano.

di Giorgio Martini, Francesco
  1967 *Trattati*, edited by C. Maltese, Il Polifilo. Milano.

Frascari, Marco
  1985 "Carlo Scarpa in Magna Graecia." *AA Files*, 9,
        p. 3–9.

Krier, Leo
  1984 "Houses, Palaces, Cities." *A.D.*, 54, 7–8,
        pp. 15–96.

Magagnato, Licisco (ed.)
  1982 *Carlo Scarpa a Castelvecchio*, Comunita°. Milano.

Pietropoli, Guido
  1983 "Invitacio° al viatge." *Quaderns*, 158, pp. 4–8.

Ripa, Carlo
  1675 *Iconologia*. Venezia.

Vitruvio
  1960 *Architettura*, edited by S. Ferri. Palumbo. Roma.

Clowns: Apollinaire's writings on Picasso

Orphée[1]

Admirez le pouvoir insigne
Et la noblesse de la ligne
Elle est la voix que la lumière fit entendre
Et dont parle Hermès Trismégiste en son Pimandre
　　　　　Guillaume Apollinaire, Le Bestiaire

Picasso met Guillaume Apollinaire in a bar on the rue d'Amsterdam around 1904, when both were in their mid-twenties, and they were friends until the poet's death in 1918.[2] In *Le Poète assassiné* (1916, I, 231–364), Apollinaire presents a fictional account of that meeting: At the end of a cold, dark corridor, the poet Cronimental knocks on a strange door. When it opens, he sees the Bird of Benin, a painter dressed in workman's blue and barefoot, surrounded by paintings as a shepherd by his flock. And "there was in the sudden light the creation of two beings and their immediate marriage."[3]

In 1907, Apollinaire attributed to Matisse the statement—one that reflected the poet's own belief—that the artist is formed in his confrontation and struggle with other artistic personalities, with other scripts and other arts. All "plastic scripts"—the Greek, the Cambodian, the African—as well as arts related to painting, Apollinaire wrote, could help the painter discover his own personality.[4] In Apollinaire's terms, Picasso's greatest encounter was perhaps with African art. Although relatively little was known in the early years of the century about the statues or the cultures

Figure 1. Raoul Dufy, *Orphée*, 1911. Illustration for "Orphée" in Apollinaire's *Le Bestiaire ou cortège d'Orphée*. © SPADEM, Paris/VAGA, New York, 1987.

that produced them,[5] the African works interested Picasso both for their formal and their magic qualities. Few poets of his time were as attuned as Apollinaire to African and Oceanic art.[6] His greatest artistic "struggle" was not with these arts, however; it was with Picasso's painting. Like André Salmon and other poets of their

1. "Orphée," in Guillaume Apollinaire, *Oeuvres poétiques*, ed. Marcel Adéma and Michel Décaudin (Paris: Gallimard, 1965), p. 3. Reprinted with permission of © Editions Gallimard.

2. Accounts of Apollinaire's early friendship with Picasso include Marcel Adéma, *Guillaume Apollinaire: le mal-aimé* (Paris: Plon, 1952), pp. 74–78; Guillaume Apollinaire, *Oeuvres complètes*, 4 vols. (Paris: André Balland et Jacques Lecat, 1965–1966), IV, 274–275; Roger Shattuck, *The Banquet Years: The Origins of the Avant-garde in France, 1885–World War I*, revised ed. (1969: rpt. Salem, New Hampshire: Ayer, 1984), pp. 262–264 (Shattuck notes that various dates, from 1903 to 1906, have been given to Picasso and Apollinaire's first meeting); Fernande Olivier, *Picasso et ses amis* (Paris: Stock, 1933), pp. 38–40, 71–75, et passim.

3. Apollinaire, *The Poet Assassinated and Other Stories*, trans. Ron Padgett (San Francisco: North Point Press, 1984), pp. 27–28.

4. Apollinaire, *Oeuvres complètes*, IV, 85–86. The passage contains Apollinaire's first allusion to African art. Most subsequent references to the *Oeuvres complètes* appear in the text and note simply volume and page.

5. See Apollinaire, *Apollinaire on Art: Essays and Reviews 1902–1918*, The Documents of 20th Century Art, ed. LeRoy C. Breunig, trans. Susan Suleiman (New York: Viking, 1972), p. 471; Apollinaire, *Oeuvres complètes*, II, 496. Most subsequent references to AoA appear in the text.

6. For discussion of Picasso's "primitivism" (the term reflects a Western concern and is not necessarily descriptive of the varied works to which it is applied), and especially his interest in non-Western art, see William Rubin, "Picasso," in *"Primitivism" in 20th Century Art: Affinity of the Tribal and the Modern*, ed. William Rubin, 2 vols. (Boston: Little, Brown, 1984), I, 241–343. André

generation raised on the nineteenth-century myth of the "poète-voyant," Apollinaire regarded Picasso as something of a shaman or a seer.[7] Picasso's art challenged Apollinaire, as African art challenged Picasso, because the poet considered it magic — and because it was at once familiar and other. And although Apollinaire is perhaps best known as a defender of Cubism and the avant-garde, it was the paintings he saw when he first visited Picasso's atelier, the works of the Circus (early Rose) Period (1905), that intrigued him most and longest of all.[8] Protean and liminal figures, Picasso's clowns would guide Apollinaire in a voyage through painting that led from Symbolism to the "primitivism" of Iberia and Africa, to the ghostly canvases of Hermetic Cubism and the harlequinade sleights of hand of Synthetic Cubism, and, beyond where Picasso himself wished to go, to abstraction and "pure painting."

Meyer Schapiro has described Picasso's *Young Acrobat on a Ball* (1905) as an isolated and alienated "performer" concerned with the manipulation of form. The painting looks forward to Cubism, Schapiro notes, but also, more immediately, to Picasso's interest in non-Western art, in the art of "tribal" peoples scorned by European society except as entertainers and admired only by artists.[9] The aestheticism and primitivism that color Apollinaire and Picasso's early work spring from a common nineteenth-century source: artists' perception of the failure of bourgeois society on the one hand, and, on the other, the failure of traditional Western myth to rescue the world from the vulgar and the banal. Myth is ubiquitous in the modern West, Mircea Eliade has written, but it is secularized, camouflaged, and in disrepair.[10] Apollinaire's poetry is suffused with nostalgia for myth and legend and religion, but "many of those gods have died," he wrote in 1903. "Great Pan Love Jesus Christ / Are all quite dead and tomcats howl."[11] One nineteenth-century response to this sense of spiritual crisis was an attempt to create secret and sacred spaces through art. Another was the idealization of a variety of so-called "primitive" sources that represented freedom from convention and an imagined return to innocence. In this vein, Rimbaud and Baudelaire identified the artist with the child; Gauguin left Europe for Tahiti; Champfleury wrote, "The idol cut on a tree-trunk by savages is nearer to Michelangelo's 'Moses' than most of the statues in the annual Salons. . . ."[12] And Rimbaud claimed that he loved "absurd paintings . . . stage settings, clowns' backdrops, signboards, popular colored prints, old-fashioned literature, church Latin, erotic books without proper spelling, novels of our grandmothers' time, fairy tales, little books for children, silly refrains, [naive] rhythms."[13]

Apollinaire's *Alcools* (1913), with its folktales and magic, its wandering children and gypsies and clowns, is heir to the diffuse primitivism of the nineteenth century. And, as Phoebe Pool has shown, Picasso's early work is related to the international "cult of

---

Malraux attributes to Picasso a number of evocative statements regarding African art and especially its sacred and magic qualities in *Picasso's Mask*, trans., June Guicharnaud (New York: Holt, Rinehart & Winston), pp. 10–13, et passim. For discussion of Apollinaire's interest (primarily as expressed in his criticism) in various kinds of primitivism, including African and Oceanic art, naive and folk art, and the childlike, see Katia Samaltanos, *Apollinaire: Catalyst for Primitivism, Picabia, and Duchamp*, Studies in the Fine Arts: The Avant-Garde, 45 (Ann Arbor: UMI Research Press, 1984). See also Jean-Claude Blachère, *Le Modèle nègre: aspects littéraires du mythe primitiviste au XXᵉ siècle chez Apollinaire–Cendrars–Tzara* (Dakar: Nouvelles Editions Africaines, 1981).

7. See *Apollinaire on Art*, pp. 196, 280; André Salmon, *La Jeune Peinture française* (Paris: Albert Messein, 1912), p. 52; LeRoy C. Breunig, "Picasso's Poets," *Yale French Studies*, no. 21 (1958), p. 8; Scott Bates, *Guillaume Apollinaire*, Twayne's World Authors Series, 14 (New York: Twayne, 1967), p. 68, et passim.

8. Alfred Barr distinguishes between the Circus Period, which is the first phase of the Rose Period (and the one under consideration here) and the first "Classic" Period, which begins mid-1905 and ends mid-1906. See Alfred Barr, Jr., *Picasso: Fifty Years of His Art* (New York: Museum of Modern Art, 1974), pp. 34–40. I generally follow Barr's classification of Picasso's painting.

9. See Meyer Schapiro, *Modern Art: 19th and 20th Centuries: Selected Papers* (New York: George Braziller, 1978), pp. 203–204.

10. See Mircea Eliade, "Les Mythes du monde moderne," *La Nouvelle N. R. F.*, 9, September 1953, p. 453. Also see Eliade, *Images and Symbols: Studies in Religious Symbolism*, trans. Philip Mairet (New York: Sheed & Ward, 1961), pp. 17–18.

11. Apollinaire, "La Chanson du mal-aimé," in *Alcools*, trans. Anne Hyde Greet (Berkeley: University of California Press, 1965), p. 23.

12. Cited by Phoebe Pool in her introduction to Anthony Blunt and Phoebe Pool, *Picasso: The Formative Years* (Greenwich, Connecticut: New York Graphic Society, 1962), p. 12. See Pool's remarks on nineteenth-century primitivism and its role in Picasso's Barcelona in Blunt and Pool, p. 12. For comments on the role of the child in the works of Baudelaire and Rimbaud, see Schapiro, pp. 63–64 and Shattuck, p. 31, respectively. General treatments of primitivism and modern art include Rubin, "Primitivism," Robert Goldwater, *Primitivism in Modern Art*, revised ed. (New York: Vintage, 1967); Jean Laude, *La Peinture française (1907–1914) et l'art nègre*, 2 vols. (Paris: Klincksieck, 1968).

13. Arthur Rimbaud, "Delires II," in *A Season in Hell, The Illuminations*, trans. Enid Rhodes Peschel (New York: Oxford University Press, 1973), p. 77. (Bracketed word is my translation.)

primitivism" that reigned in the Barcelona of his youth and that was celebrated in *Arte Joven*, the journal he edited in Madrid in 1901. That primitivism, Pool suggests, may account for the many portraits of children in Picasso's Blue Period, as well as for his later interest in non-Western art.[14] But when Apollinaire and Picasso met, between the Blue Period and the African-inspired works of 1907–1908, Picasso was painting another kind of "primitive" and outsider to "civilized" society: the clown.

* * *

It is the nature of Apollinaire's encounter with Picasso's early painting that interests me. Certainly, it is because they allude to the sad, moonlit clowns of the Romantic and Symbolist eras to which Apollinaire and Picasso were heir that the Rose Period works were accessible to Apollinaire.[15] And the clown, multivalent and mysterious, creator and creation, embodiment and spirit, is a fertile image for poet and painter. The mere sharing of images and motifs, however, is not the most important feature of the relationship between literature and the plastic arts. Before Apollinaire, French poets of the mid- and late nineteenth century had already looked to other arts to explore the nondiscursive nature of their own work. As poets of the nineteenth century turned to the wordless arts, to mime, dance, music, and painting, to understand and challenge poetic language, so Apollinaire turned a poetic eye to an art of silence and stasis. In evoking Picasso's works in lyric rather than discursive terms, Apollinaire wrote poetic meditations remarkable for their subtlety and sensitivity to the painting. In dreaming of Picasso's art, he

fashioned pieces of intrinsic poetic interest; and he deepened, and ultimately changed, his understanding of both painting and poetry.

Apollinaire saw himself as an adventurer at the frontier of the ancient and the new. Picasso's circus figures too stand at a crossroads, between the Symbolist and the modern, the literary and the abstract, the figurative and the formal, the nineteenth century and the twentieth. To Robert Rosenblum, the *Family of Saltimbanques* (1905, fig. 2), with its wistful vestiges of symbol and sentiment, is "the last picture of the nineteenth century."[16] For Meyer Schapiro—and for Rosenblum as well—the *Young Acrobat on a Ball* (fig. 3) of the same year suggests a pre-Cubist artist "concerned with the adjustment of lines and masses."[17]

Apollinaire's interpretations of the Rose Period anticipate these views. In "Picasso, peintre," a lyric essay of 1905, he surrounded the familiar figures of the Rose Period with the atmosphere of magic and mystery that also washes over the works of *Alcools* (1913, III, 54–145), his first major collection of poetry. Nonetheless, Apollinaire was conscious of the radical promise of the Rose Period as early as 1905. By 1912 and 1913, when he was active in defending Cubism and other avant-garde painting, he was all the more aware of that potential. And in "Un Fantôme de nuées" (III, 184–186), a poem of 1913, he contemplates the saltimbanques in the light of a new day. Placing the poem in "Ondes," the opening section of *Calligrammes* (1918, III, 157–289)—his second and more experimental major volume of verse—Apollinaire recalls the clowns to life, much as Picasso had in *Family of Saltimbanques*, to bid them a tentative adieu, and to proclaim his dedication to a new aesthetic.[18] Apollinaire alluded to the Circus paintings in at least five poetic works published between 1905 and 1917. Of these, "Picasso, peintre" and "Un Fantôme de nuées" deal most directly with the painting and are most interesting for the light they shed on Apollinaire's developing understanding of art.[19]

14. See Pool, p. 12.

15. For discussion of Picasso's Rose Period clowns, see Theodore Reff, "Harlequins, Saltimbanques, and Fools," *Artforum*, 19, no. 2 (1971), 31–43; Reff, "Themes of Love and Death in Picasso's Early Work," in *Picasso in Retrospect*, eds. Roland Penrose and John Golding (New York: Praeger, 1973), pp. 28–46. More general treatments of nineteenth- and twentieth-century clowns include Georges Doutrepont, *Les Types populaires de la littérature française* (Paris: Albert Dewit, 1927), II, 55–67, 191–206, 560 et passim; Jean Starobinski, *Portrait de l'artiste en saltimbanque* (Genève: Skira, 1970); Robert F. Storey, *Pierrot: A Critical History of a Mask* (Princeton: Princeton University Press, 1978), pp. 93–155; Martin Green and John Swan, *The Triumph of Pierrot: The Commedia dell'Arte and the Modern Imagination* (New York: Macmillan, 1986). For a description of the great mime Jean-Gaspard Deburau, who created the prototype of the alienated, moonlit clown of the Romantic and Symbolist eras, see Charles Baudelaire, "De l'essence du rire," in *Oeuvres complètes*, ed. Yves Florenne (Paris: Le Club français du livre, 1966), I, 547.

16. Robert Rosenblum, *Cubism and Twentieth Century Art* (New York: Abrams, 1966), p. 12.

17. Schapiro, pp. 203–204. See Rosenblum, p. 10.

18. "Ondes" (III, 159–192), the first and most experimental section of *Calligrammes*, includes poems written between 1912 and the declaration of war in 1914.

19. English translations of "Picasso, peintre," in *Apollinaire on Art*, pp. 14–16, and of "Un Fantôme de nuées," in *Calligrammes: Poems of Peace and War (1913–1916)*, trans. Anne Hyde Greet (Berkeley: University of California Press, 1980), pp. 81–87, are contained in an appendix to this essay. Apollinaire also alludes to the

Figure 2. Picasso, *Family of Saltimbanques*, 1905. National Gallery of Art, Washington, D.C.; Chester Dale Collection.

Baudelaire's suggestion that the best review of a painting might be a poem is admirably illustrated by the lyric prose of "Picasso, peintre."[20] The essay, written on the occasion of Picasso's exhibition at the Galeries Serrurier, incorporates an astonishingly detailed reading of the painting, not only of its general atmosphere and images, but also of its specific works and subtle evolutions. In so doing, it stands in complex relation to the painting, as a good illustration does to a text.[21]

Admittedly the reverie of a poet, "Picasso, peintre" has the virtue of engaging and extending the canvas without reducing it to a set of fixed meanings or robbing it of suggestion—of what the nineteenth-century poets called music, and Gauguin and other nineteenth-century painters called poetry.[22] According to Daix and Boudaille, "Picasso liked Apollinaire's essay . . . very much. When we recently showed him the photostat, he

---

circus paintings in "Saltimbanques" and "Crépuscule" of *Alcools* (III, 75, 97), and "Pablo PIcasso," a "lyric ideogram" of 1917, included in *Apollinaire on Art*, pp. 450–451.

20. See Baudelaire, I, 282. I discuss Baudelaire's remark in relation to Apollinaire's essay in Eberiel, "Guillaume Apollinaire: Poetic Encounters with Painting," diss. Harvard 1979, pp. 11–12. Others who have used Baudelaire's comment to describe the essay are Harry Buckley, *Guillaume Apollinaire as an Art Critic*, Studies in the Fine Arts: Criticism, 11 (Ann Arbor: UMI Research Press, 1981), p. 21, and Samaltanos, p. 6.

21. See Gérard Bertrand, *L'Illustration de la poésie à l'époque du cubisme* (Paris: Klincksieck, 1971). Although he is discussing one of

Picasso's illustrations for Max Jacob's *Saint Matorel*, Bertrand's words might well describe "Picasso, peintre": "Comment . . . ne pas rêver sur cette merveilleuse et fugitive coincidence de la pensée plastique et de la pensée poétique, inconciliables par nature, mais pour un bref instant l'une à l'autre mystérieusement accordées." Bertrand, p. 110.

22. See letter from Paul Gauguin to Charles Morice, July 1901, cited by George Heard Hamilton, *Painting and Sculpture in Europe: 1880–1940*, the Pelican History of Art (Harmondsworth: Penguin Books, 1967), pp. 91–92. Suzanne Bernard describes the influence of music on nineteenth-century poetry in *Mallarmé et la musique* (Paris: Nizet, 1959), pp. 9–21, et passim. H. R. Rookmaaker takes up the topic of "Musicality" in *Gauguin and 19th Century Art Theory* (Amsterdam: Sweto & Zeitlinger, 1972), pp. 210–220.

read the first lines aloud with an emotion to which he does not yield easily"[23]:

> If we knew, all the gods would awaken. Born of the profound knowledge that humanity had of itself, the adored pantheisms that resembled it have gone to sleep. But despite eternal slumbers, there are eyes that reflect humanities resembling divine and joyous phantoms.

"Picasso, peintre" is not only a meditation on the paintings of the Blue and Rose periods; it is also an inquiry into the nature of art. "Picasso has looked at human images that float in the azure of our memories and that partake of the divine. . . ." Apollinaire does not isolate or comment directly on the blue monochrome of 1901 to 1904 (the Blue Period).[24] Through the poetic image, he suggests that its works were born not of optics but of mind, that although Picasso depicted the poor and outcast of Paris and Barcelona with compassion, his gaze, like those of his blind men and oddly staring youths, looks not into physical but into spiritual space. This painting, he implies, is the product of memory and thus shares a common inspiration with poetry. Art, Picasso believed during the Blue Period, was born of love and suffering, of innocence and introspection.[25]

"These children whom no one caresses understand so much. Mommy, love me a lot. They know how to jump and the feats they accomplish are [like] mental evolutions."[26] Apollinaire treats the children as a group, as he will other Blue Period figures (fig. 4). Using the children as a point of departure, he creates a fiction that is also a comment on the Blue Period. There are echoes here of the Romantic notion that art comes of suffering. The children of "Picasso, peintre" are

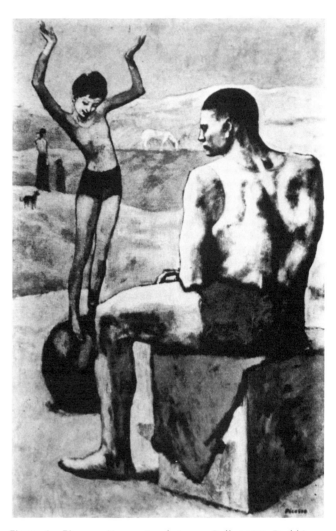

Figure 3. Picasso, *Young Acrobat on a Ball*, 1905. Pushkin Museum, Moscow. © SPADEM, Paris/VAGA, New York, 1987.

unloved, unschooled; yet out of their privation have come a rare understanding and mysterious gifts. Art, Apollinaire implies in the first lines of the essay, is the fruit of knowledge and insight. In his own work, he associates art with magic and esotericism. Picasso's children also understand, the essay notes, but their knowledge and power are more primitive and instinctive. They stop and the rain ceases to fall; nature bows before them as it did for Baudelaire's "Bohémiens en voyage,"[27] as it will for Apollinaire's "Saltimbanques" (*Alcools*, III, 97).

23. Pierre Daix and Georges Boudaille, *Picasso: The Blue and Rose Periods: A Catalogue Raisonné 1900–1906*, trans. Phoebe Pool (Greenwich, Connecticut, New York Graphic Society, 1967), p. 74.

24. Useful treatments of the Blue Period include Barr, pp. 22–31; Daix and Boudaille, pp. 51–65; George Heard Hamilton, pp. 140–144; Roland Penrose, *Picasso: His Life and Work* (New York: Icon, 1973), pp. 78–95, 98–99; Theodore Reff, "Themes of Love and Death," pp. 11–28; Jaime Sabartés, *Picasso: An Intimate Portrait*, trans. Angel Flores (New York: Prentice-Hall, 1948), pp. 58–69.

25. In discussing the Blue Period, Sabartés states: "Picasso believes that art emanates from sadness and pain. . . . That sadness lends itself to meditation, and that grief is at the depths of life." Sabartés, p. 65. Penrose, p. 92, states: " 'In the end, there is only love,' Picasso once remarked, 'and they should put out the eyes of painters as they do goldfinches to make them sing better.' " For treatment of the theme of blindness in Picasso's work, see Penrose, pp. 91–92.

26. I have added the bracketed word to Apollinaire's image to reflect more closely the French text.

27. See Baudelaire, I, 779. For discussion of the role of magic and the magician in Apollinaire, see Philippe Renaud, *Lecture d'Apollinaire* (Lausanne: L'Age d'Homme, 1969), p. 167, et passim.

It is significant that of all the blue figures, Apollinaire selects the child (rather than the *Old Guitarist*) to symbolize the artist.[28] Often, children represent primitive consciousness, and Picasso's interest in forms of primitivism began even before the Blue Period. According to Sabartés, Picasso preferred "childlike stammerings" to "academic rhetoric" in the Blue Period years and admired "primitive" art for its innocence. And "if we demand sincerity of the artist," Sabartés goes on, "we must remember that it is not to be found outside the realm of grief."[29]

Condemned to sadness and solitude, Picasso's figures, as Apollinaire portrays them, turn inward. And in the essay, the privileged among them, like the painter or the mystic, reveal truths that cannot be explained, but can be manifested in form.[30] The poor children of Apollinaire's imagination trace with their bodies the invisible and impalpable shapes of thought. Idea and emotion are embodied in symbol. And, like Mallarmé's ballerina, and the painter, the acrobat creates a poem without using the writer's tools.[31] "After all," Picasso is reported to have said, "the arts are all the same; you can write a picture in words just as you can paint sensations in a poem."[32] During the Blue Period, Picasso was influenced by the Symbolist dialogue among the arts, and by Symbolist painters who, with Gauguin, believed that suggestion was all-important in art and that the artistic sign was a manifestation of the idea.[33] Apollinaire's simile, the comparison of movement and thought, takes note of this aesthetic and marks its limitations. According to Pierre Daix, the dilemma of the Blue Period is the risk of an overly abstract symbolism on the one hand and an excessively anecdotal realism on the other.[34] In Apollinaire's image, there is a tension between symbol and idea and a persistence of anecdote that reflects this dilemma.

The Blue Period, as Apollinaire portrays it, is a realm of interiority, and Picasso's figures are presented, not only as personal symbols and as reflections of phantom images that float in a collective cultural memory, but also as fictional characters who possess thoughts and feelings and have a past. As he begins to comment on the Rose Period (fig. 5),[35] however, Apollinaire speculates less often on the social status of the figures or the states of mind behind the masks. The apparent autonomy of the figure becomes more precarious, the essay implies, the autonomy of the canvas more evident, and meaning comes to reside not only in the fiction, but also in the artistry that produced it.

A work of art, Apollinaire would write in 1908, is an "enchanting falsehood," a human fabrication with its own laws distinct from nature's (III, 783; AoA, 49). While there are many possible explanations for Picasso's interest in the clown in 1904 and 1905, it is interesting to note that clowns and acrobats belong to a theatrical tradition that celebrates artifice. In the portion of the essay devoted to the Rose Period, Apollinaire views the clowns from outside, without penetrating their thoughts. Occasionally, he seems to think of the painter as a director who shapes and places the figures to achieve a desired effect. Whereas Apollinaire began his study of the Blue Period by reflecting on the consciousness of artist and figures, he directs his first remarks on the Rose Period to the formal elements of the painting. The essay thus appears to suggest that dramatic and expressive function has been transferred from the figure to the line and colors that produce it, that emotion here is manifested not in character but in form: "The harlequins live beneath their ragged finery while the painting gathers, heats up, or whitens its colors in order to tell of the strength and the duration of passions, while the lines . . . curve, soar . . . or are cut short."

There are echoes here of the nineteenth-century notion, variously expressed by Delacroix, Baudelaire, Gauguin, Denis, and others—that line and color act on

28. It may be that the *Old Guitarist* was not among the paintings at the Galeries Serrurier. Positive identification of the paintings exhibited is not possible. See Daix and Boudaille, pp. 254–255.

29. Sabartés, p. 65. Sabartés speaks generally of "primitive painters" without mentioning any specific artist or work.

30. Unlike the mystic's truth, the painter's posits no independent existence, but is revealed only in the act of creation. "A painting," Picasso said, "is not thought out and fixed beforehand; while one is painting it, it follows the mobility of one's thoughts." Dore Ashton, ed., *Picasso and Art: A Selection of Views*, The Documents of 20th Century Art (New York: Viking, 1972), p. 29.

31. See Stéphane Mallarmé, *Oeuvres complètes*, eds. Henri Mondor and Jean-Aubry (Paris: Gallimard, 1945), p. 304.

32. Ashton, ed., p. 131.

33. See Daix and Boudaille, p. 60. Gauguin, whose work Picasso contemplated during the winter of 1903, believed, with his literary friends, that suggestion was all-important in art. "Known symbols," such as the lily, he felt, "would congeal the canvas into a melancholy reality, and the problem would no longer be a poem." Cited in Hamilton, pp. 91–92.

34. See Daix and Boudaille, p. 70.

35. Useful treatments of the Rose Period include Barr, pp. 34–43; Blunt and Pool, pp. 21–22; Daix and Boudaille, pp. 66–86; Hamilton, pp. 144–145; Penrose, pp. 110–116; Reff, "Themes of Love and Death," pp. 28–42.

the imagination independently of the representation.[36] Although Apollinaire's statement might appear to look forward to Cubist fragmentation and subordination of the figure to the picture surface or to predict the tendency toward abstraction among artists influenced by Cubism, neither Picasso nor Apollinaire had yet begun (in 1905) to abandon conventional subject matter. And in the rest of the essay, the poet emphasizes — more than many of the professional critics do, and more than he himself later would — the symbolic and mythic dimensions of the Rose Period.

Like the demiurges of *Alcools* and the clowns of nineteenth-century art, Apollinaire's saltimbanque is a privileged figure of the artist and a creature of artists' shared imagination. In "Picasso, peintre," the Rose Period is depicted as a timeless realm, not of fictional consciousness, but of mythic correspondence: "Color has the flat quality of frescoes, and the lines are firm. But placed at the outer limits of life, the animals are human and the sexes indistinct." Isolated in an obscure and deserted landscape, clothed in maillots even when they do not perform, the saltimbanques are primitive and magic figures. The clowns of the essay, all at a twilight time of life, know neither past nor future. The females, nubile, fertile, are close to the source of life. The acrobats whom they resemble are morbidly aged and withered, perhaps because they know more shadowy mysteries. Young girls have been instructed in religion by animals, and the line between human and bestial cannot be drawn: "Hybrid beasts have the consciousness of the demigods of Egypt." Although they pose in the manner of the Holy Family, the saltimbanques remind Apollinaire of the figures of Greek vase painting. And like the Greeks of Hermetic tradition, the clowns he describes are initiates. The clowns of the painting and essay do not gaze at their mates but stare into space, cast their eyes down, or perform feats of balance that are solitary rites. As Starobinski points out, the acrobat of nineteenth-century art was also a narcissistic figure; and "beauty that suffices to itself," he says, "is an androgyne."[37]

Like the children who represented the Blue Period, the clowns of "Picasso, peintre" figure their own creation. Conceived in mystery, they are born

Figure 4. Picasso, *Three Children (Petits Gueux)*, 1904. Location unknown, Zervos, I, 219. © SPADEM, Paris/VAGA, New York, 1987.

miraculously and unexpectedly. Once grown, they in turn create lovely and silent forms. "The adolescent sisters, treading and balancing themselves on the great balls of the saltimbanques, impart to those spheres the radiant movement of the planets." Picasso's *Young Acrobat on a Ball*, which Apollinaire almost certainly has in mind here, can be seen in retrospect as a figure of the pre-Cubist artist. In "Picasso, peintre," however, line and mass are not mere form: the shapes they assume are celestial. The saltimbanques' mastery borders on magic, and the globes they tread move in harmony with the universe. Apollinaire abandons the simile that linked idea and sign in his image of the Blue Period children. In the Rose Period, the poet implies, the symbol no longer stands for the reality. It *is* the

36. See Eugene Delacroix, *Journal* (Paris: Plon, 1893), I, 327; Jean Stump, "Varieties of Symbolism," in *Les Mardis: Stéphane Mallarmé and the Artists of His Circle* (Kansas: University of Kansas Museum of Art, 1966), pp. 33, 43; Schapiro, pp. 16–18; Maurice Denis, *Théories*, 4th ed. (Paris: L. Rouart et J. Watelin, 1920), p. 1.

37. See Starobinski, p. 44. The translation is mine.

Figure 5. Picasso, *Two Acrobats With a Dog*, 1905. Collection The Honorable and Mrs. William A. M. Burden, New York. © SPADEM, Paris/VAGA, New York, 1987.

reality. And the traditional figures of the Rose Period, repositories of dream, are, at the same time, perhaps no more than they reveal. "There is a genuine mystery in art," Northrop Frye notes, "and a real place for wonder. . . . But the intrinsic mystery . . . remains a mystery in itself no matter how fully known it is, and hence is not a mystery separated from what is known."[38] "Painting remains painting because it eludes . . . investigation," Picasso once commented. "It remains there like a question. And it alone gives the answer."[39]

In another poem inspired by the Rose Period, Rilke asks, "But tell me, who *are* they these acrobats, even a

little more fleeting than we ourselves. . . ."[40] The painting seems to invite the question and mock the asker. Of all the descendants of Watteau's Gilles and Deburau's Pierrot, Picasso's are perhaps the most unfathomable. Some have interpreted the figures' detachment and alienation in psychological or sociological terms; many have attributed their lack of clear relation to one another to the Rose Period's increasing rejection of anecdote and allegory.[41] When Cubism reduces Harlequin to the lozenge shapes of his costume,[42] there is relatively little temptation to interpret the canvas in sentimental terms. In the Rose Period, however, the integrity of the figure is respected and enhanced by symbolic and autobiographical allusion.[43] As a result, the lack of clear connection among the figures is puzzling and tends to be read as mystery.

The atmosphere of religious mystery in the essay may have been suggested in part by the painting's allusions to Christian art. Apollinaire was also aware, of course —as was Picasso, according to Reff—of the "primitive" and "demonic" origins of the clown.[44] Apollinaire's sense of the quasi-sacred nature of the Rose Period, moreover, seems justified in light of Picasso's later fascination with the supernatural qualities of African sculpture and with the near sacred status of all art.[45] Ultimately, however, the mysticism of "Picasso, peintre" is related to ideas and images that haunted Apollinaire before and after his encounter with Picasso. Apollinaire makes no explicit reference to any cult in "Picasso, peintre." To do so baldly would betray an art that chooses silence over speech, painting over literature. Nonetheless, throughout the essay, he uses themes and motifs associated elsewhere in his work with Hermeticism. Describing the evolution of the painting, he thus traces an initiate's voyage, from descent into a blue abyss, to death and resurrection, to

38. Northrop Frye, *Anatomy of Criticism: Four Essays* (Princeton: Princeton University Press, 1971), p. 88.

39. Ashton, ed., p. 25.

40. Rainer Maria Rilke, "The Fifth Elegy," in *Duino Elegies*, ed. and trans. J. B. Leishman and Stephen Spender (New York: W. W. Norton & Co., 1939), p. 47.

41. See Hamilton, p. 144; Barr, pp. 36–37.

42. See Reff, "Harlequins," p. 31.

43. Reff points out that the figures in *Family of Saltimbanques* were modeled after Picasso and his friends. The male figures, from left to right, resemble Picasso, Apollinaire, André Salmon, and Max Jacob. See Reff, "Harlequins," p. 42. Reff has also suggested that the figures in Picasso's *Three Musicians* (1921), painted after Apollinaire's death, were modeled after Picasso, Apollinaire, and Jacob. See Theodore Reff, "Picasso's Three Musicians: Maskers, Artists and Friends," *Art in America*, Dec. 1980, pp. 124–142.

44. See Reff, "Picasso's Three Musicians," p. 131.

45. See Malraux, pp. 11–13, Rubin, pp. 255, 335; Ashton, ed., p. 25.

the miraculous and crepuscular world of the circus paintings.

Apollinaire was drawn to the Hermetic writings, where initiation is described as knowledge and awakening, where introspection yields truths that transcend individual consciousness. He was not, however, a mystic, nor did he hesitate to distort Hermetic doctrine in the service of asserting the primacy of human creation over the divine.[46] Rather, he used the language of mysticism, as nineteenth-century poets had, to express his ideas about art. The Symbolists, according to A. G. Lehmann, confused imaginative knowledge with the irrational and thus associated art with the occult.[47] Such confusion is common, Suzanne Langer states. Artistic truth, she says, is not mystical, but it is inaccessible to discursive reason, untranslatable, and "bound to the particular form which it has taken."[48] According to Eliade, literature and spectacle play a role in modern society akin to that of myth in traditional societies, in that they transcend historical time to recover a sense of the paradisiacal and the primordial through the recreation of language.[49] The remark is interesting in light of the Symbolist concern with languages that go beyond the discursive and beyond language itself. Like his Symbolist predecessors, Apollinaire uses a quasi-religious vocabulary to express his awe of an art that articulates the ineffable and that does so without words. "The spectator who watches them must be pious," he writes of the clowns, "for they celebrate wordless rites with painstaking agility."

*   *   *

By 1913, when Apollinaire published "Un Fantôme de nuées," a poem that reconsiders both the Rose Period and his own aesthetic, contemporary painting had undergone great changes. "One cannot forever carry on one's back the body of one's father,"

Apollinaire had written in 1908 (AoA, 48). As early as 1905, Picasso had begun to abandon the sentimental vocabulary of Symbolism. In 1906, he turned to archaic Greek and Iberian sculpture for inspiration, and, in 1907, to African and Oceanic art.[50] According to André Malraux, Picasso believed the African pieces were "magic things," "intercessors." "The fetishes," Picasso reportedly said, "were weapons."[51] African art had its role in Picasso's "proto-Cubist" painting of 1907–1908, as it would in Synthetic Cubism's (1912–1921) use of disparate materials and multiple sign systems.[52] As Picasso himself would later state, however, the African sculptures were not so much "models" as "witnesses"[53] to his own metamorphoses. In 1907, he completed the powerful and disturbing Demoiselles d'Avignon, which he described as his first "exorcism-painting."[54] By the end of that year, Apollinaire had introduced Picasso to Braque. Cubism was born and, in its wake, Delaunay's Simultanism, or Orphism, as Apollinaire baptized it. The fin de siècle atmosphere that lingered in the opening years of the century had faded. Born of Symbolism, the new art surpassed and destroyed that aesthetic, and there was in the air a feeling of freedom from tradition, from imitation, from all order save that created out of chaos by the artist (AoA, 38).

This freedom, as romanticized by Apollinaire and other participants and observers, was accompanied by a sense of the primitive and exotic manifest in the vitality of new forms, the vibrance of new colors. Matisse, Apollinaire noted, created a luminous and hedonistic art of bold colors freed not only from verisimilitude, but also from the symbolism and mysticism of his predecessors (AoA, 330–331). Once the Rose Period had ended, Picasso dealt a further blow to realism with the depiction of hulking figures stalking through forests of jagged shapes. And Rousseau, Apollinaire wrote, painted lush paradises of a reality so overwhelming to their creator that he was forced to open the window to breathe (AoA, 349). In the years that preceded the war, Paris no longer seemed so gray and muddy to its artist/chroniclers as it had to Baudelaire's exiles, nor paradise so far.[55] The spirits of

46. See Louis Ménard, trans. Hermès Trismégiste: traduction complète (Paris: Didier, 1866). For discussion of Apollinaire's treatment of Hermetic materials, see Marie-Jeanne Durry, Guillaume Apollinaire: Alcools, 3 vols. (Paris: Société d'Editions d'Enseignement Supérieur, 1956–1964), I, 156–157. For remarks on the gnostic and mystic atmosphere of "Picasso, peintre," see Starobinski, p. 126; Bates, p. 68. See also "Jung on Picasso," trans. Patrick O'Brian, in O'Brian, Pablo Ruíz Picasso (New York: Putnam, 1966), p. 490.

47. See A. G. Lehmann, The Symbolist Aesthetic in France, 2d ed. (Oxford: Basic Blackwell, 1968), p. 108.

48. Susanne K. Langer, Philosophy in a New Key: A Study in the Symbolism of Reason, Rite, and Art, 3rd ed. (Cambridge: Harvard University Press, 1974), p. 260.

49. See Eliade, "Les Mythes," pp. 454–457.

50. See Rubin, pp. 242–86, et passim.

51. Malraux, Picasso's Mask, pp. 10–11.

52. See Rubin, "Picasso," in Rubin, ed., pp. 241–343. Lévi-Strauss contrasts Cubist and primitive sign systems in G. Charbonnier, Conversations with Claude Lévi-Strauss, trans. John and Doreen Weightman (London: Jonathan Cape, 1971), pp. 72–78.

53. Cited in Rubin, p. 260.

54. Cited in Malraux, Picasso's Mask, p. 11.

55. See "Le Cygne," in Baudelaire, I, 952–953.

Africa, of Chagall's Vitebsk, and of Oceania were in the air. And no less exuberant spirits were to be found in indigenous marvels, in the fantasies of folk art and the equally fantastic creatures of technology: airplanes and dirigibles, towers and wheels. Even the shards of café interiors, bits of newsprint, scraps of oilcloth, bottle labels, took on new wonder in Cubist painting. With Sonia Delaunay's invention of Simultaneous books and dresses, "astral" cushions, and "halo depth" lamps (AoA, 337), once-ordinary objects became receptacles of light and color. The same color rhythms were present in the painting of Robert Delaunay, in rainbows and prisms both abstract and astral. Delaunay claimed to have rediscovered "the childhood of all art,"[56] and Apollinaire's choice of the word *Orphism* to describe Delaunay's painting is felicitous, says Jean Cassou, for it evokes an age even before the most primitive, when the first god is the poet who "awakens to things, names them, and sings their praises."[57] There was, in the myth of the new that Apollinaire helped create, a mood of utopia very different from the dream worlds of Symbolism. Unlike Mallarmé's clown, martyr to the artificial, the painters of Apollinaire's circle could announce without shame, "J'ai troué dans le mur de toile une fenêtre."[58] More precisely, they looked through a Paris windowpane onto a world that, neither mythological nor mundane, was a kaleidoscope of the seen and the imagined.

There is a popular element in much of this art, in Cubists' depiction of café interiors, in Delaunay's representation of urban motifs—ballplayers and Ferris wheels—borrowed from picture postcards and photographs.[59] And it is only seemingly paradoxical that painters open to the world around them created an art radically lacking in what is popularly termed "realism." Artists now felt free to open their eyes because the real world was suffused with imagination and because, once they had abandoned illusionism, they no longer feared being mere imitators or transcribers. When Cubism broke definitively with perspective and shattered the traditional categories of figure and ground, the canvas itself began to assume the status of an object in the world rather than a mirror held up to it.[60] Painting had all but dispensed with fiction. If spectators could wonder naively at the thoughts and feelings of Picasso's blue figures, they would not think to muse on the past lives of the *Demoiselles d'Avignon*. As fiction dissolved into form, the meaning of art began to reside not in mystery but in presence. Painting, Apollinaire believed, had begun to approach music in its liberation from the perceived tyranny of the subject (AoA, 197). And it is again only seemingly paradoxical that poets, including Apollinaire, found inspiration in an art increasingly disdainful of the impure, that is, of the literary.

So too Apollinaire's art had evolved, in part as a result of its confrontation with painting. The influence of the plastic arts on his work is most evident in "Ondes," the first section of *Calligrammes* (1918). In *Alcools* (1913), only "Zone" (III, 55–60)—the first poem in the volume, although the last to be composed—invites comparison with avant-garde painting. "Zone's" celebration of the naive faith of childhood, of Christ the aviator, and of the childish grace of a young industrial street suggests something of the primitivism of the time. So too do billboards screeching like jungle parrots. The poem's ironic proclamation of the poetry of signboards and handbills and the prose of newspapers may allude to Cubist iconography. And the Eiffel Tower—a shepherdess of bleating bridges in the poem—was a favorite image of Rousseau and Robert Delaunay. But "Zone" is above all a regretful and tentative farewell to the poet's youth and to the dusky and autumnal world of *Alcools*, with its atmosphere of myth and magic. At the end of "Zone," after a walk that takes him across Paris and deep into the geography of his childhood, the poet returns at dawn to his room, to sleep among fetishes, "inferior Christs of obscure hopes," in a world about to be severed from the past. For the final sunrise of *Alcools* brings not the rebirth of the old myths promised in "Picasso, peintre," but their death: "Farewell farewell / Sun slit throat."

Adieu Adieu
Soleil cou coupé

"You are weary at last of this ancient world."[61] So begins "Zone" and *Alcools*. With the completion of his

56. Robert Delaunay, *Du Cubisme à l'art abstrait:* documents inédits publiés par Pierre Francastel, ed. (Paris: SEVPEN, 1957), p. 113.

57. Jean Cassou, *Préface à l'Exposition Robert Delaunay mai–septembre 1957* (Editions des Musées Nationaux, 1957), cited in S. I. Lockerbie, "Qu'est-ce que l'Orphisme d'Apollinaire," in *Apollinaire et la Musique*, Actes du colloque de Stavelot, 27–29, August 1967, "Les Amis d'Apollinaire" (Stavelot: Minard, 1967), p. 82. The translation is mine.

58. See "Le Pitre châtié," in Mallarmé, p. 31.

59. See Gustav Vriesen and Max Imdahl, *Robert Delaunay: Light and Color*, trans. Maria Pelikan (New York: Abrams, 1969), p. 28.

60. For discussion of the notion of "le tableau objet," see John Golding, *Cubism: A History and an Analysis* (Boston: Boston Book & Art Shop, 1968), p. 93.

61. Apollinaire, III, 60; Apollinaire, *Alcools*, trans. Greet, pp. 13, 3.

first major volume of poetry, a new era in Apollinaire's life had begun. "If we knew, the gods would awaken," reads the first line of "Picasso, peintre." The old world, slumbering in "Picasso, peintre," dying in *Alcools*, has nearly slipped away in "Ondes." And Apollinaire's poetry reveals a new concern with the art and life of the present. The Eiffel Tower of "Ondes" is no longer an ironic symbol of ancient pastoral, as it was in "Zone." In "Lettre-Océan" (III, 174–177), a "lyric ideogram" of 1914, it sends out messages like telegraph waves to the poet's brother in Mexico and to the world. The squeaking of the poet's new shoes, bits of conversation, sounds of buses, and cries of twentieth-century sirens "Hou Hou ou ou" circle a central point, "300 meters high." In "Liens" (III, 159), another poem of the period, the pattern formed by vertical and horizontal lines, by rain-combed smoke and submarine cables, is reminiscent of a Cubist grid and of Cubist rimes. And the "poèmes-conversation," with their juxtaposed bits of speech, have been likened to the pasted fragments of collage and to Duchamp's "ready-mades."[62] "A travers l'Europe" (III, 190–191) is dedicated to Marc Chagall, painter of Paris and Vitebsk. And Robert Delaunay's presence can be felt throughout the poetry of "Ondes," not only in "Tour" (III, 190), dedicated to the painter, and in "Les Fenêtres" (III, 160–161), written for a catalogue of his painting, but also, more surprisingly, along with Picasso's in "Un Fantôme de nuées," which deals ostensibly with saltimbanques, thin and shadowy, red and rose.

"I very much like my poems written after *Alcools*," Apollinaire would write in 1915 from the war front. "They are the result of a completely new esthetic whose energies I have not since been able to recapture" (IV, 493, trans. mine). In his analyses of "Un Fantôme de nuées," Philippe Renaud has suggested that the poem announces this new aesthetic.[63] I would add that the poem alludes to three

of the Circus pictures, all painted in 1905, and that it is a reevaluation, not only of Apollinaire's own work, but also of the Rose Period.

Unlike "Picasso, peintre," which began with an invocation of the gods, "Un Fantôme" starts with a simple prose statement: "Since it was the day before July fourteenth / Around four in the afternoon / I went down to the street to see the clowns." Even the ordinary can be marvelous, Apollinaire suggests in "Sur les Prophéties" (III, 178–179), another poem in "Ondes." It is not a question of religion or mysticism, he says, but of observation. Surveying the scene as through a movie camera, the poet of "Un Fantôme" seizes on the circular shape of the crowd, the spherical weights of the barbells, and the movement of fingers "rolling a cigarette bitter and delicious like life." The gesture of the fingers is banal, the object produced no less so, yet the cigarette burns with a fire as efficacious as the metaphysical flames of *Alcools* (III, 113–115). Transformed by fire and human breath, the cigarette becomes pure essence, as stains on the rugs the clowns spread out become notes of music. Intrigued by notions of pure art inherited from nineteenth-century aesthetics, Apollinaire, like Mallarmé, uses burning tobacco as a sign of purification.[64] In an essay of 1912 entitled "On the Subject in Modern Painting," he had suggested that the increasingly abstract painting of his contemporaries would someday be to more traditional art as music is to poetry. The new art would not, however, destroy the old. Music, after all, had not supplanted literature, nor had the "acrid taste of tobacco replace[d] the savor of food." (AoA, 197–198). Rather than contemplating a mystic interior landscape, as he had in "Crépuscule," one of the poems in *Alcools* inspired by the Rose Period, the poet of "Un Fantôme" focuses on the sights before him until they disappear, like the little clown of the piece, into harmony and form.

It is striking that Apollinaire returned to the saltimbanques when he was most active in defending Cubism and Orphism, and when his exuberance for the avant-garde was evident in his poetry. Apollinaire does not change his high opinion of the Rose Period in 1913, but he does call into question the vision he had earlier brought to that troubling and elusive art. Standing mute at the threshold of this century, bathed in the uncertain light of the last, Picasso's clowns were enigmatic. As subject, they were fragile, and that fragility haunted the poet. In "Picasso, peintre," Apollinaire had spoken of the mysteries of the Rose

62. See Durry, II, 203; Renaud, *Lecture*, pp. 259, 320, 345, 377, 378, et passim.

63. See Philippe Renaud, " 'Ondes,' ou les métamorphoses de la musique," in *Apollinaire et la musique*, pp. 21–31; Renaud, *Lecture*, pp. 277–280, et passim. For discussion and debate concerning Apollinaire's "changement de front" in "Ondes," see Renaud, *Lecture*, pp. 214–221, 272–277, et passim; Claude Debon, *Guillaume Apollinaire après Alcools*, Bibliothèque des Lettres Modernes, 31, 2 vols. (Paris: Minard, 1981), I, 30, et passim; Michel Décaudin, "Le 'Changement de front' d'Apollinaire, *Revue des Sciences Humaines*, NS 60 (October–December 1950), 255–256; Michel Décaudin, *La Crise des valeurs symbolistes: vingt ans de poésie française 1895–1914* (Toulouse: Editions Privat, 1960), pp. 484–491.

64. See "Toute l'âme résumée . . ." in Mallarmé, p. 73.

Period. In an essay published in 1912, he remarks instead on the calm and grace of their objective form (AoA, 196).

In "Un Fantôme de nuées," the clowns are no longer privileged merely by virtue of their character or heritage. The pseudo-Hermetic world of "Picasso, peintre" is no more. And morbidity, no longer a sign of initiation, is an emblem of the disintegration of the figure. Of the three clowns in "Un Fantôme de nuées" based on Picasso's *Family of Saltimbanques* (fig. 2), one decomposes, another dissolves, a third is a hoodlum. As for Apollinaire's organ grinder, he is closer in spirit to the madmen of the Blue Period and "Picasso, peintre" than to Picasso's *Organ-Grinder* (1905, fig. 6). He is perhaps also, as Renaud suggests, an ironic double of the poet of *Alcools* and the traditional lyric poet.[65] Swarming with the past, dreaming of the future, he grinds out a strange and dissonant lament. He is savage, not in the fashion of the "primitive" peoples whose sophisticated art Apollinaire and Picasso admired,[66] but in the more frightening manner of the once "civilized." His face, like an ill-tended garden, is grown over with ancestral cinder. And when he hides his grizzled visage in his hands, fingers are "foetuses" growing out of his beard. Instead of ennobling Picasso's *Organ-Grinder* as he did other Rose Period figures in "Picasso, peintre," Apollinaire makes of the old musician (far from grotesque in the painting) a monster, and a prisoner, of time.

"Un Fantôme," however, does not depict the Rose Period merely as a source of decay and superannuation. From under the ashen shadow of the old musician appears a little saltimbanque, a delicate new life:

> And when he balanced on a sphere
> His thin body became such delicate music that none of the
>   onlookers could resist it
> . . .
> And that music of shapes
> Destroyed the music of the mechanical organ
> That the man with the ancestor-covered face was
>   grinding out

Sitting at the feet of Picasso's organ-grinder is a small boy. The little saltimbanque of the poem is modeled in

part on that figure. But where Picasso's clown is silent and immobile, Apollinaire's does not come to life until he begins to move.

The child's mastery may surprise those who, hearing his "brief cries," "redskin cries," thought him a tiny savage, a fauve. Other artists too—sculptors of Africa and Oceania—were considered primitive by some, Apollinaire noted elsewhere. Yet they too created works the poet described as graceful and delicate. The little clown looks back to the primitivism of Rimbaud's "Bateau ivre," with its shouting redskins, and may suggest the "primitivism" of non-Western art.[67] But the figure stands above all for the primitive and childlike in modern Western art. "I want to be as though newborn," Klee had written in 1902, "knowing . . . nothing about Europe . . . to be almost primitive."[68] For Apollinaire, Picasso was heir to Michelangelo, but he was also "a newborn child" who "orders the universe with a brutality that knows . . . how to be gracious" (AoA, 196, 280). The little clown is an innocent and a "primitive," but not in the manner of the young boys and adolescent girls of "Picasso, peintre." His art is not born of pain or memory, knowledge or emotion. It is an art of pure movement and presence.

Facing the crowd the organ grinder had been too self-absorbed to see, the little saltimbanque makes a gesture reminiscent of a sign of benediction. Here, however, symbol is eclipsed by a new preoccupation with shape and motion. Once he steps on the ball, the clown's movements lose nearly all conventional meaning. The source of the image is *Young Acrobat on a Ball* (fig. 3), the painting Apollinaire had evoked eight years earlier in "Picasso, peintre." In "Un Fantôme," however, the adolescent sisters of the essay, initiates in mystical rites, have been replaced by a wild little boy. And the feat, to which Apollinaire had assigned great metaphysical weight, is portrayed as a triumph of lightness and balance. No longer identified with the cosmos, save by its harmonious rhythms, the ball is simply a sphere, and the little clown's art is synonymous with the movement of his delicate form.

65. See Renaud, " 'Ondes,' " p. 29.

66. See *Apollinaire on Art*, p. 244. For Apollinaire's comments on African and Oceanic Art, see Apollinaire, II, 494–497; IV, 274, 375–377; *Apollinaire on Art*, pp. 225, 243–246, 470–471. A previously unpublished remark by Apollinaire on the subject is

included in Samaltanos, p. 13. For general comments on Apollinaire and primitivism, see Samaltanos; Blanchère, pp. 25–70. In the *Poète assassiné*, a fictionalized Picasso is called "l'oiseau du Bénin" (I, 255). The name suggests Picasso's interest in African art and alludes more specifically to a sculpture in Apollinaire's small collection of African and Oceanic art. See Samaltanos, pp. 29–32.

67. See Arthur Rimbaud, "Le Bateau ivre," in *Oeuvres*, ed. Suzanne Bernard (Paris: Garnier Frères, 1960), p. 128.

68. *Paul Klee* (New York: Museum of Modern Art, 1945), p. 8.

In the Blue Period, as Apollinaire portrayed it in "Picasso, peintre," the human figure embodied mind. In the Rose, he implied in that essay, meaning resided not only in the figure, but also in line and color that "tell the force and duration of passion." The child's art in "Un Fantôme," however, represents neither ideas nor emotions. Like the notes of the "purest" music, the lines of the most abstract painting, his gestures do not represent objects or ideas, yet they echo the rhythm of the universe, radiating like light, transforming the world. If the little clown is a charmed figure, it is because of what he creates, and because his arrival, "la veille du quatorze juillet," marks a tenuous emancipation of art from the precious baggage of the past. The little clown, like his fellows, is an outsider, and a descendant of ancient wanderers, but he is fresh and newborn. Where his predecessors stood immobile in a misty and timeless landscape, he appears on a Paris street corner and performs for all the populace, not merely the initiated or an elect, an art of exquisite harmony and grace.

"An entirely new art is thus being evolved," Apollinaire had written in his 1912 article on "The Subject," "an art that will be to painting, as painting has hitherto been envisaged, what music is to literature. It will be pure painting, just as music is pure literature" (AoA, 197). Discussion of the purity and nonreferentiality of music in its relation to poetry was commonplace in the late nineteenth century, as were formalist notions of painting. But Apollinaire witnessed what he believed to be the gradual disappearance of the image from painting itself. And while he may have been less than accurate in 1912, when he associated Picasso's work with abstraction (AoA, 198), other painters influenced by Cubism, among them Delaunay, were perhaps evolving toward an art where "the subject no longer counts or if it counts it counts for very little" (AoA, 197). Robert Delaunay elaborated his aesthetic notions in the course of long conversations with Apollinaire, and it is likely that his ideas inform the esthetic of "Un Fantôme."[69] Ultimately, however, Apollinaire associated abstraction with many artists. In

Figure 6. Picasso, *The Organ-Grinder*, 1905. Kunsthaus, Zurich. © SPADEM, Paris/VAGA, New York, 1987.

the article of 1912 on "The Subject," he tells the story of Apelles and Protogenes, who vied in drawing lines so fine and subtle that they gave more pleasure than representations of gods and goddesses (AoA, 198). As early as 1908, Apollinaire had criticized art that slavishly imitates the anthropomorphic and the natural, that is, divine Creation. For Apollinaire, abstraction seems to have stood both for the liberation of human creativity from the divine and for the possibility of transcendence in the absence of religious myth.[70]

69. Apollinaire played an important role in presenting Delaunay's ideas to the public, especially in two essays of 1912, both written with the aid of notes provided by the painter (AoA, 259–265). The essays, Francastel notes, constitute "une sorte de dialogue du peintre et du poète sur les thèmes fournis par le premier." See Francastel's comment in Delaunay, p. 145. Delaunay's notion of pure art, his equation of painting and music, and his description of inferior art as mechanical, successive, and destructive, are echoed in Apollinaire's

portraits of the little clown and the organ grinder. See Delaunay, 149, 157, et passim. For more detailed analysis of the role of Delaunay's work in Apollinaire's poetry, see Eberiel, "Apollinaire," pp. 108–164.

70. Abstract art was not without metaphysical impulse. No longer

When Apollinaire wrote "Un Fantôme," he had not truly given up traditional myths, nor had he abandoned an art of memory and emotion and character. But he had begun to seek the marvelous and the sublime in new, less sentimental and anthropomorphic creations. There are glimpses in "Un Fantôme de nuées" of what a poetic equivalent of the child's music might be. Yet, in many respects, the poem is a quite traditional work of symbolic exposition reminiscent of Baudelaire's "Vieux Saltimbanque."[71] And although the little clown's arrival heralds the advent of an art both more abstract and more realistic than the old, it is elsewhere in Calligrammes that one finds that promise fulfilled.[72]

"I am here to judge the long debate," Apollinaire would write in 1918, the year of his death. "Between tradition and invention / Between Order and Adventure" ("La Jolie Rousse").[73] In his biography of Apollinaire, Marcel Adéma suggests that Apollinaire, Picasso, and Max Jacob, through their friendship and collaboration, invented a new aesthetic.[74] Still, it is interesting to remember that when they met, neither Apollinaire nor Picasso was working in a truly avant-garde mode. Poised on the brink of modernism, they had not yet broken with the art of the past. In the years that followed the Rose Period, Apollinaire, through his criticism, and most especially his poetry, would explore what seemed to be infinite new artistic possibilities: "Be indulgent when you compare us / To those who were the perfection of order / We who look for adventure everywhere."[75] From Montmartre, in the sunset of western myth and the twilight of Symbolism,

Apollinaire and Picasso would go to the Trocadéro to confront strange and new figures of magic. But before that, still under the spell of an earlier century, they went with their friends to the Cirque Médrano, to see the clowns.[76]

Appendix I

GUILLAUME APOLLINAIRE
Young Artists: Picasso the Painter*

If we knew, all the gods would awaken. Born of the profound knowledge that humanity had of itself, the adored pantheisms that resembled it have gone to sleep. But despite eternal slumbers, there are eyes that reflect humanities resembling divine and joyous phantoms.

Those eyes are attentive like flowers that wish ever to contemplate the sun. O fecund joy, there are men who see with those eyes!

Picasso has looked at human images that floated in the azure of our memories and that partake of the divine to the damnation of metaphysicians. How pious are his skies stirred by the movement of wings, his lights heavy and low like the lights of grottoes.

There are children who have wandered without learning the catechism. They stop and the rain dries up. "Look! There are people who live in these hovels, and they are poorly dressed." These children whom no one caresses understand so much. Mommy, love me a lot! They know how to jump and the feats they accomplish are mental evolutions.

These women who are no longer loved remember. They are tired of ironing their brittle ideas today. They do not pray; their devotion is to their memories. They huddle in the twilight like an ancient church. These women are giving up, and their fingers are eager to weave crowns of straw. At daybreak, they disappear, they have consoled themselves in silence. They have passed through many doors: mothers protected the

---

content with classic and anthropomorphic representation, the artists of his time, Apollinaire felt, sought new sources of the ideal and the sublime: "Wishing to attain the proportions of the ideal and not limiting themselves to humanity, the young painters offer us works that are more cerebral than sensible. They are moving further and further away from the old art of optical illusions and literal proportions, in order to express the grandeur of metaphysical forms. That is why today's art, although it does not emanate directly from specific religious beliefs, nevertheless possesses several of the characteristics of great art, that is to say, of religious art" (AoA, 223).

71. See Baudelaire, III, 35–37.

72. The more avant-garde poems of "Ondes" include "Les Fenêtres" (III, 160–161), written for a catalogue of Delaunay's exhibition at the gallery of Der Sturm in 1912; "Lundi rue Christine" (III, 172–173, with its references to Cubism, and the "lyric ideogram" "Lettre-Océan" (III, 174–177).

73. Apollinaire, Calligrammes, trans. Greet, p. 343.

74. See Adéma, p. 75.

75. Apollinaire, "La Jolie Rousse," in Calligrammes, trans. Greet, pp. 343, 345.

76. See Olivier, p. 155.

I would like to thank Francesco Pellizzi for his comments and suggestions.

* "Young Artists: Picasso the Painter," in Apollinaire, Apollinaire on Art: Essays and Reviews 1902–1918, The Documents of 20th Century Art, ed. LeRoy C. Breunig, trans. Susan Suleiman (New York: Viking, 1972), pp. 14–16. Reprinted with permission of © Editions Gallimard.

cradles so that the newborn babes would not be ill favored; when they leaned over, the little children smiled to know them so kind.

They have often given thanks, and their forearms trembled like their eyelids.

Enveloped in icy mists, the old men wait without pondering, for children alone ponder. Stirred by faraway lands, by the quarrels of animals, and by hardened tresses, these old men can beg without humility.

Other beggars have been worn out by life. They are the cripples, the disabled, and the knaves. They are astonished at having reached the goal that has remained blue yet is no longer the horizon. Growing old, they have become mad like kings with too many herds of elephants carrying miniature citadels. There are travelers who confuse flowers with stars.

Grown old the way oxen die at twenty-five, young men have carried infants suckled by the moon.

In pure sunlight, women remain silent, their bodies are angelic and their glances tremble.

In the face of danger, their smiles become internal. They await fear to confess innocent sins.

For the space of one year, Picasso lived this painting, wet and blue like the humid depths of the abyss, and pitiful.

Pity made Picasso more harsh. The public squares held up a hanged man stretching himself against the houses above oblique passers-by. These tortured men were waiting for a redeemer. The cord swung away, miraculously; on the mansard roofs, the windowpanes blazed with the flowers of the windows.

In bedrooms, poor painters drew fleecy nudes by lamplight. The women's shoes abandoned near the bed suggested tender haste.

Calm descended after this frenzy.

The harlequins live beneath their ragged finery while the painting gathers, heats up, or whitens its colors in order to tell of the strength and the duration of passions, while the lines outlining the costume curve, soar up, or are cut short.

Paternity transfigures the harlequin in a square room while his wife bathes herself with cold water and admires herself, as slender and frail as her husband, the puppet. A neighboring fireplace sends some warmth into the caravan. Lovely songs mingle in the air and soldiers pass elsewhere, cursing the day.

Love is good when it is adorned and the habit of living in one's own home redoubles the paternal sentiment. The child brings together the father and the wife, whom Picasso sees as glorious and immaculate.

The expectant mothers were no longer expecting the child, perhaps because of certain chattering crows and evil omens. Noël! They gave birth to future acrobats amid the familiar monkeys, the white horses, and the bearlike dogs.

The adolescent sisters, trading and balancing themselves on the great balls of the saltimbanques, impart to those spheres the radiant movement of the planets. These girlish adolescents, children still, have the anxieties of innocence; animals teach them the religious mysteries. Some harlequins accompany the aura of the women and resemble them, neither male nor female.

Color has the flat quality of frescoes, and the lines are firm. But placed at the outer limits of life, the animals are human and the sexes indistinct.

Hybrid beasts have the consciousness of the demigods of Egypt; the cheeks and brows of taciturn clowns are withered by morbid sensibilities.

One cannot confuse these saltimbanques with mere actors on a stage. The spectator who watches them must be pious, for they celebrate wordless rites with painstaking agility. This is what distinguishes this painter from the Greek potters, whom his drawing sometimes calls to mind. On the painted vases, bearded, verbose priests sacrificed resigned animals bound to no destiny. In these paintings virility is beardless, but it manifests itself in the muscles of the skinny arms and flat cheekbones, and the animals are mysterious.

Picasso's penchant for the fleeting trait transforms and penetrates and produces almost unique examples of linear drypoints, in which the general aspect of the world is not altered by the light that modifies forms by altering colors.

More than all the poets, sculptors, and other painters, this Spaniard stings us like a sudden chill. His meditations are laid bare in silence. He comes from far away, from the richness of composition and brutal decoration of the Spaniards of the seventeenth century.

Those who have known him remember fiery outbursts that were already more than mere experiments.

His perseverance in the pursuit of beauty has led him on his way. He has seen himself ethically more of a Latin, rhythmically more of an Arab.

(La Plume, May 15)

Appendix II

GUILLAUME APOLLINAIRE
Phantom of Clouds*

Since it was the day before July fourteenth
Around four in the afternoon
I went down to the street to see the jugglers

Those people who give open-air performances
Are beginning to be rare in Paris
In my youth you saw many more of them
They've nearly all gone to the provinces

I took the Boulevard Saint-Germain
And in a little square between Saint-Germain des-Prés and
    Danton's statue
I found the jugglers

The crowd surrounding them was silent and resigned to
    waiting
I found a place in the circle where I could see everything
Tremendous weights
Belgian cities raised at arm's length by a Russian worker
    from Longwy
Hollow black dumbbells whose stem is a frozen stream
Fingers rolling a cigarette as bittersweet as life

A number of dirty rugs covered the ground
Rugs with wrinkles that won't come out
Rugs that are almost entirely dust-colored
And with some yellow or green stains persistent
Like a tune that pursues you

Do you see the man who's savage and lean
His father's ashes sprouted in his graying beard
And he bore his whole heredity in his face
He seemed to be dreaming about the future
Turning his barrel organ all the while
Its lingering voice lamented in marvelous
Glug-glugs squawks and muffled groans

The jugglers didn't move
The oldest wore a sweater the rose-violet color you see
    in the fresh cheeks of young girls who are dying

That rose nestles above all in the creases surrounding their
    mouths
Or near their nostrils
It's a rose full of treachery

Thus he bore on his back
The lowly hue of his lungs

Arms arms everywhere mounted guard

The second juggler
Wore only his shadow
I watched him for a long time
His features escape me entirely
He's a headless man

Then there was another who resembled a tough thug
With a kind heart and a dirty mind
With his baggy trousers and garters to hold up his socks
Didn't he look dressed up like a pimp

The music stopped and there were negotiations with the
    public
Who sou by sou threw down on the rug the sum of two
    and a half francs
Instead of the three francs the old man had set as the price
    of the show

But when it was clear no one was going to give any more
They decided to begin the performance
From beneath the organ appeared a tiny juggler dressed
    in pulmonary pink
With fur at his wrists and ankles
He gave little cries
And saluted by gracefully lifting his forearms
And spreading wide his fingers

One leg back ready to kneel
He saluted the four points of the compass
And when he balanced on a sphere
His thin body became such delicate music that none of
    the onlookers could resist it
A small inhuman sprite
Each of them thought
And that music of shapes
Destroyed the music of the mechanical organ
That the man with the ancestor-covered face was grinding
    out

The tiny juggler turned cartwheels
With such harmony
That the organ stopped playing
And the organist hid his face in his hands

---

* "Phantom of Clouds," in Apollinaire, *Calligrammes: Poems of Peace and War* (1913–1916), trans. Anne Hyde Greet, with an introduction by S. I. Lockerbie and commentary by Anne Hyde Greet and S. I. Lockerbie (Berkeley: University of California Press, 1980), pp. 81–87. Reprinted with permission of University of California Press.

His fingers resembled descendants of his destiny
Miniscule fetuses appearing in his beard
New cries like Redskins
Angelic music of the trees
Vanishing of the child

The jugglers raised the huge dumbbells at arm's length

They juggled with weights

But every spectator searched in himself for the miraculous child
Century oh century of clouds

List of authors

ENRICO CASTELLI is an Associate of the Istituto di Etnologia e Antropologia Culturale of the University of Perugia, Italy.

ERIK COHEN is a Professor of Sociology and Social Anthropology at The Hebrew University of Jerusalem.

ROSEMARY EBERIEL is Assistant Professor in French at Agnes Scott College, Decatur, Georgia.

MARCO FRASCARI is an Associate Professor in the College of Architecture, Georgia Institute of Technology, Atlanta, Georgia.

STEPHEN HOUSTON is Assistant Professor of Anthropology at Yale University.

DAVID LEATHERBARROW is a Professor at the Graduate School of Fine Arts of the University of Pennsylvania.

MARY ELLEN MILLER is Associate Professor in the Department of the History of Art, at Yale University.

PAUL MUS (1902–1969) was a member of the Ecole Française d'Extrême-Orient (1927–1946). In 1945–47 he was an adviser to the French authorities in Indochina. In 1946 he was elected Professor to the Collège de France; later he was also "visiting professor" at Yale University.

CARLO SEVERI is a Research Associate at the Centre National de la Recherche Scientifique and a Member of the Laboratoire d'Anthropologie Sociale of the Collège de France, Paris.

SERGE THION is a Research Fellow at the Centre National de la Recherche Scientifique, Paris.

Res 15 Spring 1988

Contents of upcoming issue

Res

Anthropology and aesthetics

RES is a journal of anthropology and comparative aesthetics dedicated to the study of the object, in particular cult and belief objects and objects of art. The journal brings together, in an anthropological perspective, contributions by philosophers, art historians, and critics, linguists, architects, artists, and others. Its field of enquiry is open to all cultures, regions, and historical periods.

RES also seeks to make available previously unpublished documents — both textual and iconographic — of importance for the theory of the arts.

RES appears twice a year, in the spring and in the autumn. Subscriptions are filled only on a calendar-year basis. Back years are available at current subscription prices:

$26 (£19) per year for individuals
$50 (£35) per year for institutions
$100 per year for sustaining subscriptions

Orders, which must be accompanied by payment, should be sent to a bookseller or subscription agent or directly to Cambridge University Press, 32 East 57th Street, New York, NY 10022 (for the United States and Canada) or to Cambridge University Press, The Edinburgh Building, Shaftesbury Road, Cambridge CB2 2RU, Great Britain (for all other countries). Claims for missing issues should be made immediately after receipt of the subsequent issue of the journal.